Text Structures
From the Masters

Text Structures From the Masters
At a Glance

Students enter the title of their piece here, so it's front and center as they write.

The text structure is essentially an outline of the historical document that appears on the opposite page. Students use the words in these boxes to create their own "kernel essay" below.

PLANNING PAGE

Name: _____

TITLE OF YOUR PIECE

TEXT STRUCTURE

Why Something Goes Viral

| one effect these have on people | my example of one that went viral | another version of it | what makes people stop, notice, and share |

Jane Addams

KERNEL ESSAY

1. _____

2. _____

3. _____

4. _____

SUGGESTIONS FOR QUICK LIST:

What goes viral these days?
• videos • songs • pictures • messages
What went viral before computers?
• stories • tales • fables • ghost stories
List some examples.

MY QUICK LIST OF TOPICS:

1. _____
2. _____
3. _____
4. _____
5. _____

Students write one sentence for each of the text structure boxes above, leaving them with a "kernel" of an essay to expand upon as they write.

Here, we've brainstormed some ideas to get students thinking about their own pieces.

This space invites students to jot down topics they might like to explore in their kernel essay.

Engaging historical documents from notable Americans inspire students to "try on" the same writing structures used by these masters of the craft.

"A Modern Day Devil Baby"
(*American Journal of Sociology, 20(1)*, 117–118)

Jane Addams, 1914

There is a theory that women first evolved and used the fairy story, that combination of wisdom and romance, in an effort to tame her mate and to make him a better father to her children. The stories finally became a rude creed, or rather rule of conduct, which softened the treatment men accorded to women.

These first pitiful efforts of women became so widespread and so powerful that we have not yet escaped their influence. We had remarkable experience at Hull House this year of the persistence of one of these tales which has doubtless had its taming effects through the centuries upon recalcitrant husbands and fathers. It burst upon us one day in the persons of three Italian women who, with excited rush into Hull House, demanded to see the devil-baby. No amount of denial convinced them that it was not there for they knew exactly what it was like, with its cloven hoofs, its pointed ears, and its diminutive tail. It had been able to speak as soon as it was born and was most shockingly profane. For six weeks the messages, the streams of visitors from every part of the city and suburbs to this mythical baby, poured all day long and so far into the night that the regular activities were almost swamped. The Italian version, with a hundred variations, dealt with a pious Italian girl married to an atheist who vehemently tore a holy picture from the bedroom wall, saying that he would quite as soon have a devil in the house as that, whereupon the devil incarnated himself in the child. As soon as the devil-baby was born, it ran about the table shaking its finger in deep reproach at its father, who finally caught it and in fear and trembling brought it into Hull House. When the residents there, in spite of the baby's shocking appearance, in order to save its soul took him to church for a baptism, they found the shawl was empty, and the devil-baby, fleeing from the water, ran lightly over the backs of the pews.

The Jewish version, again with variations, was to the effect that the father of six daughters said before the birth of the seventh child that he would rather have a devil than another girl, whereupon the devil-baby promptly appeared. The story was not only used to tame restless husbands, but mothers threatened their daughters that if they went to dance halls or out to walk with strange young men they would be eternally disgraced by devil-babies. Simple, round-eyed girls came to Hull House to see if this were true, many of them quite innocent of the implications in the warning. Save for a red automobile which occasionally figured in the story, and a stray cigar, the tale was mediaeval and unrelieved as if it had been fashioned a thousand years ago in response to the imperative need of anxious wives and mothers. It had fastened itself to a poor little deformed creature, born in an obscure street, destined in its one breath of life to demonstrate the power of an old wives' tale among thousands of people in modern society who are living in a corner of their own, their vision fixed, their intelligence held by some iron chain of silent habit. Or did the incident rather make clear that the love of the marvelous will not die, and that romance springs unexpectedly from the most uncongenial soil?

Students enter their names and the titles of their essays here, establishing ownership of their work.

Samples of completed planning pages demonstrate students' writing moves as they emulate the masters.

The title of the text structure, repeated here, serves as an anchor to focus students on the theme.

The text structure framework remains, capturing the essence of the source document and the framework for each student essay.

Authentic, student-crafted kernel sentences bring new life to the text structures.

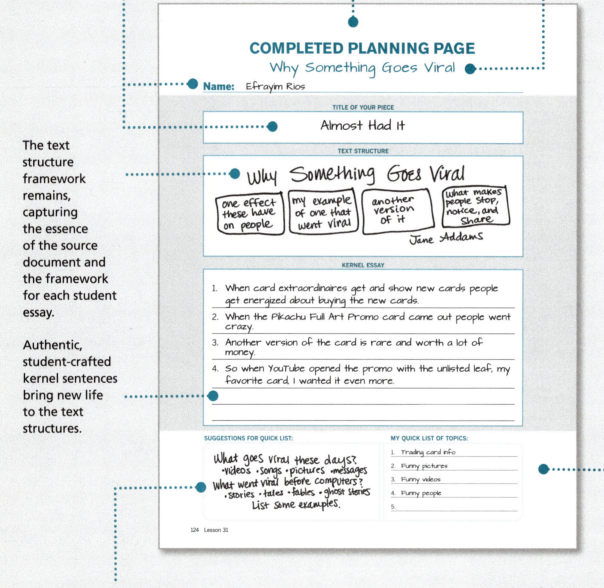

COMPLETED PLANNING PAGE
Why Something Goes Viral

Name: Efrayim Rios

TITLE OF YOUR PIECE

Almost Had It

TEXT STRUCTURE

Why Something Goes Viral

| one effect these have on people | my example of one that went viral | another version of it | what makes people stop, notice, and share |

Jane Addams

KERNEL ESSAY

1. When card extraordinaires get and show new cards people get energized about buying the new cards.
2. When the Pikachu Full Art Promo card came out people went crazy.
3. Another version of the card is rare and worth a lot of money.
4. So when YouTube opened the promo with the unlisted leaf, my favorite card, I wanted it even more.

SUGGESTIONS FOR QUICK LIST:

What goes viral these days?
• videos • songs • pictures • messages
What went viral before computers?
• stories • tales • fables • ghost stories
List some examples.

MY QUICK LIST OF TOPICS:

1. Trading card info
2. Funny pictures
3. Funny videos
4. Funny people
5.

Pointed suggestions and questions get students' gears moving as they write.

Samples of the student-generated ideas that sit at the heart of the writing are found in this section.

FULL ESSAY
Why Something Goes Viral

ALMOST HAD IT

I was lying on the bed browsing YouTube and there it was. No . . . it couldn't be. It, it, it was Pikachu Promo Full Art Yaw Squid. It was an unlisted leaf, my all time favorite Poker tuber had a pre-release on the one, the only, the Pikachu Prom Full Art Box! I decided to pick that video instead of the other great videos. When Ando (the unlisted leaf's name) opened the box, he was screaming in happiness. Ahhhhhhhh. Then all of the sudden, he started jumping for joy! After the video, I looked on eBay to try and get the card, but it was $750. Another version came when that happened. Yikes!! "That's past our budget Effie," my mom griped. "Okay, mom!"

In conclusion, the card was a viral sensation! What made me stop, and other people, too, was the unlisted leaf, of course!

Efrayim Rios, Grade 5

Students' "full essays" represent the final product that comes out of their process of brainstorming, kernelizing, and fleshing out their thinking and writing.

KERNEL ESSAYS BY STUDENTS
Can't We Just Get Along?

BABY BROTHER—AVI STOP!

1. I am speaking up because it needs to stop, Avi, you are too too cute.
2. We agreed to offer you, Avi, all the monster trucks if you stop.
3. We fear that you are cute, too cute for the mind to process.
4. Stop being cute so we can live better.

   Jakob Tawil, Grade 6

HOMEWORK

1. Right now, we have way too much homework.
2. We participate in class every day, take our tests, and are more than willing to work in groups on projects.
3. But, we're scared to talk to teachers about it because they think their class is the most important and they get insulted.
4. So, we are going to start talking to teachers more often, and we'd like teachers to let each other know when kids have a lot of homework for them.

   Jerry Tartlin, Grade 8

REVOLUTIONARY WAR

1. Currently, the patriots don't have a chance against the British, because we don't have enough soldiers.
2. We want to fight, but we can't fight like the British (in approaching lines) because we lose all our men in one battle.
3. But, we're scared to try something different, because it is not really humane.
4. So, if the British force us to keep fighting, we will have to resort to secretive and manipulative warfare.

   Gary Henley, Grade 8

CIVIL WAR

1. We are in grave danger of losing this fight, because we are sick and running out of supplies.
2. We just want the South to offer freedom to the slaves and keep trading with us.
3. But, we're scared that they are never going to give up on slavery, because it helps their economy.
4. So, you don't have to trade with us if you don't want to, but we will continue to fight for slavery, even if we all die trying.

   Patrick O'Neil, Grade 8

LABOR REFORMS

1. We are working way too many hours in a day under bad conditions.
2. We want to work and will work hard for our factories.
3. But, if we can't slow down, we won't be healthy enough to work anymore.
4. So, if we can't cut back on our hours, we will strike.

   Midge Erbach, Grade 8

Some lessons showcase student planning pages alongside the resulting student essay.

PLANNING PAGE + ESSAY
How Bullying Works

THE TRAIL OF TEARS

The Trail of Tears started in Georgia and it went on to Tennessee, Alabama, North Carolina and Florida. That's where they found the Native Americans. The person who decided this was President Jackson who passed the Indian Removal Act and they sent the Native Americans to the western states. The reason they did that was because we had territory in the south and we did not want them to be there.

The Americans demanded that the Native Americans leave their territories right away and the new Americans were really rude and forceful to the Native Americans. They didn't want them on their land and thought that the Native Americans were unfamiliar and alien people who occupied land that white settlers wanted. Some of the northern states also did not want the Native Americans in their land, like Illinois and Wisconsin. The bloody Black Hawk War in 1832 opened up millions of acres of land to white settlements.

In my opinion I didn't think the Native Americans liked that and they were going to refuse to leave but the Americans had that covered already and they told them, "If you guys refuse we will kill you," and I guess that the Native Americans were terrified of the Americans.

In my case I feel that the Native Americans reacted by thinking that this was not right. "We were here first and they can't take our land. We lived here longer than them and first come first serve." But I guess that didn't really matter.

Not a lot of Native Americans survived moving to the Indian Territories. By 1840, ten thousand had been driven off of their land in the southeastern states and forced to move across the Mississippi to Indian Territory. The government promised that their new land would be permanent and they would not kick them out of their homes, but the Indian country shrank and shrank as the whites moved in. By 1907 Oklahoma became a state and Indian Territory was gone for good.

In my opinion I wished we would have not done that. We could have learned more from the Native Americans.

Genesis Thomas, Grade 8

To Bert Shoopman, USNA Class of '53, and his beautiful wife Dixie,

with gratitude and deep affection

—GB

To Jessica, Jason, Midge and Mom, with love

—JK

Text Structures
From the Masters

50 Lessons and
Nonfiction Mentor Texts
to Help Students

WRITE THEIR WAY IN

&

READ THEIR WAY OUT

of Every Single
Imaginable Genre

Grades 6–10

Gretchen Bernabei
Jennifer Koppe

Foreword by Tom Newkirk

CL CORWIN
LITERACY

FOR INFORMATION:

Corwin

A SAGE Company

2455 Teller Road

Thousand Oaks, California 91320

(800) 233-9936

www.corwin.com

SAGE Publications Ltd.

1 Oliver's Yard

55 City Road

London EC1Y 1SP

United Kingdom

SAGE Publications India Pvt. Ltd.

B 1/I 1 Mohan Cooperative Industrial Area

Mathura Road, New Delhi 110 044

India

SAGE Publications Asia-Pacific Pte. Ltd.

3 Church Street

#10-04 Samsung Hub

Singapore 049483

Publisher: Lisa Luedeke

Editorial Development Manager: Julie Nemer

Assistant Editor: Emeli Warren

Editorial Assistant: Nicole Shade

Production Editor: Melanie Birdsall

Copy Editor: Jared Leighton

Typesetter: C&M Digitals (P) Ltd.

Proofreader: Alison Syring

Interior Designer: Gail Buschman

Cover Designer: Rose Storey

Marketing Manager: Rebecca Eaton

Printed in the United States of America

Library of Congress Cataloging-in-Publication Data

Names: Bernabei, Gretchen, author. | Koppe, Jennifer, author.

Title: Text structures from the masters : 50 lessons and nonfiction mentor texts to help students write their way in and read their way out of every single imaginable genre, grades 6–10 / Gretchen Bernabei, Jennifer Koppe ; foreword by Tom Newkirk.

Description: Thousand Oaks, California : Corwin, 2016.

Identifiers: LCCN 2015040187 | ISBN 978-1-5063-1126-5 (pbk. : alk. paper)

Subjects: LCSH: Composition (Language arts)—Study and teaching (Middle school) | Composition (Language arts)—Study and teaching (Secondary) | English language—Composition and exercises—Study and teaching (Middle school) | English language—Composition and exercises—Study and teaching (Secondary)

Classification: LCC LB1631 .B3926 2016 | DDC 372.62/3—dc23 LC record available at http://lccn.loc.gov/2015040187

This book is printed on acid-free paper.

SUSTAINABLE FORESTRY INITIATIVE

Certified Chain of Custody

Promoting Sustainable Forestry

www.sfiprogram.org

SFI-01268

SFI label applies to text stock

16 17 18 19 20 10 9 8 7 6 5 4 3 2 1

Contents

Note: *In this book, the lessons are organized chronologically, according to the publication date of the associated source document.*

Visit the companion website at
https://resources.corwin.com/textstructures
for downloadable planning pages, text structures,
and other resources.

Foreword

Structure is surely one of the unsexiest topics in writing instruction. Unlike *voice* or *image* or *dialogue*, which seem more connected to human experience, structure implies limitations, formats, a world of rules and restrictions. It is so . . . mandatory with its obligatory textual organs: the introduction (with thesis), its body paragraphs, and its conclusion, which cartoonist Sandra Boynton once portrayed as the heavy tail of a dinosaur that goes over ground that has already been covered. Sometimes additional rules are piled on: a fixed number of sentences for each paragraph or even templates for writing the sentences. No wonder exposition has such a bad name. It's like living your life tied to a chair.

The message we send to students, even in the Common Core era, is that argument is a matter of claim and evidence. This is true to a point, but there is more to do; we have more options than this. Essays in particular—real essays, that is—can go in a variety of directions as a writer explores a topic. Essays can take side routes, tell stories, invite in multiple voices, make comparisons, invoke humor, repeat with variations, describe problems (as I have done to start), and speculate on solutions (as I will). Writers really have a much bigger tool bag, or a *repertoire* of moves, that can keep a reader engaged.

That repertoire is what this book is about. Gretchen Bernabei breathes life into the concept of structure, bringing it closer to the idea of "form," as Kenneth Burke defined it: "an arousing and fulfillment of desire." Now that *is* sexy. Readers move through time, invited along by the writer who builds expectations, tension, and curiosity, which are resolved or satisfied in the writing. This is a form of seduction. Peter Elbow has put it dermatologically: Form is all about an itch that needs to be scratched.

The process is analogous to what we experience when we listen to music, another art form that moves through time. A while back, I watched a tape of Leonard Bernstein's Norton lecture from 1973, titled "The Unanswered Question." A good part of his lectures deal with tonality. He would play a chord or sequence of notes and demonstrate how three notes in sequence would create the desire for that fourth. And when it came, you felt a satisfaction. Form is embodied. We desire it and take pleasure in it, and when texts lack form, we can feel it. We become restless and fidgety; we get up and get a cup of coffee. The attraction, the pull, the forward motion of the text has been lost.

Gretchen Bernabei takes us beyond the conventional limiting, reductive, and frankly boring approach to teaching structure. She asks students to work inductively—to derive possible structures from examining mentor texts, and the more structures the better. Instead of that one format that students are given—you know the five-paragraph theme—she gives us fifty and doesn't pretend that this is a complete list. She changes the landscape students can work in from one of a poverty of options to one of wonderful excess. She shows us that as writers, we are playing a game with lots of moves.

Another key feature of her approach is to visually demonstrate these forms as a set of text boxes that progress forward. For example, we could see Martin Luther King Jr.'s "I Have a Dream" speech as this progression:

The unfulfilled promise of freedom and dignity to all Americans.	Actions we must take in the present to achieve this goal.	A vision of the future.

Gretchen gives us something like an x-ray device for looking at texts, one that allows us to see and later emulate the forward movement of exemplary texts. She invites students to represent these core structures in short kernels that represent the major moves of the essay or argument.

Almost 30 years ago, during a blessed year on the English faculty at the University of Hawaii, I wrote a long essay on the essay, trying to "reclaim" it as a flexible instrument of thought. I remember working on it in my office on early Sunday mornings before we would take our kids to the beach. In one sentence, I wrote that essays tracked "the movement of the mind." I can't say that I put a lot of thought into that sentence; it seemed to fit.

I could not have predicted how Gretchen Bernabei, in this and her earlier books, could illuminate the teaching potential of that simple idea—how she would create strategies I could not have imagined when I wrote that sentence. I feel honored to have played a part in her ongoing exploration of the structure and possibilities of exposition.

—Tom Newkirk
University of New Hampshire, Emeritus

Acknowledgments

Thank you to our teaching visionaries in publishing, Lisa Luedeke and Maura Sullivan. We're grateful for your trust, your leadership, and your friendship. You're funny, too. And to our Corwin team, our sincere gratitude: Melanie Birdsall, Emeli Warren, Julie Nemer, Gail Buschman, Rose Storey, and our new and already-cherished friend, Rebecca Eaton.

Warmest gratitude to the following teachers who helped us try out ideas and gather samples and permission forms and who offered unflagging enthusiasm: Serena Stasa, Kelley Burnett, Iris Estrada, Nancy Gibson, Shelby Strebeck, Erica Goforth, Kip Nettles, Cynthia Labutta, Brittney Longacre, Stephanie Biggs-Scribner, Rachel Rhodes, Kristina Bertrand, Daina Land, Anne Doyle, Jennifer Culver, Rita Lasuzzo, Leigh Ballard, Shelley Fisette, Kasey L. Turner, Leslie Hopkins-Huntress, Elizabeth Perez, Susie Youngblood, Stephanie Cash, Richard Franco, Kat Roark, Heather Farmer Dean, Sarah Wiley, Linda Steitle, Brianna Johnson, Sheila Richards, Adrian Viccellio, and Peggy Williams.

To Kathryn Davis and Tracy Smith and the rest of the staff at our school, the Eleanor Kolitz Hebrew Language Academy, thank you for your encouragement and support and for your advice.

Thank you to our middle school students, who were willing to experiment, analyze, compose, and persist, even when they got tired. You have inspired us, challenged us, and richly entertained us, and we will not forget you.

Thank you to Judi Reimer, both our anchor and fresh breeze. And thank you, Dave and Allison, for doing without her for so many hours.

For Gretchen's buds: Kimberly Sue Grauer, Mary Sue Shoopman King, Tim Martindell, Patricia Gray, Dottie Hall, Tracy Winstead, Marian Jones, Chris Goode, Sally Aguirre; and family, Johnny, Matilde, and Julian.

For Jennifer's friends: Katherine Campbell, Dawn Harris, Sigal Russo, Sara Locke, and Lori Sindewald.

Finally, our most humble gratitude to Susan Diaz of NEISD. This book rings with voices you brought to us.

Introduction

"Historical documents are boring."

"School writing won't actually benefit my personal life."

If your students think either of these things, then you need this book.

Often, students think that pieces of writing aren't connected to anything else, to any other human voices. But in truth, all public writing is part of a bigger conversation.

Consider this idea from Thomas Newkirk (2014):

> All important decisions and debates are located in time. Key events precede any act of rhetoric; indeed, they create the need for speaking (or writing); they provoke it. Something has happened (or not happened), something has been said (or not said), some problem is unmet, some calamity has occurred. There is then a case to be made for a kind of response—a plan of action, a new understanding of the situation, a challenge to accepted wisdom. Then often, there is a look to the future—"so what"—what advantage do we gain by this change, this proposal, this alteration (often a place for appeals to emotion, hope, vision)? Where do we go from here? As I state it here, it sounds formulaic, but in great speeches, like the one Martin Luther King gave just before his assassination, the "Moutaintop" speech, it can be profoundly uplifting. It follows the arc of human desire. (p. 115)

Newkirk also describes "an itch."

> An itch to say something.
> To find out something.
> To change something.
> To explain something.

Below, consider the different desires to express something.

THE ITCH	
To say, "I feel your pain"	To say, "We're both wrong; we're both right"
To pick up the pieces	To explain a controversial decision
To give a pep talk	To give parting advice to your replacement
To make a team promise	To say "Bon voyage"
To comfort a friend in pain	To craft a problem-solution message
To say "No, thank you"	To reflect at a milestone moment

These are common, universal, and human messages. Each has its own special kind of itch or desire; each requires its own distinct kind of handling. They are all messages from human beings to other human beings. And they don't really look like the kinds of messages students expect to read at school, nor to write at school. They are, instead, the kinds of messages that we struggle to actually deliver to other people in real life.

Now consider the purposes of the following historical documents:

HISTORICAL DOCUMENT	THE ITCH
JFK's Berlin speech	To say, "I feel your pain."
FDR's Pearl Harbor message	To pick up the pieces
JFK's inaugural address	To give a pep talk
Mayflower Compact	To make a team promise
Henry James letter	To comfort a friend in pain
Indians of the Six Nations letter	To say, "No, thank you."
Lincoln's second inaugural address	To say, "We're both wrong; we're both right"
Emancipation Proclamation	To explain a controversial decision
MacArthur's farewell speech	To give parting advice to your replacement
Scott Carpenter's letter from dad	To say "Bon voyage"
Declaration of Independence	To craft a problem-solution message
Gettysburg Address	To reflect at a milestone moment

In this book you will find 50 mentor texts, drawn from early American history through the present, with accompanying lessons.

You'll notice that we organized the lessons chronologically, by date of the historical piece.

Each lesson comes with a planning sheet and several examples of student writing. On the planning sheet, you'll find the text structure of the historical document, a place for students to brainstorm topics for their own essays, and space to write their kernel essays.

What is a *kernel essay*? A kernel essay is created using a text structure from another piece of writing, like the one on the planning page below. This particular structure is from JFK's inaugural address, but a kernel essay can be created from *any* text structure. First, students brainstorm their own topics to use with the structure. Then, they use the structure to guide them as they write one sentence for each box in the structure. The structure, when imitated, provides students with a kernel of an essay.

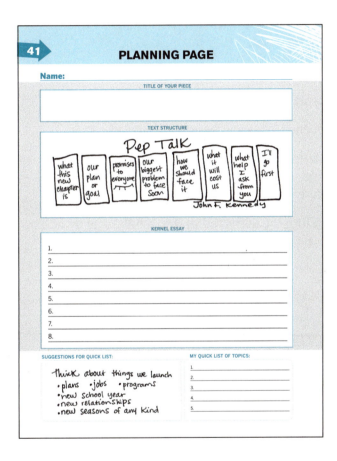

Q: What am I supposed to do with these lessons?

A: There are a couple of different approaches. The lessons can be used for a writing activity or as a reading activity.

Below are examples of the two different processes.

1. It's a writing activity.

Use the text structure, and write your own kernel essay.

The students can use the quick lists and text structures on the planning page to write about their own lives, topics that they're interested in exploring, or topics that you're currently studying as a class.

Procedure:

- Have students create a quick list from their own lives.

- Have them choose a topic from the quick list.

- Using the text structure on the planning page as a guide, have them try writing a kernel essay about their topic by writing *one sentence for each box of the text structure.*

- Have them turn the kernel essay into a full essay by adding details to the kernel sentences (which will become paragraphs).

Here's an example:

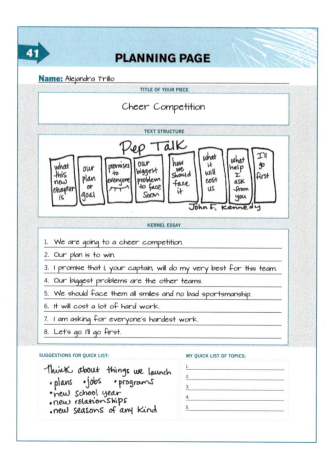

In her kernel essay, Alejandra addresses her cheer team with a pep talk. She writes one sentence for each step in the text structure. Every student can write kernel essays, from our most sophisticated to our most struggling writers. All they need is a structure, and the world offers structures for any occasion. Imagine knowing that you took the same steps taken by John Fitzgerald Kennedy when he became president. And imagine knowing that your message was no less real.

Kernel essays are a useful step for kids who write well, and for struggling students (and their teachers), kernel essays are practically magic. Add some details, and the sentences become paragraphs. The kernel becomes an essay.

Soon, students ask permission to change the words in the text structure slightly, to rearrange the boxes, or to delete a box that doesn't work with their content. As soon as these questions emerge, you can breathe well and know that the students are learning to use a structure, not be controlled by it. And when they ask to invent their own structures, it's time for celebration.

> When students ask to invent their own structures, it's time for celebration.

Whether the student stops at the kernel essay stage or develops the kernel essay into a full-blown essay, the exercise is worthwhile as a composing experience, giving him or her practice at the mental gymnastics of filling someone else's form with his or her own content, with no special tools.

They don't even need the "special paper" but can write kernel essays on regular paper, as this student did.

2. It's a reading exercise.

Kernelize the original document.

Use the text structure to kernelize the historical document, and write the kernel essay of the document.

Here is how. First, they read the text structure. Next, they read the document, looking for the parts of the text structure. For instance, if they are preparing to read JFK's inaugural address, it will help them to read the text structure first.

This will give students an idea of the parts of JFK's speech, an idea of what to look for.

Next, they read the document, navigating by using the text structure as a kind of map. Students chunk the text; that is, they circle the parts of the document, underlining words or phrases that clue them to the chunk of text and how it relates to the structure.

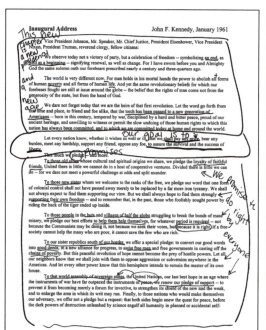
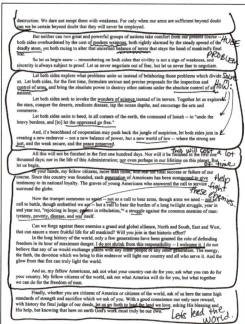

When students use the text structure to find the parts, they are ready to write summary sentences for each of the parts, as Alejandra did on the next page.

PLANNING PAGE

41

Name: Alejandra Trillo

TITLE OF YOUR PIECE

John F. Kennedy - Inaugural Address

TEXT STRUCTURE

Pep Talk

| what this new chapter is | our plan or goal | promises to everyone | our biggest problem to face soon | how we should face it | what it will cost us | what help I ask from you | I'll go first |

John F. Kennedy

KERNEL ESSAY

1. This is a start of a new world & presidency.
2. Our goal is to assure the survival and success of liberty.
3. We promise loyalty and friendliness to our allies.
4. Some people don't want peace.
5. We should face it calmly.
6. It will cause some burdens.
7. I'm asking our citizens for help.
8. Let's go.

SUGGESTIONS FOR QUICK LIST:

Think about things we launch
• plans • jobs • programs
• new school year
• new relationships
• new seasons of any kind

MY QUICK LIST OF TOPICS:

1. _____
2. _____
3. _____
4. _____
5. _____

This process is called *kernelizing* the text, or converting the text to a *kernel essay*, with one summary sentence per box in the text structure.

When students kernelize difficult texts, they find it simple to kernelize easier texts. They actually begin to read with author's steps in mind.

But we have yet another way that we like to use it.

Use the kernel essay before reading the original document.

We have discovered something wonderful. When we ask students to use the text structures from these documents *before* reading the original document—to write their own experiences first—they have a different understanding when they do turn to read the original document. Some students have described the experience as "stepping into the shoes" of that other person, the author. And as Thomas Newkirk might say, to feel his or her "itch."

They read more deeply.

They relate more empathically.

They write more powerfully.

And in experiencing these compelling, surprising human messages from notable Americans, they fall in love with our country even more.

Reference

Newkirk, T. N. (2014). *Minds made for stories: How we really read and write informational and persuasive texts*. Portsmouth, NH: Heinemann.

Lessons

PLANNING PAGE

Name: _____

TITLE OF YOUR PIECE

TEXT STRUCTURE

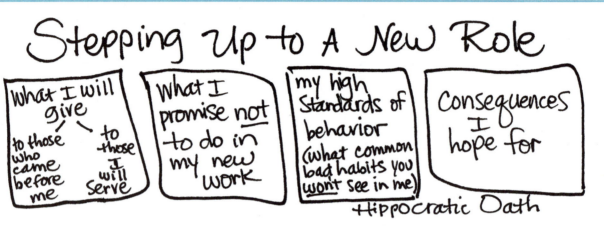

KERNEL ESSAY

1. _____

2. _____

3. _____

4. _____

_____

SUGGESTIONS FOR QUICK LIST:

New roles, new responsibility
Now I'm a ___.
- babysitter
- cook
- teenager
- driver
- athlete
- sister
- leader
- fourth grader

MY QUICK LIST OF TOPICS:

1. _____

2. _____

3. _____

4. _____

5. _____

Hippocratic Oath

I swear by Apollo the physician, and Aesculapius the surgeon, likewise Hygeia and Panacea, and call all the gods and goddesses to witness, that I will observe and keep this underwritten oath, to the utmost of my power and judgment.

I will reverence my master who taught me the art. Equally with my parents, will I allow him things necessary for his support, and will consider his sons as brothers. I will teach them my art without reward or agreement; and I will impart all my acquirement, instructions, and whatever I know, to my master's children, as to my own; and likewise to all my pupils, who shall bind and tie themselves by a professional oath, but to none else.

With regard to healing the sick, I will devise and order for them the best diet, according to my judgment and means; and I will take care that they suffer no hurt or damage.

Nor shall any man's entreaty prevail upon me to administer poison to anyone; neither will I counsel any man to do so. Moreover, I will get no sort of medicine to any pregnant woman, with a view to destroy the child.

Further, I will comport myself and use my knowledge in a godly manner.

I will not cut for the stone, but will commit that affair entirely to the surgeons.

Whatsoever house I may enter, my visit shall be for the convenience and advantage of the patient; and I will willingly refrain from doing any injury or wrong from falsehood, and (in an especial manner) from acts of an amorous nature, whatever may be the rank of those who it may be my duty to cure, whether mistress or servant, bond or free.

Whatever, in the course of my practice, I may see or hear (even when not invited), whatever I may happen to obtain knowledge of, if it be not proper to repeat it, I will keep sacred and secret within my own breast.

If I faithfully observe this oath, may I thrive and prosper in my fortune and profession, and live in the estimation of posterity; or on breach thereof, may the reverse be my fate!

PLANNING PAGE + ESSAY
Stepping Up to a New Role

JOHNSONITE OATH: TO BE A JAGUAR

I swear by my family, all members that I will work tirelessly in these years to fulfill the path you have set me on. It is my greatest desire to uphold my name, and as God is my witness I will recall and keep this oath to protect and serve my fellow students.

I will revere my fellow students who similarly work to uphold the honor of what it means to be a Jaguar. Likewise with my peers, I will persevere to demonstrate my resolve and determination in learning and comprehending the lessons our teachers and mentors intend to relay.

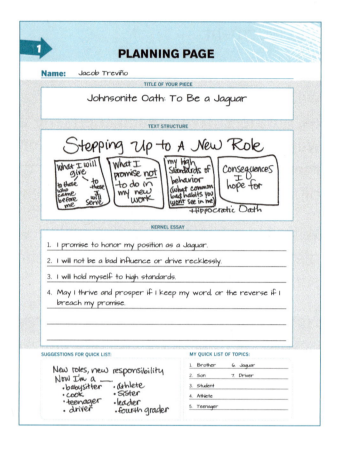

Additionally, I will not guide or instruct this institution's posterity in methods that could harm the valuable learning environment surrounding us. Moreover, I will put no other individuals in danger while operating a motor vehicle. This right was not afforded to me for the purpose of endangering others, as it is a responsibility of a student to do no harm.

Any damage I could inflict I should hope would return upon me in the event that I fail to uphold this promise. I cannot take lightly the gravity of my situation. I have been set up to fail, and it is my duty to overcome.

Henceforth I swear under God's watchful eye and those of my fellow students that I will work unerringly and with my utmost power to maintain the title of Jaguar, and all honors associated with it. "If I faithfully observe this oath, may I thrive and prosper in my fortune and profession, and live in the estimation of posterity; or on breach thereof, may the reverse be my fate!"

Jacob Treviño, Grade 9

PLANNING PAGE + ESSAY
Stepping Up to a New Role

FINALLY THIRTEEN

Given these past twelve years of my life, I think it's time to grow up and see the world in a broader perspective. I will try my best to seek opportunities that favor in my best interest. Thus being my number one intention for the next six years.

As the years move on I will keep myself out of dangerous situations and stand up for what I believe is right. I am entitled to my own opinions and I will not be afraid to share my thoughts, as most matured teenagers do already. Now that I am in the older division of age I will help the lower ages despite their own immaturities getting in the way. To those I will serve of the younger ages, I can show them the routes of the crazy life that is to come for them.

These new years are ahead and at points I may feel in over my head. I promise not to be disrespectful to my peers and show them in uncaring ways. I will not impart on using narcotics or alcohol under any influence whatsoever. May I not take part in the teenage flow of disrespecting my parents who have helped me travel this far in my journey of teenage years. If my plans do not go the way I plan, I hope to be treated like any other teenager. I want to have respect and a decent consequence, because yes, I am finally thirteen.

Connie Kickirillo, Grade 9

PLANNING PAGE

Name: _____

TITLE OF YOUR PIECE

TEXT STRUCTURE

Can't We Just Get Along?

| my reason for speaking up right now | We offer you cooperation in these ways ⌃ | But we fear you because... | What you must do so that we can live peacefully |

Chief Powhatan

KERNEL ESSAY

1. _____

2. _____

3. _____

4. _____

_____

_____

SUGGESTIONS FOR QUICK LIST:

Constant, daily conflicts
• someone "under our skin"
• advocating for ourselves
• Establishing ground rules

MY QUICK LIST OF TOPICS:

1. _____
2. _____
3. _____
4. _____
5. _____

Speech to Captain John Smith   **Chief Powhatan, 1609**

Powhatan, an Algonquin leader, delivered this stirring speech to John Smith, the leader of the Virginia Colony.

I am now grown old, and must soon die; and the succession must descend, in order, to my brothers, *Opitchapan, Opekankanough*, and *Ca-tataugh*, and then to my two sisters, and their two daughters. I wish their experience was equal to mine; and that your love to us might not be less than ours to you. Why should you take by force that from us which you can have by love? Why should you destroy us, who have provided you with food? What can you get by war? We can hide our provisions, and fly into the woods; and then you must consequently famish by wronging your friends. What is the cause of your jealousy? You see us unarmed, and willing to supply your wants, if you will come in a friendly manner, and not with swords and guns, as to invade an enemy. I am not so simple, as not to know it is better to eat good meat, lie well, and sleep quietly with my women and children; to laugh and be merry with the English; and, being their friend, to have copper, hatchets, and whatever else I want, than to fly from all, to lie cold in the woods, feed upon acorns, roots, and such trash, and to be so hunted, that I cannot rest, eat, or sleep. In such circumstances, my men must watch, and if a twig should but break, all would cry out, "*Here comes Capt. Smith*"; and so, in this miserable manner, to end my miserable life; and, Capt. Smith, this *might* be soon your fate too, through your rashness and unadvisedness. I, therefore, exhort you to peaceable councils; and, above all, I insist that the guns and swords, the cause of all our jealousy and uneasiness, be removed and sent away.

KERNEL ESSAYS BY STUDENTS
Can't We Just Get Along?

1. I don't like being abandoned but you won't listen.
2. I'll be nice, do what you ask and I won't get mad at you.
3. I get mad because you won't listen to my request.
4. All I want is for you to wait for me.

Kaitlyn Postell, Grade 6

_____

FROM TITANIA TO OBERON

1. I'm amazed at all the thunder and lightning, and I don't think we should be fighting.
2. You're my Oberon, and you may go with us to sing our fairy songs, to eat fairy food, and to revel through the night.
3. But you're so jealous and irrational about that little boy I have! It makes you crazy.
4. So give it up, and enjoy looking at him while you're with me. Ok?

Anna Surach, Grade 9

_____

FROM AGATHA TO SOPHIA, FROM
THE SCHOOL FOR GOOD AND EVIL

1. You're getting more and more obsessed with revenge.
2. I am trying to do whatever it takes to get us both out of here.
3. But you're not even looking like yourself any more.
4. Can you please see some reason here, and abandon your revenge plots so that we can move ahead?

Anael Weinstein, Grade 7

FROM MARY TO COLIN,
FROM *THE SECRET GARDEN*

1. You're so sour, and you're acting like a baby.
2. I don't even have to come to your room, or tell you about what Dickon and I are doing every day, but I do.
3. But you are the "young master" of this house, and you have power over the servants, so tantrums can get us in trouble.
4. You have to stop screaming, stop being so spoiled, and listen to our plan.

Kim Berber, Grade 5

_____

SORTING OUT THE BEDROOM

1. We are still arguing about where things go in our bedroom.
2. We offered to cooperate with the beds and dressers.
3. But we are worried, because you want our clothes in the same closet.
4. So, the only way I'll share a closet is if we each get a side, and she's not allowed to borrow my stuff.

Jenny Hopkins, Grade 12

_____

RECESS

1. Right now, there are too many older kids at recess.
2. We want the older kids to have time outside to play.
3. But we are scared of the older kids because they throw balls too hard and take our gaga and basketball areas when they are at recess.
4. So, if you allow the big kids time outside, please tell them to give the elementary kids at least one play area that they don't take over and to be careful throwing balls.

Katy Campbell, Grade 4

KERNEL ESSAYS BY STUDENTS
Can't We Just Get Along?

BABY BROTHER—AVI STOP!

1. I am speaking up because it needs to stop, Avi, you are too too cute.
2. We agreed to offer you, Avi, all the monster trucks if you stop.
3. We fear that you are cute, too cute for the mind to process.
4. Stop being cute so we can live better.

Jakob Tawil, Grade 6

HOMEWORK

1. Right now, we have way too much homework.
2. We participate in class every day, take our tests, and are more than willing to work in groups on projects.
3. But, we're scared to talk to teachers about it because they think their class is the most important and they get insulted.
4. So, we are going to start talking to teachers more often, and we'd like teachers to let each other know when kids have a lot of homework for them.

Jerry Tartlin, Grade 8

REVOLUTIONARY WAR

1. Currently, the patriots don't have a chance against the British, because we don't have enough soldiers.
2. We want to fight, but we can't fight like the British (in approaching lines) because we lose all our men in one battle.
3. But, we're scared to try something different, because it is not really humane.
4. So, if the British force us to keep fighting, we will have to resort to secretive and manipulative warfare.

Gary Henley, Grade 8

CIVIL WAR

1. We are in grave danger of losing this fight, because we are sick and running out of supplies.
2. We just want the South to offer freedom to the slaves and keep trading with us.
3. But, we're scared that they are never going to give up on slavery, because it helps their economy.
4. So, you don't have to trade with us if you don't want to, but we will continue to fight for slavery, even if we all die trying.

Patrick O'Neil, Grade 8

LABOR REFORMS

1. We are working way too many hours in a day under bad conditions.
2. We want to work and will work hard for our factories.
3. But, if we can't slow down, we won't be healthy enough to work anymore.
4. So, if we can't cut back on our hours, we will strike.

Midge Erbach, Grade 8

PLANNING PAGE

Name:

TITLE OF YOUR PIECE

TEXT STRUCTURE

Team Promise

| what group we are | what we are doing | what we promise to each other | how we are signing and sealing our promise |

Mayflower Compact

KERNEL ESSAY

1. _____

2. _____

3. _____

4. _____

   _____

SUGGESTIONS FOR QUICK LIST:

What groups do you belong to?
What goals do you share?
- School groups
- Sports teams
- family groups
- friend groups

MY QUICK LIST OF TOPICS:

1. _____
2. _____
3. _____
4. _____
5. _____

Mayflower Compact   November 11, 1620

In the name of God, Amen.

We, whose names are underwritten, the loyal subjects of our dread Sovereigne Lord, King James, by the grace of God, of Great Britaine, France and Ireland king, defender of the faith, etc. having undertaken, for the glory of God, and advancement of the Christian faith, and honour of our king and country, a voyage to plant the first colony in the Northerne parts of Virginia, doe by these presents solemnly and mutually in the presence of God and one of another, covenant and combine ourselves together into a civill body politick, for our better ordering and preservation, and furtherance of the ends aforesaid; and by virtue hereof to enacte, constitute, and frame such just and equal laws, ordinances, acts, constitutions and offices, from time to time, as shall be thought most meete and convenient for the generall good of the Colonie unto which we promise all due submission and obedience.

In witness whereof we have hereunder subscribed our names at Cape-Cod the 11 of November, in the year of the raigne of our sovereigne lord, King James, of England, France and Ireland, the eighteenth, and of Scotland the fiftie-fourth. Anno Dom. 1620.

John Carver	Edward Tilley	Degory Priest
William Bradford	John Tilley	Thomas Williams
Edward Winslow	Francis Cooke	Gilbert Winslow
William Brewster	Thomas Rogers	Edmund Margeson
Issac Allerton	Thomas Tinker	Peter Browne
Myles Standish	John Rigdale	Richard Britteridge
John Alden	Edward Fuller	George Soule
Samuel Fuller	John Turner	Richard Clarke
Christopher Martin	Francis Eaton	Richard Gardiner
William Mullins	James Chilton	John Allerton
William White	John Crackston	Thomas English
Richard Warren	John Billington	Edward Dotey
John Howland	Moses Fletcher	Edward Leister
Stephen Hopkins	John Goodman	

PLANNING PAGE + ESSAY
Team Promise

THE STUDENT COMPACT

In the name of God, please save us all.

We, the students of the school, the "disruptive" members under our dreaded totalitarian ruler Patrick Aguillon, principal of North Central High School, have begun, for our families, future, and education, a long and arduous journey to gain a high school education, (I sure hope God is with us all,) and suffer together under one roof

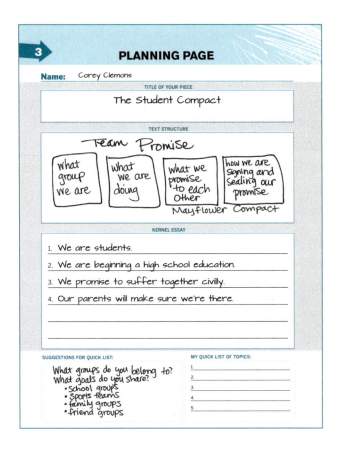

for hours on end to "better" ourselves, and learn to behave civilly as adults, and follow all rules given to us (to some extent) in order for <u>everybody</u> to learn for the next four years.

Our parents have (without much of our consent) enrolled us at this school, with our education beginning the 25th of August, in the year of the rule of our totalitarian Dictator, Principal Patrick Aguillon, of North Central High School, 2014.

Corey Clemons, Grade 9

KERNEL ESSAYS BY STUDENTS
Team Promise

1. We are the Churchill Pep Squad team.
2. We are in the middle of training for camp.
3. We promise to try our best to have fun.
4. We are sealing this promise with a contract.

Alejandra Trillo, Grade 8

———————

1. I'm in a group of three friends, Potato (Karissa), Maddy, and Banana (Me).
2. Our friendship and good teamwork have caused us to join brains in a teach-the-class history project.
3. We have promised ourselves to do our homework of reading 8 pages of our history book.
4. Maddy has made a lovely masterpiece portrait of my face and in the back we have made a contract that we all signed to make sure we do our homework or else never draw again.

Deniff Lara, Grade 7

———————

1. We are the 7th grade group.
2. We are in the middle of laughing and having fun.
3. We promise to be friends and laugh a lot.
4. We are signing and sealing our promises by staying close and never letting go.

Jessicalynn Jackson, Grade 7

1. I am in Youth Group.
2. We are in the middle of planning to go to South Padre in the spring or summer and raise a lot of money.
3. We promise to raise money and not keep the money.
4. We sealed our promise by signing a paper.

Juliette Urrutia, Grade 8

———————

1. We are a group of HCYO, Hill Country Youth Orchestra.
2. We are now in the middle of practicing for our spring performance.
3. We (should) promise to each other that we will practice our parts on our free time and not in class.
4. We put our instruments in one hand and the other hand over our hearts, and pledge the pledge we have agreed to.

Nina De La Torre, Grade 8

PLANNING PAGE

Name: _____

TITLE OF YOUR PIECE

TEXT STRUCTURE

Humble Request for Help

| Here is my view | Here is what we have accomplished | Here are ways we have made progress | But these things are causing problems | So here is what I wish you would do | Humble thanks |

E.W. - Plymouth Plantations

KERNEL ESSAY

1. _____
2. _____
3. _____
4. _____
5. _____
6. _____

SUGGESTIONS FOR QUICK LIST:

From someone on the front lines to one of the bosses
- worker to boss
- child to parent
- performer to agent
- voter to elected representative

MY QUICK LIST OF TOPICS:

1. _____
2. _____
3. _____
4. _____
5. _____

A true Relation of things very re-markable at the Plantation of Plymouth in New-England since their first arrival.

TO ALL WELL-WILLERS AND FURTHERERS OF Plantations in New-England: especially to such as ever have or desire to assist the people of Plymouth in their just pro-ceedings, Grace, and Peace, be multiplied.

Right Honorable and Worshipful Gentlemen, or whatsoever:

Since it hath pleased God to stir you up to be instruments of his glory, in so honorable an enterprise as the enlarging of his Majesty's Dominions, by planting his loyal subjects in so healthful and hopeful a country as New England is; where the Church of God being seated in sincerity, there is no less hope of converting the Heathen of their evil ways, and converting them to the true knowledge and worship of the living God, and so consequently the salvation of their souls by the merits of Jesus Christ, then elsewhere though it be much talked on, and lightly or lamely prosecuted. I therefore think it but my duty to offer the view of our proceedings to your worthy considerations, having to that end composed them together thus briefly as you see; wherein to your great encouragement, you may behold the good providence of God working with you in our preservation from so many dangerous plots and treacheries, as have been intended against us; as also in giving his blessing so powerfully upon the weak means we had, enabling us with health and ability beyond expectation, in our greatest scarcities, and possessing the hearts of the savages with astonishment and fear of us, whereas if God had let them loose, they might easily have swallowed us up, scarce being an handful in comparison of those forces they might have gathered together against us, which now by God's blessing will be more hard and difficult, in regard our number of men is increased, our town better fortified, and our store better victualed. Blessed therefore be his name, that hath done so great things for us, and hath wrought so great a change amongst us.

Accept I pray you my weak endeavors, pardon my unskillfulness, and bear with my plainness in the things I have handled. Be not discouraged by our former necessities, but rather encouraged with us, hoping that as God hath wrought with us in our beginning of this worthy Work, undertaken in his name and fear, so he will by us accomplish the same to his glory and our comfort, if we neglect not the means. I confess it hath not been much less chargeable to some of you, then hard and difficult to us, that have endured the brunt of the barrel, and yet small profits returned; only by God's mercy we are safely seated, housed, and fortified, by which means a great step is made unto gain, and a more direct course taken for the same, then if at first we had rashly and covetously fallen upon it.

Indeed, three things are the overthrow and bane (as I may term it) of plantations:

1. The vain expectation of present profit, which too too commonly taketh a principal seat in the heart and affections though God's glory, etc., is preferred before it in the mouth with protestation.

2. Ambition in their Governors and Commanders, seeking only to make themselves great, and slaves of all that are under them, to maintain a transitory base honor in themselves, which God oft punisheth with contempt.

3. The carelessness of those that send over supplies of men unto them, not caring how they be qualified: so that oft times they are rather the Image of Men endued with bestial, yea, diabolical affections, then the Image of God, endured with reason, understanding, and holiness. I pray God I speak not these things experimentally, by way of complaint of our own condition, but having great cause on the contrary part to be thankful to God for his mercies towards us: but rather, if there be any too desirous of gain, to entreat them to moderate their affections, and consider that no man expecteth fruit before the tree be grown; advising all men, that as they tender their own welfare so to make choice of such to maintain and govern their affairs, as are approved not to be seekers of themselves, but the common good of all for whom they are employed; and beseeching such as have the care of transporting men for the supply and furnishing of plantations, to be truly careful in sending such as may further and not hinder so good an action. There is no godly honest man, but will be helpful in his kind, and adorn his profession with an upright life and conversation, which Doctrine of manners ought first to be preached by giving good example to the poor savage heathens amongst whom they live. On the contrary part, what great offense hath been given by many profane men who being but seeming Christians, have made Christ and Christianity stink in the nostrils of the poor infidels, and so laid a stumbling block before them: but we be to them by whom such offenses come.

These things I offer to your Christian considerations, beseeching you to make a good construction of my simple meaning, and take in good part this ensuing relation, dedicating myself and it evermore unto your service: beseeching God to crown our Christian and faithful endeavors with his blessings temporal and eternal.

Yours in this service,
ever to be commanded:

E.W.

KERNEL ESSAYS BY STUDENTS
Humble Request for Help

1. I see the world being destroyed.
2. We have tried to save the oxygen.
3. We have stopped cutting down as <u>many</u> trees.
4. But people filled with greed are causing problems.
5. I wish we'd stop destroying forests.

Lauren Messer, Grade 7

TOPIC: WRITTEN AS GUY MONTAG, CHARACTER FROM THE NOVEL *FAHRENHEIT 451*

1. Books shouldn't be burned.
2. I've managed to save a few of them.
3. I'm also understanding it more every day.
4. But people are starting to notice.
5. I need help to make our ways change.
6. Thank you to everyone who helps.

Miriam Stein, Grade 7

PLANNING PAGE

Name: _____

TITLE OF YOUR PIECE

TEXT STRUCTURE

No, thank you

| what you have offered | but here is a difference between us | How this Same offer has backfired on me in the Past | So... no thank you | my counter-offer |

Indians of the Six Nations

KERNEL ESSAY

1. _____

2. _____

3. _____

4. _____

5. _____

_____

SUGGESTIONS FOR QUICK LIST:

Any recommendation or offer that you don't want
- unwanted gifts
- new/healthy/foreign food
- job offers • books • movies

MY QUICK LIST OF TOPICS:

1. ....
2. ....
3. ....
4. ....
5. ....

Letter to William and Mary College

The Indians of the Six Nations, 1744

In 1744, the Indians of the Six Nations sent this bold letter to the College of William and Mary, responding to an invitation from the college to send their men to the college for a "proper" education.

Sirs,

We know that you highly esteem the kind of learning taught in Colleges, and that the Maintenance of our young Men, while with you, would be very expensive to you. We are convinc'd, therefore, that you mean to do us Good by your Proposal; and we thank you heartily. But you, who are wise, must know that different Nations have different Conceptions of things; and you will therefore not take it amiss, if our Ideas of this kind of Education happen not to be the same with yours. We have had some Experience of it. Several of our Young People were formerly brought up at the Colleges of the Northern Provinces; they were instructed in all your Sciences; but, when they came back to us, they were bad Runners, ignorant of every means of living in the Woods, unable to bear either Cold or Hunger, knew neither how to build a Cabin, take a Deer, or kill an Enemy, spoke our Language imperfectly, were therefore neither fit for Hunters, Warriors, nor Counsellors; they were totally good for nothing. We are, however, not the less oblig'd by your kind Offer, tho' we decline accepting it; and, to show our grateful Sense of it, if the Gentlemen of Virginia will send us a Dozen of their Sons, we will take care of their Education; instruct them in all we know, and make Men of them.

COMPLETED PLANNING PAGE
No, Thank You

Name: Josh Levin

TITLE OF YOUR PIECE

Nighttime Roof

TEXT STRUCTURE

No, Thank You

| what you have offered | but here is a difference between us | How this same offer has backfired on me in the past | So... no thank you | my counter-offer |

Indians of the Six Nations

KERNEL ESSAY

1. My friend offered to get on my roof at night.

2. I'm afraid of heights and you're not.

3. I got on his roof and fell off.

4. I don't want to, please.

5. We can go inside and play my Xbox instead?

SUGGESTIONS FOR QUICK LIST:

Any recommendation or offer that you don't want
- unwanted gifts
- new/healthy/foreign food
- job offers • books • movies

MY QUICK LIST OF TOPICS:

1.
2.
3.
4.
5.

KERNEL ESSAYS BY STUDENTS

No, Thank You

1. My cousin gave me a $50 gift card and offered to get me a Victoria's Secret gift card.
2. I don't like Victoria's Secret.
3. This reminds me of the time my aunt got me a Make-Your-Own Bracelet kit.
4. I told her No, Thank You and she laughed.
5. I think that she should skip that idea.

Zoe Falk, Grade 6

---

1. My friend offered me to hide out in the car.
2. You might like doing that, I don't.
3. It would backfire because my mom would yell at me.
4. So I said "NO, I'm gonna get in trouble!"
5. I said, "How about you go in my car?"

Kandice Hernandez, Grade 6

---

1. You asked if I'll buy camping equipment with you.
2. But I hate camping.
3. Last time I did that, eight tents fell on me.
4. So No, thank you.
5. Let's buy clothes instead.

Maggie Davis, Grade 8

PLANNING PAGE

Name: _____

TITLE OF YOUR PIECE

```



```

TEXT STRUCTURE

Lighting a Fire Under a Procrastinator

| You don't want to —, but I do. | We both want —, and your way of getting it is… | But my observations have shown me… | What we've tried that hasn't worked | Here are our assets/ strengths right now… | What is happening while we do nothing | Let's go. |

Patrick Henry

KERNEL ESSAY

1. _____

2. _____

3. _____

4. _____

5. _____

6. _____

7. _____

SUGGESTIONS FOR QUICK LIST:

When have you had an urge to act? When have you had an urge for change?
- resolutions
- new habits
- taking bold steps
- changing your appearance

MY QUICK LIST OF TOPICS:

1. _____
2. _____
3. _____
4. _____
5. _____

Speech

Delivered March 23 at St. John's Church, Richmond, Virginia

MR. PRESIDENT: No man thinks more highly than I do of the patriotism, as well as abilities, of the very worthy gentlemen who have just addressed the House. But different men often see the same subject in different lights; and, therefore, I hope it will not be thought disrespectful to those gentlemen if, entertaining as I do, opinions of a character very opposite to theirs, I shall speak forth my sentiments freely, and without reserve. This is no time for ceremony. The question before the House is one of awful moment to this country. For my own part, I consider it as nothing less than a question of freedom or slavery; and in proportion to the magnitude of the subject ought to be the freedom of the debate. It is only in this way that we can hope to arrive at truth, and fulfill the great responsibility which we hold to God and our country. Should I keep back my opinions at such a time, through fear of giving offence, I should consider myself as guilty of treason towards my country, and of an act of disloyalty toward the majesty of heaven, which I revere above all earthly kings.

Mr. President, it is natural to man to indulge in the illusions of hope. We are apt to shut our eyes against a painful truth, and listen to the song of that siren till she transforms us into beasts. Is this the part of wise men, engaged in a great and arduous struggle for liberty? Are we disposed to be of the number of those who, having eyes, see not, and, having ears, hear not, the things which so nearly concern their temporal salvation? For my part, whatever anguish of spirit it may cost, I am willing to know the whole truth; to know the worst, and to provide for it.

I have but one lamp by which my feet are guided; and that is the lamp of experience. I know of no way of judging of the future but by the past. And judging by the past, I wish to know what there has been in the conduct of the British ministry for the last ten years, to justify those hopes with which gentlemen have been pleased to solace themselves, and the House? Is it that insidious smile with which our petition has been lately received? Trust it not, sir; it will prove a snare to your feet. Suffer not yourselves to be betrayed with a kiss. Ask yourselves how this gracious reception of our petition comports with these war-like preparations which cover our waters and darken our land. Are fleets and armies necessary to a work of love and reconciliation? Have we shown ourselves so unwilling to be reconciled, that force must be called in to win back our love? Let us not deceive ourselves, sir. These are the implements of war and subjugation; the last arguments to which kings resort. I ask, gentlemen, sir, what means this martial array, if its purpose be not to force us to submission? Can gentlemen assign any other possible motive for it? Has Great Britain any enemy, in this quarter of the world, to call for all this accumulation of navies and armies? No, sir, she has none. They are meant for us; they can be meant for no other. They are sent over to bind and rivet upon us those chains which the British ministry have been so long forging. And what have we to oppose to them? Shall we try argument? Sir, we have been trying that for the last ten years. Have we anything new to offer upon the subject? Nothing. We have held the subject up in every light of which it is capable; but it has been all in vain. Shall we resort to entreaty and humble supplication? What terms shall we find which have not been already exhausted? Let us not, I beseech you, sir, deceive ourselves. Sir, we have done everything that could be done, to avert the storm which is now coming on. We have petitioned; we have remonstrated; we have supplicated; we have prostrated ourselves before the throne, and have implored its interposition to arrest the tyrannical hands of the ministry and Parliament. Our petitions have been slighted; our remonstrances have produced additional violence and insult; our supplications have been disregarded; and we have been spurned, with contempt, from the foot of the throne. In vain, after these things, may we indulge the fond hope of peace and reconciliation. There is no longer any room for hope. If we wish to be free, if we mean to preserve inviolate those inestimable privileges for which we have been so long contending, if we mean not basely to abandon the noble struggle in which we have been so long engaged, and which we have pledged ourselves never to abandon until the glorious object of our contest shall be obtained, we must fight! I repeat it, sir, we must fight! An appeal to arms and to the God of Hosts is all that is left us!

They tell us, sir, that we are weak; unable to cope with so formidable an adversary. But when shall we be stronger? Will it be the next week, or the next year? Will it be when we are totally disarmed, and when a British guard shall be stationed in every house? Shall we gather strength by irresolution and inaction? Shall we acquire the means of effectual resistance, by lying supinely on our backs, and hugging the delusive phantom of hope, until our enemies shall have bound us hand and foot? Sir, we are not weak if we make a proper use of those means which the God of nature hath placed in our power. Three millions of people, armed in the holy cause of liberty, and in such a country as that which we possess, are invincible by any force which our enemy can send against us. Besides, sir, we shall not fight our battles alone. There is a just God who presides over the destinies of nations; and who will raise up friends to fight our battles for us. The battle, sir, is not to the strong alone; it is to the vigilant, the active, the brave. Besides, sir, we have no election. If we were base enough to desire it, it is now too late to retire from the contest. There is no retreat but in submission and slavery! Our chains are forged! Their clanking may be heard on the plains of Boston! The war is inevitable and let it come! I repeat it, sir, let it come.

It is in vain, sir, to extenuate the matter. Gentlemen may cry, Peace, Peace but there is no peace. The war is actually begun! The next gale that sweeps from the north will bring to our ears the clash of resounding arms! Our brethren are already in the field! Why stand we here idle? What is it that gentlemen wish? What would they have? Is life so dear, or peace so sweet, as to be purchased at the price of chains and slavery? Forbid it, Almighty God! I know not what course others may take; but as for me, give me liberty or give me death!

Source: Wirt, William. *Sketches of the Life and Character of Patrick Henry.* (Philadelphia) 1836, as reproduced in *The World's Great Speeches,* Lewis Copeland and Lawrence W. Lamm, eds., (New York) 1973

PLANNING PAGE + ESSAY
Lighting a Fire Under a Procrastinator

TIME OF PROCRASTINATION: TO KILL A TEAM PROJECT

So guys, we have needed to do this project for 2 weeks now. We have only done small amounts of it. You might want to play video games instead. But if we want to pass we must complete this.

I know you guys want the project finished. I also know you don't want to do the work for it. Sitting around doing nothing is only hurting us all. We need to work together to get this done.

From what I've seen, you guys are smart enough to finish this thing. Also from my experience, we can easily get this done before the deadline and we can work so fast you can get on with whatever you were doing when we started this project.

We have already tried to do it a little at a time. That never works. We always do almost nothing and just screw around for 10 minutes. We must do it all in one sitting or else it won't work.

Currently, we have all of the supplies, tools, info, and people required to finish the project in one sitting. We are smart, intuitive and creative people. We all have the skill to do this.

In reality, we have much of the project done and it's so easy to finish the rest of the project.

So let's get started. Let's knock the rest of it out and get this thing so perfect, the teacher will think we cheated! LET'S finish this!

Caleb Castle, Grade 9

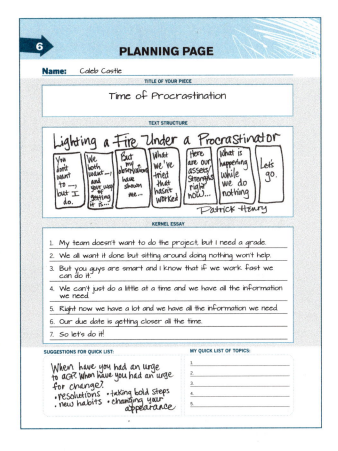

PLANNING PAGE — 6

Name: Caleb Castle

TITLE OF YOUR PIECE
Time of Procrastination

TEXT STRUCTURE

Lighting a Fire Under a Procrastinator
- You don't want to —, but I do.
- We both want —, and your way or getting it is...
- But my observations have shown me...
- What we've tried that hasn't worked
- Here are our assets/strengths right now...
- What is happening while we do nothing
- Let's go.

Patrick Henry

KERNEL ESSAY

1. My team doesn't want to do the project, but I need a grade.
2. We all want it done but sitting around doing nothing won't help.
3. But you guys are smart and I know that if we work fast we can do it.
4. We can't just do a little at a time and we have all the information we need.
5. Right now we have a lot and we have all the information we need.
6. Our due date is getting closer all the time.
7. So let's do it!

SUGGESTIONS FOR QUICK LIST:
When have you had an urge to act? When have you had an urge for change?
- resolutions
- new habits
- taking bold steps
- changing your appearance

MY QUICK LIST OF TOPICS:
1.
2.
3.
4.
5.

PLANNING PAGE

Name: _____

TITLE OF YOUR PIECE

TEXT STRUCTURE

How Bullying Works

where they see you (or find you)	What they demand from you	what they will do if you refuse	how people usually react

Janet Schaw

KERNEL ESSAY

1. _____

2. _____

3. _____

4. _____

_____

_____

SUGGESTIONS FOR QUICK LIST:

People push other people to do things. When have you seen this?
- bullies at School
- rules you disagree with

MY QUICK LIST OF TOPICS:

1. _____
2. _____
3. _____
4. _____
5. _____

June 17, 1775

At present the martial law stands thus: "an officer or a committeeman enters a plantation with his posse."

The alternative is proposed: "Agree to join us [Whigs] and your persons and properties are safe . . . if you refuse, we are directly to cut up your corn, shoot your pigs, burn your houses, seize your Negroes, and perhaps tar and feather yourself."

Not to choose the first requires more courage than they are possessed of, and I believe this method has seldom failed with the lower sort.

Source: Janet Schaw, *Journal of a Lady of Quality,* June 1775. Schaw was a Scot visiting her brother, a merchant, in Wilmington, North Carolina, where she was strongly critical of the local Whig regime.

PLANNING PAGE + ESSAY
How Bullying Works

THE TRAIL OF TEARS

The Trail of Tears started in Georgia and it went on to Tennessee, Alabama, North Carolina and Florida. That's where they found the Native Americans. The person who decided this was President Jackson who passed the Indian Removal Act and they sent the Native Americans to the western states. The reason they did that was because we had territory in the south and we did not want them to be there.

The Americans demanded that the Native Americans leave their territories right away and the new Americans were really rude and forceful to the Native Americans. They didn't want them on their land and thought that the Native Americans were unfamiliar and alien people who occupied land that white settlers wanted. Some of the northern states also did not want the Native Americans in their land, like Illinois and Wisconsin. The bloody Black Hawk War in 1832 opened up millions of acres of land to white settlements.

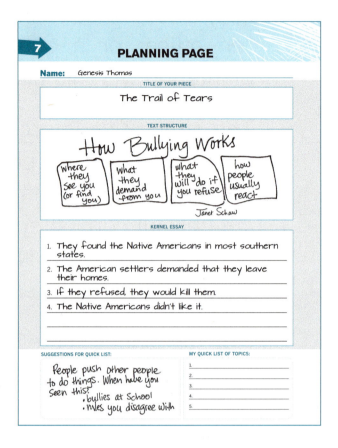

In my opinion I didn't think the Native Americans liked that and they were going to refuse to leave but the Americans had that covered already and they told them, "If you guys refuse we will kill you," and I guess that the Native Americans were terrified of the Americans.

In my case I feel that the Native Americans reacted by thinking that this was not right. "We were here first and they can't take our land. We lived here longer than them and first come first serve." But I guess that didn't really matter.

Not a lot of Native Americans survived moving to the Indian Territories. By 1840, ten thousand had been driven off of their land in the southeastern states and forced to move across the Mississippi to Indian Territory. The government promised that their new land would be permanent and they would not kick them out of their homes, but the Indian country shrank and shrank as the whites moved in. By 1907 Oklahoma became a state and Indian Territory was gone for good.

In my opinion I wished we would have not done that. We could have learned more from the Native Americans.

Genesis Thomas, Grade 8

KERNEL ESSAYS BY STUDENTS
How Bullying Works

TOPIC: TAKING THE STAAR TEST

1. They find you in your classroom.
2. They force you to take multiple tests.
3. If you don't you can't go to high school.
4. People complain but in the end, take the tests.

Maggie Davis, Grade 8

TOPIC: LA LLORONA: THE LEGENDARY WEEPING WOMAN: HOW LA LLORONA MAKES CHILDREN BEHAVE

1. La Llorona says, "I know where you live, because I shelter you!"
2. She demands that you behave or else . . .
3. If you refuse, La Llorona will come for you.
4. People are scared of her, so children do behave.

Jacob Torres, Grade 8

TOPIC: DON'T PLAY HOOKY

1. You're sitting at home skipping school and a letter comes in the mail or in an email.
2. "Don't skip school and play hooky when you aren't sick!" it says.
3. "Or else you'll have to go to court and maybe even jail!"
4. So you go to school and never play hooky again.

Kaitlyn Postell, Grade 6

TOPIC: KIDS BULLYING

1. They'd find you in the janitor's closet eating lunch.
2. They want your lunch money.
3. If the target would refuse, they will shove the person in a toilet and humiliate them.
4. Kids that stand around don't react to tell a teacher that could actually help.

Kassandra B. Martinez, Grade 6

1. Reporters catch you doing something.
2. The reporters will demand something from you.
3. If you refuse they will threaten to put you on the Internet.
4. Most celebrities will give reporters what they want in order for their secrets to be safe.

Tamara Weiss, Grade 7

PLANNING PAGE

Name: _____

TITLE OF YOUR PIECE

TEXT STRUCTURE

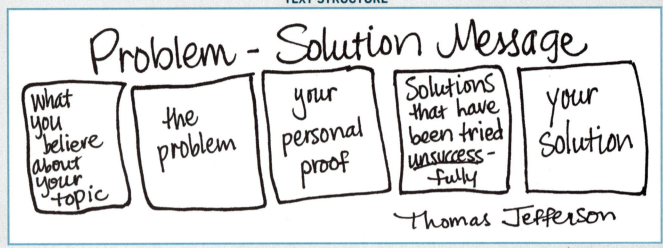

Problem - Solution Message

| What you believe about your topic | the problem | your personal proof | Solutions that have been tried <u>unsuccess</u>-fully | your Solution |

Thomas Jefferson

KERNEL ESSAY

1. _____

2. _____

3. _____

4. _____

5. _____

SUGGESTIONS FOR QUICK LIST:

If you could solve any problem, what would it be? It could be serious or minor. It could be in a store, a neighborhood, the world.

MY QUICK LIST OF TOPICS:

1. _____

2. _____

3. _____

4. _____

5. _____

Declaration of Independence

IN CONGRESS, July 4, 1776.

The unanimous Declaration of the thirteen united States of America,

When in the Course of human events, it becomes necessary for one people to dissolve the political bands which have connected them with another, and to assume among the powers of the earth, the separate and equal station to which the Laws of Nature and of Nature's God entitle them, a decent respect to the opinions of mankind requires that they should declare the causes which impel them to the separation.

We hold these truths to be self-evident, that all men are created equal, that they are endowed by their Creator with certain unalienable Rights, that among these are Life, Liberty and the pursuit of Happiness.— That to secure these rights, Governments are instituted among Men, deriving their just powers from the consent of the governed,—That whenever any Form of Government becomes destructive of these ends, it is the Right of the People to alter or to abolish it, and to institute new Government, laying its foundation on such principles and organizing its powers in such form, as to them shall seem most likely to effect their Safety and Happiness. Prudence, indeed, will dictate that Governments long established should not be changed for light and transient causes; and accordingly all experience hath shewn, that mankind are more disposed to suffer, while evils are sufferable, than to right themselves by abolishing the forms to which they are accustomed. But when a long train of abuses and usurpations, pursuing invariably the same Object evinces a design to reduce them under absolute Despotism, it is their right, it is their duty, to throw off such Government, and to provide new Guards for their future security.—Such has been the patient sufferance of these Colonies; and such is now the necessity which constrains them to alter their former Systems of Government. The history of the present King of Great Britain is a history of repeated injuries and usurpations, all having in direct object the establishment of an absolute Tyranny over these States. To prove this, let Facts be submitted to a candid world.

He has refused his Assent to Laws, the most wholesome and necessary for the public good.

He has forbidden his Governors to pass Laws of immediate and pressing importance, unless suspended in their operation till his Assent should be obtained; and when so suspended, he has utterly neglected to attend to them.

He has refused to pass other Laws for the accommodation of large districts of people, unless those people would relinquish the right of Representation in the Legislature, a right inestimable to them and formidable to tyrants only.

He has called together legislative bodies at places unusual, uncomfortable, and distant from the depository of their public Records, for the sole purpose of fatiguing them into compliance with his measures.

He has dissolved Representative Houses repeatedly, for opposing with manly firmness his invasions on the rights of the people.

He has refused for a long time, after such dissolutions, to cause others to be elected; whereby the Legislative powers, incapable of Annihilation, have returned to the People at large for their exercise; the State remaining in the mean time exposed to all the dangers of invasion from without, and convulsions within.

He has endeavoured to prevent the population of these States; for that purpose obstructing the Laws for Naturalization of Foreigners; refusing to pass others to encourage their migrations hither, and raising the conditions of new Appropriations of Lands.

He has obstructed the Administration of Justice, by refusing his Assent to Laws for establishing Judiciary powers.

He has made Judges dependent on his Will alone, for the tenure of their offices, and the amount and payment of their salaries.

He has erected a multitude of New Offices, and sent hither swarms of Officers to harrass our people, and eat out their substance.

He has kept among us, in times of peace, Standing Armies without the Consent of our legislatures.

He has affected to render the Military independent of and superior to the Civil power.

He has combined with others to subject us to a jurisdiction foreign to our constitution, and unacknowledged by our laws; giving his Assent to their Acts of pretended Legislation:

For Quartering large bodies of armed troops among us:

For protecting them, by a mock Trial, from punishment for any Murders which they should commit on the Inhabitants of these States:

For cutting off our Trade with all parts of the world:

For imposing Taxes on us without our Consent:

For depriving us in many cases, of the benefits of Trial by Jury:

For transporting us beyond Seas to be tried for pretended offences

For abolishing the free System of English Laws in a neighbouring Province, establishing therein an Arbitrary government, and enlarging its Boundaries so as to render it at once an example and fit instrument for introducing the same absolute rule into these Colonies:

For taking away our Charters, abolishing our most valuable Laws, and altering fundamentally the Forms of our Governments:

For suspending our own Legislatures, and declaring themselves invested with power to legislate for us in all cases whatsoever.

He has abdicated Government here, by declaring us out of his Protection and waging War against us.

He has plundered our seas, ravaged our Coasts, burnt our towns, and destroyed the lives of our people.

He is at this time transporting large Armies of foreign Mercenaries to compleat the works of death, desolation and tyranny, already begun with circumstances of Cruelty & perfidy scarcely paralleled in the most barbarous ages, and totally unworthy the Head of a civilized nation.

He has constrained our fellow Citizens taken Captive on the high Seas to bear Arms against their Country, to become the executioners of their friends and Brethren, or to fall themselves by their Hands.

He has excited domestic insurrections amongst us, and has endeavoured to bring on the inhabitants of our frontiers, the merciless Indian Savages, whose known rule of warfare, is an undistinguished destruction of all ages, sexes and conditions.

In every stage of these Oppressions We have Petitioned for Redress in the most humble terms: Our repeated Petitions have been answered only by repeated injury. A Prince whose character is thus marked by every act which may define a Tyrant, is unfit to be the ruler of a free people.

Nor have We been wanting in attentions to our Brittish brethren. We have warned them from time to time of attempts by their legislature to extend an unwarrantable jurisdiction over us. We have reminded them of the circumstances of our emigration and settlement here. We have appealed to their native justice and magnanimity, and we have conjured them by the ties of our common kindred to disavow these usurpations, which, would inevitably interrupt our connections and correspondence. They too have been deaf to the voice of justice and of consanguinity. We must, therefore, acquiesce in the necessity, which denounces our Separation, and hold them, as we hold the rest of mankind, Enemies in War, in Peace Friends.

We, therefore, the Representatives of the united States of America, in General Congress, Assembled, appealing to the Supreme Judge of the world for the rectitude of our intentions, do, in the Name, and by Authority of the good People of these Colonies, solemnly publish and declare, That these United Colonies are, and of Right ought to be Free and Independent States; that they are Absolved from all Allegiance to the British Crown, and that all political connection between them and the State of Great Britain, is and ought to be totally dissolved; and that as Free and Independent States, they have full Power to levy War, conclude Peace, contract Alliances, establish Commerce, and to do all other Acts and Things which Independent States may of right do. And for the support of this Declaration, with a firm reliance on the protection of divine Providence, we mutually pledge to each other our Lives, our Fortunes and our sacred Honor.

PLANNING PAGE + ESSAY
Problem-Solution Message

NATURAL DISASTERS

I believe that natural disasters are horrible because they kill a lot of people. For example, the earthquake in Nepal, a natural disaster, was horrible because it killed millions of people and buildings fell to the ground.

Whenever there is a natural disaster sometimes we don't have enough money to clean up all the junk. Sometimes we just leave it there without cleaning up the destruction because the country doesn't have enough money.

Floods, tornados and wildfires are very bad but the earthquake in Nepal was the worst of all. It destroyed everything and Nepal doesn't have enough money to fix everything.

We tried to build buildings and houses that are earthquake-proof. They did not succeed because they didn't have the money and the right supplies to make buildings or houses that are earthquake-proof.

We should make a fundraiser so people can donate money and other stuff to raise the money to clean up all the junk. The reason why is because natural disasters occur everywhere and most of the time we don't have the money.

Nica Maryanchik, Grade 6

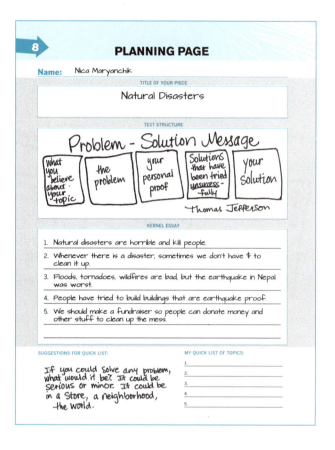

8 PLANNING PAGE

Name: Nica Maryanchik

TITLE OF YOUR PIECE
Natural Disasters

TEXT STRUCTURE

Problem - Solution Message

| What you believe about your topic | the problem | your personal proof | Solutions that have been tried unsuccessfully | your solution |

Thomas Jefferson

KERNEL ESSAY

1. Natural disasters are horrible and kill people.
2. Whenever there is a disaster, sometimes we don't have $ to clean it up.
3. Floods, tornadoes, wildfires are bad, but the earthquake in Nepal was worst.
4. People have tried to build buildings that are earthquake proof.
5. We should make a fundraiser so people can donate money and other stuff to clean up the mess.

SUGGESTIONS FOR QUICK LIST:
If you could solve any problem, what would it be? It could be serious or minor. It could be in a store, a neighborhood, the world.

MY QUICK LIST OF TOPICS:
1.
2.
3.
4.
5.

PLANNING PAGE

Name: _____

TITLE OF YOUR PIECE

TEXT STRUCTURE

Time for a Real Solution

| Everyone agrees we need to change this one thing | But here is what has been stopping us | Reasons why the change would work now | What happens if we fix this only temporarily (for now) | how we should fix it for the long-term |

Thomas Paine

KERNEL ESSAY

1. _____

2. _____

3. _____

4. _____

5. _____

_____

SUGGESTIONS FOR QUICK LIST:

For the problem that just keeps growing… and growing… when some kind of change is needed…
• behaviors • laws • habits • boundaries

MY QUICK LIST OF TOPICS:

1. _____

2. _____

3. _____

4. _____

5. _____

Of the Present Ability of America: With Some Miscellaneous Reflections

I HAVE never met with a man, either in England or America, who hath not confessed his opinion, that a separation between the countries would take place one time or other: And there is no instance in which we have shown less judgment, than in endeavoring to describe, what we call, the ripeness or fitness of the continent for independence.

As all men allow the measure, and vary only in their opinion of the time, let us, in order to remove mistakes, take a general survey of things, and endeavor if possible to find out the VERY time. But I need not go far, the inquiry ceases at once, for the TIME HATH FOUND US. The general concurrence, the glorious union of all things, proves the fact.

'Tis not in numbers but in unity that our great strength lies: yet our present numbers are sufficient to repel the force of all the world. The Continent hath at this time the largest body of armed and disciplined men of any power under Heaven: and is just arrived at that pitch of strength, in which no single colony is able to support itself, and the whole, when united, is able to do any thing. Our land force is more than sufficient, and as to Naval affairs, we cannot be insensible that Britain would never suffer an American man of war to be built, while the Continent remained in her hands. Wherefore, we should be no forwarder an hundred years hence in that branch than we are now; but the truth is, we should be less so, because the timber of the Country is every day diminishing, and that which will remain at last, will be far off or difficult to procure.

Were the Continent crowded with inhabitants, her sufferings under the present circumstances would be intolerable. The more seaport-towns we had, the more should we have both to defend and to lose. Our present numbers are so happily proportioned to our wants, that no man need be idle. The diminution of trade affords an army, and the necessities of an army create a new trade.

Debts we have none: and whatever we may contract on this account will serve as a glorious memento of our virtue. Can we but leave posterity with a settled form of government, an independent constitution of its own, the purchase at any price will be cheap. But to expend millions for the sake of getting a few vile acts repealed, and routing the present ministry only, is unworthy the charge, and is using posterity with the utmost cruelty; because it is leaving them the great work to do, and a debt upon their backs from which they derive no advantage. Such a thought's unworthy a man of honour, and is the true characteristic of a narrow heart and a piddling politician . . .

COMPLETED PLANNING PAGE
Time for a Real Solution

Name: Marcos Reyes

TITLE OF YOUR PIECE

Wounded Warriors

TEXT STRUCTURE

Time for a Real Solution

| Everyone agrees we need to change this one thing | But here is what has been stopping us | Reasons why the change would work now | What happens if we fix this only temporarily (for now) | how we should fix it for the long-term |

Thomas Paine

KERNEL ESSAY

1. Everyone agrees wounded soldiers deserve a second chance.

2. But most wounded veterans are not tended to because of the numbers coming home wounded.

3. The Wounded Warrior Project is on it!

4. We can't think a short fix will take care of it.

5. Let's use the Wounded Warrior Project to make care lasting for every soldier.

SUGGESTIONS FOR QUICK LIST:

For the problem that just keeps growing... and growing... When some kind of change is needed...
• behaviors • laws • habits • boundaries

MY QUICK LIST OF TOPICS:

1.
2.
3.
4.
5.

FULL ESSAY
Time for a Real Solution

WOUNDED WARRIORS

Everyone agrees that wounded warriors deserve our respect, appreciation, and good care. Every wounded warrior deserves a second chance, every single last one of them.

But some wounded warriors never get a second chance. Some come out of the wars wounded and are forgotten. This is what I think is unfair.

Why does this happen? Our country has been at war constantly for years now, and many injuries involve amputation, in greater number than ever before. The veterans' facilities in the United States have not been ready to handle that many injured men and women.

This problem must have a solution. The Wounded Warrior Project has been working to solve that problem. Right now, school kids all over the country are learning about this program. This is causing many people to feel that no soldier should be neglected, given help that isn't useful, or be placed in jobs that aren't appropriate.

If we only take care of our veterans for a short time, we might feel better, but have we actually solved the problem?

We need to donate our time to this program and maybe even donate money to this and any organization that helps our warriors. Every single last one of our warriors needs us.

Marcos Reyes, Grade 8

Name: _____

TITLE OF YOUR PIECE

TEXT STRUCTURE

Letter from Home

| things I wish you would tell me about | news from here | changes in the feelings here | one thing I wish you would do | why I wish you'd do that |

Abigail Adams

KERNEL ESSAY

1. _____

2. _____

3. _____

4. _____

5. _____

SUGGESTIONS FOR QUICK LIST:

A letter to someone who is far away, someone you care about. Maybe you felt like you are watching their adventure from the sidelines, watching with a burning curiosity

MY QUICK LIST OF TOPICS:

1. _____

2. _____

3. _____

4. _____

5. _____

Letter to Her Husband John Adams

Abigail Adams, 1775

Braintree, March 31, 1776

I wish you would ever write me a Letter half as long as I write you; and tell me if you may where your Fleet are gone? What sort of Defence Virginia can make against our common Enemy? Whether it is so situated as to make an able Defence? Are not the Gentery Lords and the common people vassals? Are they not like the uncivilized Natives Brittain represents us to be? I hope their Riffel Men, who have shewn themselves very savage and even Blood thirsty, are not a specimen of the Generality of the people.

I am willing to allow the Colony great merit for having produced a Washington, but they have been shamefully duped by a Dunmore.

I have sometimes been ready to think that the passion for Liberty cannot be Eaquelly Strong in the Breasts of those who have been accustomed to deprive their fellow Creatures of theirs. Of this I am certain: that it is not founded upon the generous and Christian principal of doing to others as we would that others should do unto us.

Do not you want to see Boston; I am fearful of the small pox, or I should have been in before this time. I got Mr. Crane to go to our House and see what state it was in. I find it has been occupied by one of the Doctors of a Regiment, very dirty, but no other damage has been done to it. The few things which were left in it are all gone. Crane has the key, which he never delivered up. I have wrote to him for it and am determined to get it cleaned as soon as possible and shut it up. I look upon it a new acquisition of property, a property which one month ago I did not value at a single Shilling, and could with pleasure have seen it in flames.

The Town in General is left in a better state than we expected, more oweing to a percipitate flight than an Regard to the inhabitants, tho some individuals discovered a sense of honour and have left the rent of the Houses in which they were for the owners and the furniture unhurt, or if damaged sufficient to make it good.

Others have committed abominable Ravages. The Mansion House of your President is safe and the furniture unhurt, whilst both the House and the Furniture of the Solisiter General have fallen a prey to their own merciless party. Surely the very Fiends feel a Reverential awe for Virtue and patriotism, whilst they Detest the paricide and traitor.

I feel very differently at the approach of spring to which I did a month ago. We knew not then whether we could plant or sow with safety, whether when we had toiled we could reap the fruits of our own industry, whether we could rest in our own Cottages, or whether we should not be driven from the sea coasts to seek shelter in the wilderness, but now we feel as if we might sit under our own vine and eat the good of the land.

I feel a gaieti de Coar to which before I was a stranger. I think the Sun looks brighter, the Birds sing more melodiously, and Nature puts on a more chearfull countanance. We feel a temporary peace, and the poor fugitives are returning to their deserted habitations.

Tho we felicitate ourselves, we sympathize with those who are trembling lest the Lot of Boston should be theirs. But they cannot be in similar circumstances unless pusilanimity and cowardise should take possession of them. They have time and warning given them to see the Evil and shun it.—I long to hear that you have declared an independancy—and by the way, in the new Code of Laws which I suppose it will be necessary for you to make, I desire you would Remember the Ladies, and be more generous and favourable to them than your ancestors. Do not put such unlimited power into the hands of the Husbands. Remember, all Men would be tyrants if they could. If perticuliar care and attention is not paid to the Laidies, we are determined to foment a Rebelion, and will not hold ourselves bound by any Laws in which we have no voice, or Representation.

That your Sex are Naturally Tyrannical is Truth so thoroughly established as to admit no dispute, but such of you as wish to be happy willingly give up the harsh title of Master for the more tender and endearing one of Friend. Why, then, not put it out of the power of the vicious and the Lawless to use us with cruelty and indignity with impunity. Men of Sense in all Ages abhor those customs which treat us only as the vassals of your Sex. Regard us then as Beings placed by providence under your protection, and in immitation of the Supreem Being, make use of that power only for our happiness.

PLANNING PAGE + ESSAY
Letter From Home

THE LOST USB

Residency of 1107 Fox Run

San Antonio May 30th 2015

To My Brothers—Thomas and Dominic

I hope you're not busy.

I am in dire need; I have a report due tomorrow which I have saved on a USB device—lost somewhere in my room.

The teacher who assigned this essay dictated that it must be a typed, 2-page report on the importance of preserving the Earth's natural resources. I have decided to bravely tell my teacher that my report is on my USB device at home and I will get the report to her tomorrow.

I <u>really</u> need your aid to search through my room and clean it up so I can find the USB and print out the report.

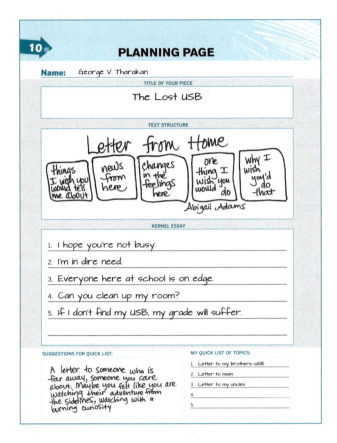

If I am not able to find the USB and print the report out I will receive a <u>zero</u> for both a test and a project grade. Additionally, my parents will ground me because it is such a major assignment that I did not turn in. If you dismiss my plea I will try to retype as much of the report as I can, but it definitely won't be as good as the original nor will it be worthy of an A grade.

George V. Tharakan
Freshman Student

P.S. There is a chance that the USB may be on my desk somewhere, so that'll narrow down our search.

George V. Tharakan, Grade 9

PLANNING PAGE + ESSAY
Letter From Home

NELSON MANDELA (DEATH) (WRITTEN AS JACOB ZUMA, CURRENT PRESIDENT OF SOUTH AFRICA)

Dear Dad,

Today was the saddest day I've encountered in my whole life. The people in South Africa share the pain with me too. The sky is no more blue like it always was, the people aren't like they were. Everything has changed since you left. All we have are memories of when we've spent together.

I wish you'd tell me everything about your greatest accomplishments in life, instead of what the world already knows, like what was I to you? Was I one of your accomplishments in life? Were you proud of me? Or did I disappoint you?

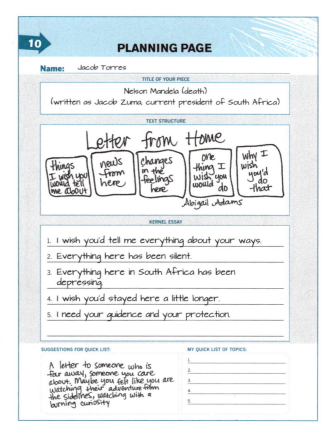

Everything in South Africa has been very silent since the tragedy that shook the whole world. What used to be Africa, is no more. Everything is much more depressing since your absence. But we know that you're in a better place up there, than down here.

Everything in South Africa has lost its color. What once used to be green grass and blue sky have now turned to grey and black, metaphorically. You were the sun to this nation; you motivated people when they were down. We all miss you, *Tata,* very much.

What I wish you've done is stay a little longer, but we both know that is not our decision. But in a couple of years I'll see you, and we'll be together with grandma and grandpa, and everyone else we know.

But for now I pray you to protect me from all bad up there, and give me guidance to life. Guide me to greatness dad. With all love and respect.

Sincerely,
Jacob Zuma

Jacob Torres, Grade 8

PLANNING PAGE

Name: _____

TITLE OF YOUR PIECE

```
┌─────────────────────────────────────────────┐
│                                               │
│                                               │
│                                               │
│                                               │
└─────────────────────────────────────────────┘
```

TEXT STRUCTURE

How Bad Is It? (A Description)

| greeting (or apology for this interruption) | what the situation is / was | contributing factors (how bad is it?) Let me count the ways. | one possible solution |

Benjamin Rush

KERNEL ESSAY

1. _____

2. _____

3. _____

4. _____

_____

_____

SUGGESTIONS FOR QUICK LIST:

When "it was really bad" just won't do. When you want someone to get the full, awful picture. You could be describing a meal, a movie, a vacation, or any experience ... especially if you didn't have a choice

MY QUICK LIST OF TOPICS:

1. _____
2. _____
3. _____
4. _____
5. _____

Letter to George Washington

Benjamin Rush, 1777

Princetown [N.J.] December 26. 1777.

Sir,

I have delayed troubling your Excellency with the State of our hospitals, in hopes you would hear it from the Director General whose business it is to correspond with your Excellency upon this Subject. I beg leave therefore at last to look up to you, and through you to the congress as the only powers that can redress our greivances, or do us justice.

I need not inform your Excellency that we have now upwards of 5000 Sick in our hospitals. This number would cease to be alarming if our hospitals could afford such accommodations to the poor fellows as would ensure them a speedy recovery. But this is far from being the case. There cannot be greater calamity for a sick man than to come into our hospital at *this season* of the year. Old disorders are prolonged, and new Ones contracted among us. This last is so much the case that I am safe when I assert that a *great majority* of those who die under our hands perish with diseases caught in our hospitals. When I consider the present Army under your Excellency's command as the last hope of America; I am more alarmed, and distressed, at these facts, than I have words to express. I can see nothing to prevent the same mortality this winter among our troops that prevailed last year. Every day deprives us of four or five patients out of 500 in the hospital under my care in this place. The same complaints are heard from every quarter. The Surgeons have been blamed

for these things, but without reason. I shall briefly point out to your Excellency the real causes of them.

1. Too many sick are crouded together in One house. I have seen 20 sick men in One room ill with fevers & fluxes, large eno' to contain only 6, or 8 well men without danger to their health. Six of our Surgeons have died since the 1st of last may, from Attending the sick under these circumstances, and almost every Surgeon in the department has been ill in a greater or lesser degree with fevers caught in our hospitals. It should be the business, (as it is certainly the interest) of the Surgeons to prevent the sick being thus crouded. But unfortunately the Congress have given the *sole* power of judging of these things to the Director general & his deputies who from the nature of thier business are never Obliged to go inside of a hospital.

2. The hospitals are provided in the most scanty manner with the Stores necessary for sick people, and these are too often withheld from them from the want of checks upon the officers of the hospital whose business it is to provide & administer them. Beef and bread are by no means suitable diet for men in fevers.

3. There is a want of hospital Shirts— Sheets—& blankets to be worne by the sick. Nothing but a miracle can save the life of a Soldier who lies in a Shirt and blanket which he has worne for

four or five months before he came into the hospital.

4. There is a want of guards, and an officer to command at every hospital. It is foreign to my purpose to take notice of the inconveniences which attend a Soldier, living any time at a hospital without being Subject to military goverment. All the discipline and Sense of Subordination he acquires at camp are generally lost as soon he enters the door of our hospitals. But it is my business to mention other inconveniences which arise from our want of guards. The men by going out when they please catch colds—they sell their arms—blankets—& cloathes to buy rum, or provisions that are unsuitable for them—they plunder & insult the inhabitants, while within doors they quarrel and fight with each other—disobey their Surgeons—matrons & nurses—and thus defeat the most salutary plans that can be contrived for their recovery. An Officer with a suitable guard at every hospital I am sure would save many hundred lives, and many thousand pounds to the continent every year.

5. The medical establishment is a bad one. It gives the Director General the most *incompatible* Offices. The Offices held by him are held by no less than *three* physicians in the British hospitals who are all independant of each Other, and who by checking each Other, perfectly secure to the sick all the good Offices,

and medicinal stores that are intended for them by goverment.

Before any material change can be made in our System it will be in your Excellency's power to stop in some measure the ravages our hospitals are making upon the army by ordering the Surgeons immediately to billet such of the sick as are able to help themselves in farm houses. The air and diet of a farmer's kitchen are the best physic in the world for a Soldier worne down with the fatigues of a campaign. I have prescribed them with great Success in this neighbourhood, but my influence is not great eno' to make the practice universal thro' the department. I have found the farmers volunteer in taking the poor fellows into their houses especially when they were indulged with the Soldiers rations of Beef & bread, in exchange for the milk and vegetables they gave them. If this most necessary measure can be immediately carried into execution, I am sure it will add 3000 men to your army in the Spring who must otherwise perish in our hospitals. Perhaps the Authority of Congress may be necessary, or of the State of Pensylvania to facilitate the execution of the measure. If your Excellency will only recommend it, I am sure it will *immediately* take place.

With the most perfect esteem I have the honor to be your Excellency's most Obedient and devoted Servant

B. Rush

KERNEL ESSAYS BY STUDENTS
How Bad Is It? (A Description)

LEONATO CONFRONTS CLAUDIO (CHARACTERS IN SHAKESPEARE'S *MUCH ADO ABOUT NOTHING*)

1. Claudio and dear sir Don Pedro, pardon this intrusion.
2. Hero is dead.
3. You have killed the beautiful Hero with slander, distrust, and heartbreak.
4. You must marry who I tell you to marry.

Jessicalynn Jackson, Grade 7

BORACHIO'S LAMENT (*MUCH ADO ABOUT NOTHING*)

1. Sorry to bother you . . .
2. I'm incarcerated and feeling terrible.
3. I am guilty of fraud, slander, and meanness, but I didn't mean for anyone to die. Also the watchmen here have terrible hygiene and no brains.
4. I'll just have to hope someone punishes Jon John even worse.

Maria Jimenez, Grade 7

SIX IS STUCK IN THE DESERT

1. Sorry for the interruption.
2. I'm stuck in the desert.
3. I'm faint, hot, and thirsty.
4. Please rescue me.

Talia Delambre, Grade 7

HOMEWORK PROBLEM

1. Mom, OMG!
2. I forgot to do my homework.
3. It's really bad because I don't want to fail or be in trouble with my teacher.
4. I'll just finish it in the car.

Anael Ashkenazi, Grade 7

MONTAG AFTER HIS CITY IS DESTROYED (*FAHRENHEIT 451*)

1. I'm sorry for my interrupting.
2. But my entire city was destroyed.
3. My wife and friends and everything I know is gone.
4. I think I just have to move on.

Miriam Stein, Grade 7

PLANNING PAGE

Name: _____

TITLE OF YOUR PIECE

_____

TEXT STRUCTURE

Reprimanding a Group

Shame on you for... (doing this)	I have earned your respect, so listen...	Description of instigators	Be patient. We're not perfect. (Why)	I urge you to speak up against this behavior	People will look back on this day and admire you

George Washington

KERNEL ESSAY

1. _____

2. _____

3. _____

4. _____

5. _____

6. _____

SUGGESTIONS FOR QUICK LIST:

When a group starts to fall apart, when it feels like it's turning into an uncivilized mob, and you want to "put out the fire." Maybe it's about breaking rules, being mean, or being selfish.

MY QUICK LIST OF TOPICS:

1. _____
2. _____
3. _____
4. _____
5. _____

Speech to Angry Officers

General George Washington, 1783

Gentlemen:

By an anonymous summons, an attempt has been made to convene you together; how inconsistent with the rules of propriety, how unmilitary, and how subversive of all order and discipline, let the good sense of the army decide . . .

Thus much, gentlemen, I have thought it incumbent on me to observe to you, to show upon what principles I opposed the irregular and hasty meeting which was proposed to have been held on Tuesday last—and not because I wanted a disposition to give you every opportunity consistent with your own honor, and the dignity of the army, to make known your grievances. If my conduct heretofore has not evinced to you that I have been a faithful friend to the army, my declaration of it at this time would be equally unavailing and improper. But as I was among the first who embarked in the cause of our common country. As I have never left your side one moment, but when called from you on public duty. As I have been the constant companion and witness of your distresses, and not among the last to feel and acknowledge your merits. As I have ever considered my own military reputation as inseparably connected with that of the army. As my heart has ever expanded with joy, when I have heard its praises, and my indignation has arisen, when the mouth of detraction has been opened against it, it can scarcely be supposed, at this late stage of the war, that I am indifferent to its interests.

But how are they to be promoted? The way is plain, says the anonymous addresser. If war continues, remove into the unsettled country, there establish yourselves, and leave an ungrateful country to defend itself. But who are they to defend? Our wives, our children, our farms, and other property which we leave behind us. Or, in this state of hostile separation, are we

to take the two first (the latter cannot be removed) to perish in a wilderness, with hunger, cold, and nakedness? If peace takes place, never sheathe your swords, says he, until you have obtained full and ample justice; this dreadful alternative, of either deserting our country in the extremest hour of her distress or turning our arms against it (which is the apparent object, unless Congress can be compelled into instant compliance), has something so shocking in it that humanity revolts at the idea. My God! What can this writer have in view, by recommending such measures? Can he be a friend to the army? Can he be a friend to this country? Rather, is he not an insidious foe? Some emissary, perhaps, from New York, plotting the ruin of both, by sowing the seeds of discord and separation between the civil and military powers of the continent? And what a compliment does he pay to our understandings when he recommends measures in either alternative, impracticable in their nature?

I cannot, in justice to my own belief, and what I have great reason to conceive is the intention of Congress, conclude this address, without giving it as my decided opinion, that that honorable body entertain exalted sentiments of the services of the army; and, from a full conviction of its merits and sufferings, will do it complete justice. That their endeavors to discover and establish funds for this purpose have been unwearied, and will not cease till they have succeeded, I have not a doubt. But, like all other large bodies, where there is a variety of different interests to reconcile, their deliberations are slow. Why, then, should we distrust them? And, in consequence of that distrust, adopt measures which may cast a shade over that glory which has been so justly acquired; and tarnish the reputation of an army which is celebrated through all Europe, for its fortitude and patriotism? And for what is this done? To

Speech to Angry Officers (Continued) — General George Washington, 1783

bring the object we seek nearer? No! most certainly, in my opinion, it will cast it at a greater distance.

For myself (and I take no merit in giving the assurance, being induced to it from principles of gratitude, veracity, and justice), a grateful sense of the confidence you have ever placed in me, a recollection of the cheerful assistance and prompt obedience I have experienced from you, under every vicissitude of fortune, and the sincere affection I feel for an army I have so long had the honor to command will oblige me to declare, in this public and solemn manner, that, in the attainment of complete justice for all your toils and dangers, and in the gratification of every wish, so far as may be done consistently with the great duty I owe my country and those powers we are bound to respect, you may freely command my services to the utmost of my abilities.

While I give you these assurances, and pledge myself in the most unequivocal manner to exert whatever ability I am possessed of in your favor, let me entreat you, gentlemen, on your part, not to take any measures which, viewed in the calm light of reason, will lessen the dignity and sully the glory you have hitherto maintained; let me request you to rely on the plighted faith of your country, and place a full confidence in the purity of the intentions of Congress; that, previous to your dissolution as an army, they will cause all your accounts to be fairly liquidated, as directed in their resolutions, which were published to you two days ago, and that they will adopt the most effectual measures in their power to render ample justice to you, for your faithful and meritorious services. And let me conjure you, in the name of our common country, as you value your own sacred honor, as you respect the rights of humanity, and as you regard the military and national character of America, to express your utmost horror and detestation of the man who wishes, under any specious pretenses, to overturn the liberties of our country, and who wickedly attempts to open the floodgates of civil discord and deluge our rising empire in blood.

By thus determining and thus acting, you will pursue the plain and direct road to the attainment of your wishes. You will defeat the insidious designs of our enemies, who are compelled to resort from open force to secret artifice. You will give one more distinguished proof of unexampled patriotism and patient virtue, rising superior to the pressure of the most complicated sufferings. And you will, by the dignity of your conduct, afford occasion for posterity to say, when speaking of the glorious example you have exhibited to mankind, "Had this day been wanting, the world had never seen the last stage of perfection to which human nature is capable of attaining."

General George Washington
March 15, 1783

KERNEL ESSAYS BY STUDENTS
Reprimanding a Group

YOU'RE GROUNDED! (AS MOM)

1. How dare you toilet paper the neighbors' house!
2. I am your mother so you listen to me.
3. Your friends might've put you up to this.
4. Don't you walk away from me. There's more I need to say.
5. If your friends put you up to this, next time say NO!
6. Now for the rest of your life you'll look back and say "Dang! That was stupid!"

Ben Brody, Grade 7

GUY MONTAG (A CHARACTER IN THE NOVEL *FAHRENHEIT 451*) REPRIMANDS SOCIETY

1. Shame on you for ruining society and burning books.
2. I am a fireman that understands we're wrong so listen.
3. They are taking away our opinions and thoughts.
4. I hope you realize how wrong you are.
5. People will look back and admire the courage of people who listen.

Miriam Stein, Grade 7

LEONATO YELLING AT CLAUDIO (CHARACTERS IN *MUCH ADO ABOUT NOTHING*)

1. Shame on you for thinking my daughter was unfaithful to you!
2. Since you were going to be my son-in-law, you respect me.
3. Don John is the bastard brother.
4. My daughter (Hero) is not really dead.
5. Don't say anything.
6. If you don't say anything, you will be admired.

Tamara Weiss, Grade 7

BENEDICK (FROM *MUCH ADO*) AND HIS PROBLEM WITH LOVE

1. Claudio, all of you people in love are crazy.
2. I am your friend and have fought wars with you, so trust me.
3. Hero is short, plain, and a female!
4. Don't be in such a hurry to marry.
5. Go on strike with me about marriage.
6. All the bachelors will be proud of you.

Maria Viramontes, Grade 7

PLANNING PAGE

Name: _____

TITLE OF YOUR PIECE

TEXT STRUCTURE

Purposes of an Action

who we are	why we are doing this (more than one) ⊓⊓⊓	what we are doing

Preamble to the Constitution

KERNEL ESSAY

1. _____

2. _____

3. _____

_____

_____

_____

SUGGESTIONS FOR QUICK LIST:

Think about a time you wanted to explain why you did something (anything).
- Made a choice
- Made a move
- Went somewhere

MY QUICK LIST OF TOPICS:

1. ....
2. ....
3. ....
4. ....
5. ....

We the People of the United States, in Order to form a more perfect Union, establish Justice, insure domestic Tranquility, provide for the common defence, promote the general Welfare, and secure the Blessings of Liberty to ourselves and our Posterity, do ordain and establish this Constitution for the United States of America.

PLANNING PAGE + ESSAY
Purposes of an Action

THE WEDDING OF CLARA JANE BRYANT AND HENRY FORD

To: All who may attend
From: Clara Bryant and Henry Ford
Time: April 11, 1888 at 2pm
Where: Greenfield Township, Michigan
Subject: Sharing our love

We are inviting you to our wedding. The reason we are getting married is because we love each other, we want to spend the rest of our lives together, and our feelings for each other are very strong. People who are this deeply in love deserve to have the best wedding, so please come join us on our special day!

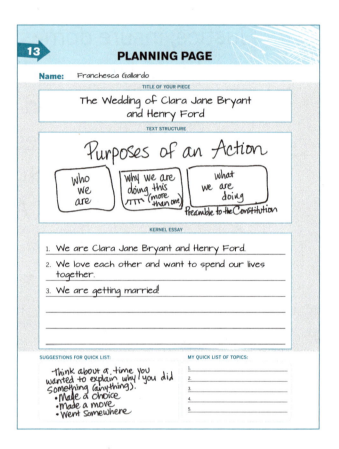

The Wedding Day

Following the wedding that will start at 2pm, we invite you to stay for the reception which will start at a quarter till 4pm. During the reception there will be food, cake, music, dancing and much more. If you would like to be part of the fun then please RSVP before the evening of April 5, 1888.

The Day After

The day after the wedding we will have a brunch at eleven the morning. The brunch will be held at Clara's parent's house on their porch. At the brunch we will be serving a variety of different foods. After the brunch Henry and Clara will be leaving for their honeymoon.

Franchesca Gallardo, Grade 8

KERNEL ESSAYS BY STUDENTS
Purposes of an Action

We are a family, including Nara, Roman, Caleb, Dad (Seth), Mom (Michelle) and me (Kayley), in order to not upset the neighbors (especially the ones below the floor of our apartment) and to not be thrown out, we tell each other to whisper and not talk loud.

Kayley Abelove, Grade 8

We, the family, in order to have a nice family meal without having to cook, to avoid doing dishes afterwards, to eat in a hurry, and to get really good pizza, are going to Grimaldi's.

Alejandra Trillo, Grade 8

We, the unicorns of every child's dreams, in order to make children happy, give children fantasies, and to make parents go crazy, will put gold at the end of all the rainbows we make, and destroy all bad dreams with our broccoli laser guns.

Nina De La Torre, Grade 8

I, a semi-athlete, in order to have fun, to relieve stress, to focus and to jump higher, am running two to four miles straight every day.

Christian Westbrook, Grade 8

JOHNSON HIGH SCHOOL CONSTITUTION PREAMBLE

We the students of Johnson High School

In order to create the perfect learning experience

Establish classroom rules and secure fair grading policy.

Provide for the Student body, Promote class unity and

Secure these successful techniques to ourselves and the students to come

Do remember and abide by these stated rules for the highest chance of graduation.

Joshua Haag, Grade 8

We are a group, rising against the bad people. We're doing this to stop everything from falling apart. We are trying our hardest to bring back peace.

Miriam Stein, Grade 7, writing as Tris from the novel *Divergent*

PLANNING PAGE

Name: _____

TITLE OF YOUR PIECE

TEXT STRUCTURE

Charm Check

| Is ___ still around? | what it looks (or looked) like | Some problems it faced | Do I/we still have it? |

Francis Scott Key

KERNEL ESSAY

1. _____

2. _____

3. _____

4. _____

_____

_____

SUGGESTIONS FOR QUICK LIST:

If you had a bracelet with charms that stand for something in your life, what would those charms be?

MY QUICK LIST OF TOPICS:

1. ....
2. ....
3. ....
4. ....
5. ....

"The Star Spangled Banner"

Francis Scott Key, 1814

Oh, say can you see by the dawn's early light

What so proudly we hailed at the twilight's last gleaming?

Whose broad stripes and bright stars thru the perilous fight,

O'er the ramparts we watched were so gallantly streaming?

And the rocket's red glare, the bombs bursting in air,

Gave proof through the night that our flag was still there.

Oh, say does that star-spangled banner yet wave

O'er the land of the free and the home of the brave?

On the shore, dimly seen through the mists of the deep,

Where the foe's haughty host in dread silence reposes,

What is that which the breeze, o'er the towering steep,

As it fitfully blows, half conceals, half discloses?

Now it catches the gleam of the morning's first beam,

In full glory reflected now shines in the stream:

'Tis the star-spangled banner! Oh long may it wave

O'er the land of the free and the home of the brave!

And where is that band who so vauntingly swore

That the havoc of war and the battle's confusion,

A home and a country should leave us no more!

Their blood has washed out their foul footsteps' pollution.

No refuge could save the hireling and slave

From the terror of flight, or the gloom of the grave:

And the star-spangled banner in triumph doth wave

O'er the land of the free and the home of the brave!

Oh! thus be it ever, when freemen shall stand

Between their loved home and the war's desolation!

Blest with victory and peace, may the heav'n rescued land

Praise the Power that hath made and preserved us a nation.

Then conquer we must, when our cause it is just,

And this be our motto: "In God is our trust."

And the star-spangled banner in triumph shall wave

O'er the land of the free and the home of the brave!

PLANNING PAGE + ESSAY
Charm Check

PEACE

Peace is not completely here,

Even the cops have us living in fear.

We lack peace where we need it the most,

It's disappeared, gone like a ghost.

Everyone wants peace, but can't seem to agree,

The peace is drowning in a raging sea.

Peace is simple, pure, and clear,

Peace takes away the pain . . . the fear.

Peace is what helps us sleep at night,

It makes everything seem right.

Peace itself doesn't have a specific view,

It has no shape, size, or hue.

Even though you can't see it,

It's something you feel.

And when you feel it,

You know it's real.

Peace went away and along came the wars,

Also to come: hatred, evil and so much more.

When people learn to listen to what others have to say,

I believe that is when peace will be here to stay.

We use violence to make peace, that just isn't right,

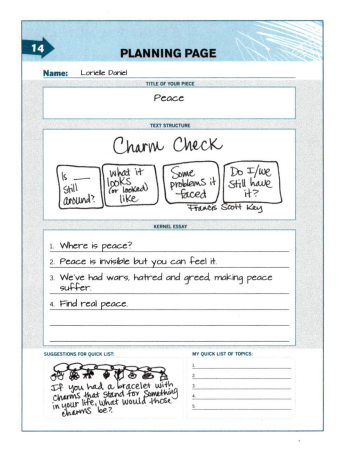

We try to make the world a better place by starting a fight.

People are concerned with only themselves,

And try to find peace in objects and wealth.

Start to find peace in the small things,

Don't focus on only money and diamond rings.

Focus on God, family, and good friends,

Find real peace. Don't pretend.

Lorielle Daniel, Grade 8

KERNEL ESSAYS BY STUDENTS
Charm Check

1. Is my violin still there?
2. It is dark brown and shiny.
3. The strings were messed up, it was stuck in a closet, and the varnish stripped off.
4. Do I still have my violin?

Talia Delambre, Grade 7

_____

1. Have you seen the Star of David?
2. It can be seen in Jewish art or in Jewish temples or all over Israel.
3. It has faced slavery, racism, and many people trying to wipe it out.
4. Will it always be here forever?
5. I sure think so.

Matheu Shiver, Grade 6

_____

1. Is Cristiano Ronaldo still playing like soccer is his life?
2. He looks like he is not sticking out to anyone any more.
3. People say bad things about him. They are probably jealous; they aren't as good as he is.
4. Will he still be playing when I'm old enough to play on his team?
5. Will he still be my idol when I'm older?

Dante Valencia, Grade 6

_____

1. Has anyone seen my shovel and bucket?
2. They were both blue and the bucket had pictures of seashells on it.
3. It hasn't been used for a few years.
4. Will I still have fun and exciting beach days?

Anael Ashkenazi, Grade 7

_____

1. Is my mom at work?
2. My mom is filled with joy, love, and laughter and always took me shopping with her.
3. She faced me, a brat, that always said no to her when she told me what to do.
4. Yes, I will always have my mom with me.

Kennedy Cantu, Grade 7

1. Are my shoes still by the front door?
2. They look gray with some blue.
3. They have been used a lot and some threads are coming out.

Dylan Totten, Grade 6

_____

1. Is my iPhone still there on my bed?
2. It has fingerprints, a blue Gameboy case, a bunch of apps, and a cool wallpaper.
3. It fell in the toilet twice, it fell down my stairs, and it was lost four times.
4. Is it still on my bed with 47% of battery?

Norman Davis, Grade 6

_____

1. Is my little seashell still in my collection box?
2. It was around here showing off its many stripes and perfect swirls on its tips along with its pearly pink skin color.
3. Even though it's not the biggest shell and it has cracks from being squished under the others, it still sings the most loveliest song of all.
4. So where is my favorite little seashell filled with songs, cracks, patterns, memories and secrets?

Deniff Lara, Grade 7

_____

1. Do I still have my little red tricycle?
2. It was a small, red tricycle that had streamers on its side.
3. On the way, it has lost a few streamers and collected dust.
4. Do I still have the love I once did for that little red tricycle?

Franchesca Gallardo, Grade 8

PLANNING PAGE

Name: _____

TITLE OF YOUR PIECE

TEXT STRUCTURE

S. O. S.

| what our Situation is right now | What is being asked of me | how I have responded | what I need from you | what will happen if I don't get help | one happy note |

William B. Travis

KERNEL ESSAY

1. _____

2. _____

3. _____

4. _____

5. _____

6. _____

SUGGESTIONS FOR QUICK LIST:

When someone asks for immediate help:
- babysitting
- car breakdowns
- Emergencies
- setting up for an event
- lock-outs

MY QUICK LIST OF TOPICS:

1. ....

2. ....

3. ....

4. ....

5. ....

"Victory or Death" Letter From the Alamo   William B. Travis, 1836

Commandancy of the The Alamo

Bejar, Feby. 24th. 1836

To the People of Texas & All Americans in the World—

Fellow Citizens & compatriots—

I am besieged, by a thousand or more of the Mexicans under Santa Anna—I have sustained a continual Bombardment & cannonade for 24 hours & have not lost a man—The enemy has demanded a surrender at discretion, otherwise, the garrison are to be put to the sword, if the fort is taken—I have answered the demand with a cannon shot, & our flag still waves proudly from the walls—<u>I shall never surrender or retreat</u>. Then, I call on you in the name of Liberty, of patriotism & everything dear to the American character, to come to our aid, with all dispatch—The enemy is receiving reinforcements daily & will no doubt increase to three or four thousand in four or five days. If this call is neglected, I am determined to sustain myself as long as possible & die like a soldier who never forgets what is due to his own honor & that of his country—**Victory or Death**.

William Barrett Travis.
Lt. Col. comdt.

P. S. The Lord is on our side—When the enemy appeared in sight we had not three bushels of corn—We have since found in deserted houses 80 or 90 bushels and got into the walls 20 or 30 head of Beeves.

Travis

PLANNING PAGE + ESSAY
S.O.S.

HONOR IN DEATH (MORSE CODE MESSAGE FROM THE TITANIC)

Captain of the RMS Titanic

About 41°-56°N, 50°-14°W

April 14th, 1912

To any ship that can hear me—

I am struck by a massive iceberg in the ice field we traverse—the water line has creeped ever higher for half an hour, but no casualties to report of. The icy waters demand a surrender, ere this ship and all her 2,000 passengers drown. I have met these demands with action and determination—I will not abandon this ship. Thus I ask of you, in the name of Honor, of decency and everything true to human nature, to come to our last known location with all haste. Five of eight compartments that made this ship "unsinkable" have ruptured, and the rest are not long to follow; we have another two hours of buoyancy left, at most. If this message goes unheeded, I will evacuate all that I can, for as long as I can, and die like a captain: I will go down with this ship. Honor in death. Godspeed.

Edward Jones Smith
Captain

P.S. We caught the damage fairly early—though there is no saving the ship, even as I write this, lifeboats are being filled, people being saved. Perhaps there is hope for us yet.

Robin Gaudette, Grade 9

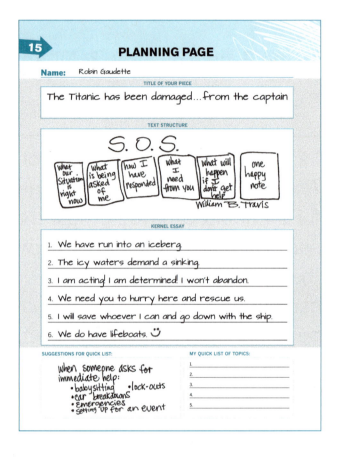

PLANNING PAGE

Name: Robin Gaudette

TITLE OF YOUR PIECE
The Titanic has been damaged...from the captain

TEXT STRUCTURE

S.O.S.

| What our situation is right now | What is being asked of me | How I have responded | What I need from you | What will happen if I dont get help | one happy note |

William B. Travis

KERNEL ESSAY
1. We have run into an iceberg.
2. The icy waters demand a sinking.
3. I am acting! I am determined! I won't abandon.
4. We need you to hurry here and rescue us.
5. I will save whoever I can and go down with the ship.
6. We do have lifeboats. ☺

SUGGESTIONS FOR QUICK LIST:
When someone asks for immediate help:
• babysitting • lock-outs
• car breakdowns
• emergencies
• setting up for an event

MY QUICK LIST OF TOPICS:
1.
2.
3.
4.
5.

KERNEL ESSAYS BY STUDENTS
S.O.S.

1. Our current situation is it's flooding outside and the yard is a lake and I'm ankle deep in water!
2. I'm being asked to help my father.
3. I have responded by saying yes and getting my rain coat on and going outside with my father to help him.
4. What he needed from me was to get the tools we needed and open the garage door and help him with whatever needed to be done.
5. What will happen if I don't help my dad is he will get angry and the house could flood.
6. One happy note is the house didn't flood and everything that was needed to be done got done and my dad was happy with me.

Matheu Shiver, Grade 6

1. I'm trying to get into the Davidson Institute, so I need to do NaNoWriMo.
2. I have to write an 8,000 word novel in 30 days.
3. I will try my best to write this novel in the correct time frame.
4. I really need you to type for me while I dictate because I can't type quickly enough to keep on track.
5. If you don't help me, I might not complete it in one month.
6. If I do finish on time, I have a chance to get into a very prestigious institute for young scholars.

Iris Hernandez, Grade 6

_____

1. I've always wanted to be a bright bulb.
2. Yet I've been told I'm simply a dim one.
3. Still I run and think with other bright bulbs.
4. Somehow I still wonder if I'm dim and if so will it turn on?
5. Yes I will tell those who see me as greater.
6. I am only human and have flaws, but maybe one day that light will turn on.

Joshua Montellano, Grade 10

PLANNING PAGE

Name:

TITLE OF YOUR PIECE

TEXT STRUCTURE

Sightseeing

| what it looks like up ahead | what it sounds like, as we get closer | signs we can see that others have been here before us | my overall impression of this spot |

Charles Dickens

KERNEL ESSAY

1.

2.

3.

4.

SUGGESTIONS FOR QUICK LIST:

When you're visiting some place for the first time
- a restaurant
- a theme park
- any tourist place
- an office
- a nature spot

MY QUICK LIST OF TOPICS:

1.
2.
3.
4.
5.

"Observations on a Steamboat Between Pittsburgh and Cincinnati," *American Notes*   Charles Dickens, 1842

Occasionally we stop for a few minutes, maybe to take in wood, maybe for passengers, at some small town or village (I ought to say city, every place is a city here); but the banks are for the most part deep solitudes, overgrown with trees, which, hereabouts, are already in leaf and very green. For miles, and miles, and miles, these solitudes are unbroken by any sign of human life or trace of human footstep; nor is anything seen to move about them but the blue jay, whose colour is so bright, and yet so delicate, that it looks like a flying flower. Through such a scene as this the unwieldy machine takes its hoarse sullen way: venting, at every revolution of the paddles, a loud high-pressure blast; enough, one would think, to waken up the host of Indians who lie buried in a great mound yonder. . . . The very river, as though it shared one's feelings of compassion for the extinct tribes who lived so pleasantly here, in their blessed ignorance of white existence, hundreds of years ago, steals out of its way to ripple near this mound: and there are few places where the Ohio sparkles more brightly than in the Big Grave Creek.

COMPLETED PLANNING PAGE
Sightseeing

I HAVE A DREAM

On August 28, 1963, Dr. Martin Luther King Jr. gave a speech about Civil Rights that will go down in history. Here is one perspective of the speech, which I wrote in the voice of a spectator.

I approached the Washington Mall (which by the way doesn't have any clothes), all I could say was wow. I repeated it over and over again.

I got closer in and I could see that this speech was going to be a huge deal. The Mall was packed to its brim, there was no room to move or walk, and there was barely any room to stand.

Once I finally found a place to stand, I stood there and took it all in. I was here with hundreds of thousands of people who wanted the same thing. Equality. I closed my eyes and listened to all of the cheering and applauding.

On the floor, I saw flyers, posters, and signs that read things like "equality," "dream," and "end racism." You could tell how many protests took place here.

Being at the Washington Mall on August 28 was surreal, before Dr. King even got up to the big stage in the front, I could tell that big things were going to happen.

Maggie Davis, Grade 8

KERNEL ESSAYS BY STUDENTS
Sightseeing

THE WESTERN WALL

1. I enter through the gate and see a ginormous wall.
2. As I enter I hear prayers, happy songs, and can see people dancing in joy.
3. As I touch and look at the wall I pray and give respect as I put my note in next to the previous people that put their note in.
4. I could feel, hear, and sense the past of this holy spot.

Jacob Fiero, Grade 8

JW MARRIOTT WATER PARK

1. It looks blue with inner tubes in the water.
2. You can hear kids screaming, laughing, and splashing.
3. There's some soda spilled on the floor over there.
4. I can't wait. It looks better than the Hilton.

Amy King, Grade 4

---

1. We were walking down the sandy, hard, concrete sidewalk that was bustling with people. We went into the SDBK store to rent kayaks, wetsuits, and snorkeling gear.
2. The employee gave us our things and said, "Here you go," and the sound of his voice cut through the murmurs, whispers, and ringing laughter of people.
3. I don't know exactly who built this shop, but I'm pretty sure it was built a while ago, maybe three, four, or five years ago. Shoppers have clearly been here.
4. I actually got to wear a wetsuit, something I'd always wished, hoped and dreamed for but never expected to actually do.

Iris Hernandez, Grade 6

SAN DIEGO ZOO

1. Olivia, my mom and Tevia waited for my dad Jakob and me. We saw maps, gift shops and flamingos.
2. I heard monkeys, buses, and crying.
3. I don't think that they will ever stop expanding the zoo with more animals and space.
4. I couldn't believe that San Diego Zoo is in the middle of the city, town, and forest.

Elliott Tawil, Grade 6

KILLING THE MICE (FROM *THE UNDERLAND CHRONICLES*)

1. Ahead we see an underground cavern with a volcano.
2. We see thousands of innocent mice being killed by toxic gasses, and we hear desperate final cries for help.
3. The history here seems clear: the Bane has ordered this to punish Regalia.
4. The rats don't seem to care!

Noah Hernandez, Grade 7

PLANNING PAGE

Name: _____

TITLE OF YOUR PIECE

```
┌─────────────────────────────────────────────────┐
│                                                   │
│                                                   │
│                                                   │
│                                                   │
└─────────────────────────────────────────────────┘
```

TEXT STRUCTURE

Tour of an Unfamiliar Place

| where we begin | what we see | what we hear | the most surprising or shocking part | who created this |

Labor Reformer

KERNEL ESSAY

1. _____

2. _____

3. _____

4. _____

5. _____

_____

SUGGESTIONS FOR QUICK LIST:

Unfamiliar places you've visited:
- hospital
- bakery
- cemetery
- X-ray office
- backstage
- factory
- arena
- kitchen
- dressing room

MY QUICK LIST OF TOPICS:

1. _____

2. _____

3. _____

4. _____

5. _____

Now let us examine the nature of the labor itself, and the conditions under which it is performed. Enter with us into the large rooms, when the looms are at work. The largest that we saw . . . is four hundred feet long, and about seventy broad; there are five hundred looms, and twenty-one thousand spindles in it. The din and clatter of these five hundred looms under full operation, struck us on first entering as something frightful and infernal, for it seemed such an atrocious violation of one of the faculties of the human soul, the sense of hearing . . .

The young women sleep upon an average six in a room; three beds to a room. There is no privacy, no retirement here; it is almost impossible to read or write alone, as the parlor is full, and so many sleep in the same chamber. A young woman remarked to us, that if she had a letter to write, she did it on the head of a band-box, sitting on a trunk, as there was not space for a table. So live and toil the young women of our country in the boarding-houses and manufactories, which the rich and influential of our land have built for them.

COMPLETED PLANNING PAGE
Tour of an Unfamiliar Place

Name: Deniff Lara

TITLE OF YOUR PIECE

Nemo's Field Trip

TEXT STRUCTURE

Tour of an Unfamiliar Place

| Where we begin | What we See | What We hear | the most surprising or shocking part | Who created this |

Labor Reformer

KERNEL ESSAY

1. My school (of fish) field trip starts off cool with my first teacher ever.

2. We see a boat, which my friends think is awesome and daring.

3. I hear my father's screams, the boat noise, and my friends.

4. The shocking consequences are that I become a captive of atrocious, unfishly creatures.

5. I guess my new friends weren't the best influence on me, and I didn't want to be a scaredy cat, so...I created this mess.

SUGGESTIONS FOR QUICK LIST:

Unfamiliar places you've visited:
- hospital
- bakery
- cemetery
- x-ray office
- backstage
- factory
- arena
- kitchen
- dressing room

MY QUICK LIST OF TOPICS:

1. Botanical gardens
2. Rapunzel--tower
3. Donkey--Shrek's Swamp
4. Dough pizzeria
5. Emily's house

KERNEL ESSAYS BY STUDENTS
Tour of an Unfamiliar Place

STATE CAPITAL

1. I first looked out the window and saw Austin. All that time being in the car was worth it.
2. I got to see the capital and go sightseeing.
3. I remember the sound of music, laughter, and people on their phones.
4. My little sis freaked out when a jumping spider landed on her.
5. I don't know who created this place, but I do know that my family made this trip possible.

Zoe Falk, Grade 6

SEEING MY BABY BROTHER

1. We walk into a big, long, clean hallway.
2. We see tiny, small, newborn babies in rooms.
3. We hear screaming, crying, and laughing.
4. I'm surprised to see that my brother has a full, red lock of hair.
5. Who makes a hospital? Taxes, fundraisers, and people.

Norman Davis, Grade 6

SCUBA DIVING

1. Splash! We went into the crystal clear ocean to see this enormous reef.
2. Swish! We meet and greet gagillions of fish and see hundreds of different species of fish.
3. I hear bubbles as I exhale through the mask.
4. Most surprising was voom! A stingray swims swiftly across the seabed!
5. The ocean was created by NATURE!!

Ilan Haas, Grade 6

ATLANTIS

1. We stepped out of the car. It was amazing, spectacular, exciting.
2. I saw sharks, fish, and dolphins in the front lobby.
3. I heard machines at work, people helping, and fish being fish.
4. I was surprised that the waterslide was gigantic, ridiculous, big.
5. The creator of this place was a genius.

Jacob Tawil, Grade 6

NEW YORK CANDY SHOP

1. I begin walking in the candy shop.
2. I see rows of assorted candy. M&Ms, candy bars, and so much more.
3. Everyone's talking, and shouting about the candy.
4. I was surprised. That was the most candy I've ever seen.
5. I don't know who created this amazing place.

Dylan Totten, Grade 6

MIAMI BEACH

1. We walked out of our condo right by the beach.
2. I see blue waters, crystal sand, and the sun shining.
3. I hear dogs barking, children laughing, and people talking.
4. I've never seen water that blue and clear.
5. This was created by the forces of nature, erosion, and God.

Norman Davis, Grade 6

PLANNING PAGE

Name: _____

TITLE OF YOUR PIECE

TEXT STRUCTURE

Breaking Into a Heated Argument

| the sides of the argument | You say this, but it's not true because... | You also say this, but it's not true because... | And you also say this, but... | So this is what will make things right... |

Sojourner Truth

KERNEL ESSAY

1. _____

2. _____

3. _____

4. _____

5. _____

_____

SUGGESTIONS FOR QUICK LIST:

Sometimes people give crazy reasons for their opinions, and you just have to disagree with the points they make. Think about shouting arguments going on in the news...

MY QUICK LIST OF TOPICS:

1. _____

2. _____

3. _____

4. _____

5. _____

"Ain't I a Woman?" Speech

Delivered at the Women's Convention in Akron, Ohio

Well, children, where there is so much racket there must be something out of kilter. I think that 'twixt the negroes of the South and the women at the North, all talking about rights, the white men will be in a fix pretty soon. But what's all this here talking about?

That man over there says that women need to be helped into carriages, and lifted over ditches, and to have the best place everywhere. Nobody ever helps me into carriages, or over mud-puddles, or gives me any best place! And ain't I a woman? Look at me! Look at my arm! I have ploughed and planted, and gathered into barns, and no man could head me! And ain't I a woman? I could work as much and eat as much as a man—when I could get it—and bear the lash as well! And ain't I a woman? I have borne thirteen children, and seen most all sold off to slavery, and when I cried out with my mother's grief, none but Jesus heard me! And ain't I a woman?

Then they talk about this thing in the head; what's this they call it? [*member of audience whispers, "intellect"*] That's it, honey. What's that got to do with women's rights or negroes' rights? If my cup won't hold but a pint, and yours holds a quart, wouldn't you be mean not to let me have my little half measure full?

Then that little man in black there, he says women can't have as much rights as men, 'cause Christ wasn't a woman! Where did your Christ come from? Where did your Christ come from? From God and a woman! Man had nothing to do with Him.

If the first woman God ever made was strong enough to turn the world upside down all alone, these women together ought to be able to turn it back, and get it right side up again! And now they is asking to do it, the men better let them.

Obliged to you for hearing me, and now old Sojourner ain't got nothing more to say.

COMPLETED PLANNING PAGE
Breaking Into a Heated Argument

Name: Jacquelyn Clendening

TITLE OF YOUR PIECE

Cross country? No.

TEXT STRUCTURE

Breaking Into a Heated Argument

| the sides of the argument | You say this, but it's not true because... | You also say this, but it's not true because... | And you also say this, but... | So this is what will make things right... |

Sojourner Truth

KERNEL ESSAY

1. You want me to run cross country, and I don't want to.

2. You say it will keep me in shape, but the time isn't well spent.

3. You say I can do it, but I wouldn't like to.

4. You say I can train extra hard, but that would take time away from soccer training/college scouts.

5. So let's compromise: I will participate in it but not to the extent you are describing.

SUGGESTIONS FOR QUICK LIST:

Sometimes people give crazy reasons for their opinions, and you just have to disagree with the points they make. Think about shouting arguments going on in the news...

MY QUICK LIST OF TOPICS:

1.
2.
3.
4.
5.

FULL ESSAY
Breaking Into a Heated Argument

EXPRESSING OPINIONS

Dad, I know you want me to do cross country but I really would not like to. I don't want to take part in it. I know that you say that it will keep me in shape but there is more effort put into it than what I receive in return.

You say that I will like it once I get into better shape. But even if I already am in shape doesn't necessarily mean I'll enjoy the extra workout. There are more important, better things that I could be doing with my time.

You also say that I can do it, but I would not like to. I'm not good at cross country. I am built like a sprinter. So therefore, I believe that I should train for sprints. I can do cross country but I would not like to take extra time to do so.

You also say that I can train extra hard for cross country. But I would not like to train extra for this. I could be training for soccer or for track. Soccer is more important to be getting better, due to the fact that I have college coaches talking to me about possibly playing for them. Therefore, the more I train for soccer, the more coaches' attention I can get.

So in order for us both to get what we want, let's meet in the middle. How about I will do cross country for its before-school practices and its meets, but I will not, however, train extra for cross country. With this free time I will now have, I can catch up on homework to get better grades, or I could get more training in for soccer or track. I could even hang out with my friends.

In conclusion, I will do cross country but I will not take extra time to go out and train for it. And with that new time that I will receive, I can train, do homework, or hang with friends.

Jacquelyn Clendening, Grade 9

PLANNING PAGE

Name: _____

TITLE OF YOUR PIECE

TEXT STRUCTURE

Controversial Decision

| what the decision is | reasons for the decision | who may disagree | request for civilized manners (not violence) | new habits this will create | why I made this decision |

Emancipation Proclamation

KERNEL ESSAY

1. _____

2. _____

3. _____

4. _____

5. _____

6. _____

SUGGESTIONS FOR QUICK LIST:

Have there been moments when someone announced a decision, knowing it would cause an outcry?

Someone was angry or outraged? Maybe the decider was you?

MY QUICK LIST OF TOPICS:

1. ....

2. ....

3. ....

4. ....

5. ....

Emancipation Proclamation   Abraham Lincoln, 1862

Whereas on the twenty-second day of September, in the year of our Lord one thousand eight hundred and sixty-two, a proclamation was issued by the President of the United States, containing, among other things, the following, to wit:

"That on the first day of January, in the year of our Lord one thousand eight hundred and sixty-three, all persons held as slaves within any State or designated part of a State the people whereof shall then be in rebellion against the United States shall be then, thenceforward, and forever free; and the Executive government of the United States, including the military and naval authority thereof, will recognize and maintain the freedom of such persons and will do no act or acts to repress such persons, or any of them, in any efforts they may make for their actual freedom.

"That the Executive will on the first day of January aforesaid, by proclamation, designate the States and parts of States, if any, in which the people thereof, respectively, shall then be in rebellion against the United States; and the fact that any State or the people thereof shall on that day be in good faith represented in the Congress of the United States by members chosen thereto at elections wherein a majority of the qualified voters of such States shall have participated shall, in the absence of strong countervailing testimony, be deemed conclusive evidence that such State and the people thereof are not then in rebellion against the United States."

Now, therefore, I, Abraham Lincoln, President of the United States, by virtue of the power in me vested as commander-in-chief of the army and navy of the United States in time of actual armed rebellion against the authority and government of the United States, and as a fit and necessary war measure for suppressing said rebellion, do, on this first day of January, in the year of our Lord one thousand eight hundred and sixty-three, and in accordance with my purpose so to do, publicly proclaimed for the full period of one hundred days from the first day above mentioned, order and designate as the States and parts of States wherein the people thereof, respectively, are this day in rebellion against the United States the following, to wit: Arkansas, Texas, Louisiana (except the parishes of St. Bernard, Plaquemines, Jefferson, St. John, St. Charles, St. James, Ascension, Assumption, Terre Bonne, Lafourche, St. Mary, St. Martin, and Orleans, including the city of New Orleans), Mississippi, Alabama, Florida, Georgia, South Carolina, North Carolina, and Virginia (except the forty-eight counties designated as West Virginia, and also the counties of Berkeley, Accomac, Northampton, Elizabeth City, York, Princess Ann, and Norfolk, including the cities of Norfolk and Portsmouth), and which excepted parts are for the present left precisely as if this proclamation were not issued.

And by virtue of the power and for the purpose aforesaid, I do order and declare that all persons held as slaves within said designated States and parts of States are, and henceforward shall be, free; and that the Executive government of the United States, including the military and naval authorities thereof, will recognize and maintain the freedom of said persons.

And I hereby enjoin upon the people so declared to be free to abstain from all violence, unless in necessary self-defence; and I recommend to them that, in all case when allowed, they labor faithfully for reasonable wages.

And I further declare and make known that such persons of suitable condition will be received into the armed service of the United States to garrison forts, positions, stations, and other places, and to man vessels of all sorts in said service.

And upon this act, sincerely believed to be an act of justice, warranted by the Constitution upon military necessity, I invoke the considerate judgment of mankind and the gracious favor of Almighty God.

PLANNING PAGE + ESSAY
Controversial Decision

BASKETBALL VS. FOOTBALL

Deciding whether to play basketball or football was a tough decision for me. I chose basketball over football this year but next year I'm giving football a try. I played football last year and it was fun, plus all the coaches are pushing me to at least try football.

Doing more than one sport is harder than it seems; that's why most people just do one. You can focus easier and learn all the plays, but with two, you have to actually study the plays and go through them more often.

There is a big downside to picking just one. The coaches, for example, will try to steer you towards the sport you didn't pick. Once they do finally break you, you're stuck with that coach and they're going to push you as hard as possible to do your best. Also, your friends will try to make you play the sport they're playing and may push you around or tease you.

Although there is an obvious choice to me, I'll still weigh the pros and cons. For basketball, there's less people on the court to communicate with, it's all about skill and stamina, and there is less pressure when playing. For football, you have to wear heavy pads, withstand a lot of pressure while being fast on your feet, and you have to risk your body pretty much every play.

If I did just pick one and quit the other, it may become a habit and I may quit other things. Quitting is never a good thing and it could lower your self-esteem as well.

Next year I'm deciding to just play basketball because in my opinion, I think I'm better at it. When weighing the pros and cons, it sounds like the better choice. I can most likely get a scholarship easier than in football because there are less people. That's why basketball, to me, is just the better choice.

Bryan Adams, Grade 9

PLANNING PAGE

19

Name: Bryan Adams

TITLE OF YOUR PIECE
Basketball vs. Football

TEXT STRUCTURE

Controversial Decision

what the decision is | reasons for the decision | who may disagree | request for civilized manners (not violence) | new habits this will create | why I made this decision

Emancipation Proclamation

KERNEL ESSAY

1. Deciding whether basketball or football is better
2. Because more than one sport is tough and it's easier to do one
3. The coaches or friends
4. I weigh the pros and cons
5. Quitting other things
6. To better myself in life and in my goals

SUGGESTIONS FOR QUICK LIST:
Have there been moments when someone announced a decision, knowing it would cause an outcry? Someone was angry or outraged? Maybe the decider was you?

MY QUICK LIST OF TOPICS:
1. Sports
2. Tattoo
3. Fighting
4.
5.

KERNEL ESSAYS BY STUDENTS
Controversial Decision

1. Claire and Maggie will share a room.
2. The baby needs a nursery and Norman is a guy and can't share.
3. Maggie may complain a lot.
4. Please don't complain.
5. This will mean you have less (closet) space and your room will be shared.
6. We made the decision because of the space in the house.

Maggie Davis, Grade 8

---

1. I would be for violent video games if the makers could rephrase the bad words.
2. Not having so many bad words would help children be in a better mood and they could be nicer to the people around them.
3. Jakob might disagree because he thinks it teaches kids responsibility.
4. Please be better game producers and rephrase the bad words.
5. This will cause people not to be in bad tempers and not to do bad things.
6. I feel this opinion because games can change peoples' communication thoughts.

Dante Valencia, Grade 6

1. I've decided to go on a juice fast.
2. I think it will help me be stronger, get healthier, and lose weight.
3. This may cause my friends to worry that I'm going weird.
4. Please don't talk about me to each other behind my back.
5. I think I'll start paying more attention to what I eat.
6. I made this decision after my friend made me watch a movie called "Fat, Sick, and Nearly Dead."

Margaret Hopkins, Grade 10

NEW SCHOOL UNIFORMS

1. We have decided that our school will now have uniforms.
2. This will help everyone decide what to wear and be less expensive for our parents.
3. You students may not like it.
4. We hope you will not resort to violence while you protest this decision.
5. We feel confident that you will focus on studying more and the content of people's character.
6. I made this decision to see if it helps our school achievement.

Bonnie Bissett, Grade 10

Name: _____

TITLE OF YOUR PIECE

```
```

TEXT STRUCTURE

At the Moment of a Milestone

| how this began -or- what we set out to accomplish | where we are right now and why | what others have contributed so far | what we need to do from now on |

Gettysburg Address

KERNEL ESSAY

1. _____

2. _____

3. _____

4. _____

_____

_____

SUGGESTIONS FOR QUICK LIST:

Make your personal timeline showing your milestones

|—broke my leg——started 1st grade——got my dog——earned blue belt—|

MY QUICK LIST OF TOPICS:

1. ....

2. ....

3. ....

4. ....

5. ....

Gettysburg Address

Abraham Lincoln, 1863

Four score and seven years ago our fathers brought forth on this continent, a new nation, conceived in liberty, and dedicated to the proposition that all men are created equal.

Now we are engaged in a great civil war, testing whether that nation, or any nation so conceived and so dedicated, can long endure. We are met on a great battle field of that war. We have come to dedicate a portion of that field, as a final resting place for those who here gave their lives that that nation might live. It is altogether fitting and proper that we should do this.

But, in a larger sense, we cannot dedicate—we cannot consecrate—we cannot hallow—this ground. The brave men, living and dead, who struggled here, have consecrated it, far above our poor power to add or detract. The world will little note, nor long remember what we say here, but it can never forget what they did here. It is for us the living, rather, to be dedicated here to the unfinished work which they who fought here have thus far so nobly advanced. It is rather for us to be here dedicated to this great task remaining before us—that from these honored dead we take increased devotion to that cause for which they gave the last full measure of devotion—that we here highly resolve that these dead shall not have died in vain—that this nation, under God, shall have a new birth of freedom—and that government of the people, by the people, for the people, shall not perish from the earth.

COMPLETED PLANNING PAGE
At the Moment of a Milestone

Name: Ally Soderdani

TITLE OF YOUR PIECE

The Teenage Address

TEXT STRUCTURE

At the Moment of a Milestone

| how this began -or- what we set out to accomplish | where we are right now and why | what others have contributed so far | what we need to do from now on |

Gettysburg Address

KERNEL ESSAY

1. Fourteen years ago, a mother and father had a baby.

2. Now, the baby is grown and entering high school.

3. Many loving people have contributed to her.

4. She will get married and have children and lead a purposeful life.

SUGGESTIONS FOR QUICK LIST:

Make your personal timeline showing your milestones

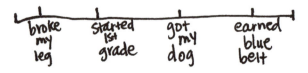

broke my leg · started 1st grade · got my dog · earned blue belt

MY QUICK LIST OF TOPICS:

1. Entering kindergarten
2. Entering high school
3. Tryouts for choir
4.
5.

FULL ESSAY
At the Moment of a Milestone

THE TEENAGE ADDRESS

A decennial and four years ago, a mother and a father brought a crying, pale baby girl into this world, made by compassion and devoted to be raised as a child of God, to be a beacon of light in the dark world.

Now this once innocent baby girl is a 14 year old pubescent teen, entering her first year of high school, learning new things and experiencing life's biggest obstacles. She is forced into the bright spotlight of awkwardness. The peers around her save a part of the stage as a place of lies, gossip, and drama, hoping that the baby girl slips into it and conforms to the ways that her parents raised her not to become. It is possible she may trip, but her loving parents pull her back up.

But, overall, we cannot forget—we cannot ignore—we cannot bypass the loving people that came into her life. The friends, old and new, who helped and assisted, have influenced the now growing teen, far more than the people who break her down. The world will little note or remember what she said, but it can never forget what she did with her friends. It is for her own children, that she plans to have when married, to be dedicated and raised to the unfinished work which she had begun in her teenage years. It is rather for her and her future husband to devote their children the task before them—of being a light and pathway for the lost and to be different from the crowd—that they highly honor God through their children's lives— that these children's lives, under God, shall have meaning and purpose and that the once baby girl, now mother's child, shall not attune to ways of this world.

Ally Soderdani, Grade 9

PLANNING PAGE

Name: _____

TITLE OF YOUR PIECE

TEXT STRUCTURE

We're Both Wrong; We're Both Right

| Here's what has been happening | Here are both sides of the conflict | We can't both be right | We share the blame | Let's heal the damage |

Abraham Lincoln

KERNEL ESSAY

1. _____

2. _____

3. _____

4. _____

5. _____

SUGGESTIONS FOR QUICK LIST:

Arguments or conflicts can be
• between two people or two groups
• over quickly or last for a long time
• over something small or over deep beliefs

MY QUICK LIST OF TOPICS:

1. _____
2. _____
3. _____
4. _____
5. _____

Second Inaugural Address

Abraham Lincoln, 1865

Fellow Countrymen:

At this second appearing to take the oath of the presidential office, there is less occasion for an extended address than there was at the first. Then a statement, somewhat in detail, of a course to be pursued, seemed fitting and proper. Now, at the expiration of four years, during which public declarations have been constantly called forth on every point and phase of the great contest which still absorbs the attention, and engrosses the energies of the nation, little that is new could be presented. The progress of our arms, upon which all else chiefly depends, is as well known to the public as to myself; and it is, I trust, reasonably satisfactory and encouraging to all.

With high hope for the future, no prediction in regard to it is ventured.

On the occasion corresponding to this four years ago, all thoughts were anxiously directed to an impending civil-war. All dreaded it—all sought to avert it. While the inaugural address was being delivered from this place, devoted altogether to saving the Union without war, insurgent agents were in the city seeking to destroy it without war—seeking to dissolve the Union, and divide effects, by negotiation. Both parties deprecated war; but one of them would make war rather than let the nation survive; and the other would accept war rather than let it perish. And the war came.

One eighth of the whole population were colored slaves, not distributed generally over the Union, but localized in the Southern part of it. These slaves constituted a peculiar and powerful interest. All knew that this interest was, somehow, the cause of the war. To strengthen, perpetuate, and extend this interest was the object for which the insurgents would rend the Union, even by war; while the government claimed no right to do more than to restrict the territorial enlargement of it. Neither party expected for the war, the magnitude, or the duration, which it has already attained. Neither anticipated that the cause of the conflict might cease with, or even before, the conflict itself should cease. Each looked for an easier triumph, and a result less fundamental and astounding. Both read the same Bible, and pray to the same God; and each invokes His aid against the other. It may seem strange that any men should dare to ask a just God's assistance in wringing their bread from the sweat of other men's faces; but let us judge not that we be not judged. The prayers of both could not be answered; that of neither has been answered fully. The Almighty has His own purposes. "Woe unto the world because of offences! for it must needs be that offences come; but woe to that man by whom the offence cometh!" If we shall suppose that American Slavery is one of those offences which, in the providence of God, must needs come, but which, having continued through His appointed time, He now wills to remove, and that He gives to both North and South, this terrible war, as the woe due to those by whom the offence came, shall we discern therein any departure from those divine attributes which the believers in a Living God always ascribe to Him? Fondly do we hope—fervently do we pray—that this mighty scourge of war may speedily pass away. Yet, if God wills that it continue, until all the wealth piled by the bond-man's two hundred and fifty years of unrequited toil shall be sunk, and until every drop of blood drawn with the lash, shall be paid by another drawn with the sword, as was said three thousand years ago, so still it must be said "the judgments of the Lord, are true and righteous altogether."

With malice toward none; with charity for all; with firmness in the right, as God gives us to see the right, let us strive on to finish the work we are in; to bind up the nation's wounds; to care for him who shall have borne the battle, and for his widow, and his orphan—to do all which may achieve and cherish a just, and a lasting peace, among ourselves, and with all nations.

KERNEL ESSAYS BY STUDENTS
We're Both Wrong; We're Both Right

AFTER WORLD WAR II

1. You attacked us and started a second world war.
2. You hate us and decided to attack one of our naval harbors, so there is victim and accuser.
3. Now it wasn't right for you to attack us and it wasn't right for us to drop atomic bombs on you.
4. We both should be disappointed in ourselves.
5. Let's come together and create a global world organization to help the wounded and promote peace.

Timothy Bates, Grade 8

BENEDICK AND BEATRICE
FROM *MUCH ADO ABOUT NOTHING*

1. Beatrice wants revenge for Hero's humiliation.
2. Beatrice wants her boyfriend to kill his best friend; he loves her but can't kill his friend for her love.
3. They can't love, stay together, and hate each other across the earth.
4. They both feel charged with guilt of loving one another, and for being loyal to their friends.
5. Later after that, Claudio and Hero are back together. They shall marry too and live merry beyond their lifetime.

Deniff Lara, Grade 7

THE CONFLICT
BETWEEN ROMEO AND JULIET

1. Romeo and Juliet had been meeting in secret because they love each other.
2. The two families hate each other, but the children are in love.
3. The lovers can't get together completely while the families are public enemies. Therefore, Romeo and Juliet are not allowed to see each other.
4. The families are wrong to continue the hate, but Romeo and Juliet are wrong to keep the secret.
5. After Romeo and Juliet were tricked into committing suicide and "being in a better place," their families might heal.

Evan Katzman, Grade 7

THE DOGBERRY INSULT
FROM *MUCH ADO ABOUT NOTHING*

1. Dogberry was called an ass by his prisoners.
2. Dogberry was mad, and Borachio and Conrad didn't care because they were in jail. Dogberry was mad because they called him that and the other person did not care.
3. They both want something so they're not going to let the other person be right.
4. The other person started all the conflict because he called Dogberry an ass, but Dogberry kept the anger going.
5. Dogberry hurt one of those persons, because he was mad.

Maria Viramontes, Grade 7

KERNEL ESSAYS BY STUDENTS
We're Both Wrong; We're Both Right

AMERICAN SUPPORT FOR CUBA (AFTER THE *USS MAINE* SUNK, KILLING 260 U.S. SOLDIERS, 1898)

1. Cuba was in the middle of trying to gain independence from Spanish rule.
2. Americans offered to work out a solution, but Cuba wanted to be free and wasn't compromising.
3. We couldn't all be right.
4. Spain and Cuba didn't want to share the blame, so the U.S. got involved.
5. Roosevelt's "Rough Riders" went in and settled the conflict.

Alessandro Capodacqua, Grade 8

LAST OF THE CHIPS

1. My brother and I are fighting over the last of the chips.
2. I think I should have them because he had more and he thinks he should have them because I had more.
3. We can't both be right because there's only a little chips left.
4. We decided to share the chips.
5. We ate the chips and peace was made.

Anael Ashkenazi, Grade 7

THE PANAMA CANAL, 1903

1. After President McKinley was shot, the new president Theodore Roosevelt started talking up the canal.
2. Roosevelt offered money to Colombia, but they refused because they didn't want their land destroyed.
3. The Colombians and Roosevelt couldn't both get what they wanted.
4. The Colombians wouldn't share the blame for the unhappy Panamanians wanting independence in this decision.
5. Theodore Roosevelt sent an army to help the Panamanians earn freedom, and they accepted the money for use of the land.

Carrie Upton, Grade 11

GUILTY? (FROM THE *GONE* NOVEL SERIES)

1. 90% of all FAYZ survivors have been involved in a crime.
2. The children had to do it to survive but the outside people say, so what?
3. Who is right?
4. Both the children and the outside people are right and wrong.
5. I think anything that has happened in the FAYZ should be forgotten.

Asher Bar-Yadin, Grade 7

PLANNING PAGE

Name: _____

TITLE OF YOUR PIECE

[blank box]

TEXT STRUCTURE

Letter to an Author

| what beliefs we share | how we are different | what you've accomplished | how I admire you |

Frederick Douglass

KERNEL ESSAY

1. _____

2. _____

3. _____

4. _____

_____

SUGGESTIONS FOR QUICK LIST:

You've seen them, but they don't know you, not that well.
- any famous person
- a fictional character
- an author
- a classmate

MY QUICK LIST OF TOPICS:

1. _____
2. _____
3. _____
4. _____
5. _____

Letter to Harriet Beecher Stowe　　　　　　　　　　**Frederick Douglass, 1868**

Dear Harriet:

I am glad to know that the story of your eventful life has been written by a kind lady, and that the same is soon to be published. You ask for what you do not need when you call upon me for a word of commendation. I need such words from you far more than you can need them from me, especially where your superior labors, and devotion to the cause of the lately enslaved of our land are known as I know them. The difference between us is very marked. Most that I have done and suffered in the service of our cause has been in public, and I have received much encouragement at every step of the way. You, on the other hand, have labored in a private way. I have wrought in the day—you in the night. I have had the applause of the crowd and the satisfaction that comes of being approved by the multitude, while the most that you have done has been witnessed by a few trembling, scarred, and foot-sore bondmen and women, whom you have led out of the house of bondage, and whose heartfelt *"God bless you"* has been your only reward. The midnight sky and the silent stars have been the witnesses of your devotion to freedom and of your heroism. Excepting John Brown—of sacred memory—I know of no one who has willingly encountered more perils and hardships to serve our enslaved people than you have. Much that you have done would seem improbable to those who do not know you as I know you. It is to me a great pleasure and a great privilege to bear testimony to your character and your works, and to say to those to whom you may come, that I regard you in every way truthful and trustworthy.

Your friend,
Frederick Douglass

KERNEL ESSAYS BY STUDENTS
Letter to an Author

MARTIN LUTHER KING JR.

1. The beliefs we share are that everyone should be treated equal.
2. I'm alive and you have passed.
3. You have changed the world.
4. I think you are very smart and you share your beliefs with everyone.

Jerry Totten, Grade 6

DEAR MYA FROM *GIRL MEETS WORLD*

1. We both believe life might not get better.
2. You're an actor and I am not.
3. In the show, you have a best friend and I just have good friends.
4. You still keep on, even when your life is bad.

Kaitlyn Postell, Grade 6

TO JACQUES COUSTEAU

1. We are alike because we both love the water.
2. We are different because you like spear fishing and I don't.
3. However, I appreciate your invention, the aqualung.
4. You're amazing for making the first underwater breathing machine.

Iris Hernandez, Grade 6

TO STAN LEE

1. We both love superheroes and comics.
2. You write the comics and I read them.
3. You've written thousands of comics.
4. I admire your creativity and ideas.

Norman Davis, Grade 6

TO ALL SINGERS!

1. Some of you believe singing songs of joy and happiness will change people's lives forever. I believe that, too.
2. Some of you sing very dirty stuff. I really hate that.
3. All of you accomplished your dream or someone else's dream for them. You made it to where you wanted to be.
4. I really love all of you because we share a lot of things like singing. I love singing!

Kassandra B. Martinez, Grade 6

1. Dear Claire, we share the belief that people (dudes in our class) are weird.
2. You are friends with everyone, but I am not.
3. You have accomplished being nice and popular.
4. I admire that you can talk to people that you don't know.

Sara Toms, Grade 7

KERNEL ESSAYS BY STUDENTS
Letter to an Author

DEAR RICHARD PAUL EVANS

1. We both share the love of intense and mind-blowing books.
2. You come up with such good ideas unlike me or other people.
3. You've written more than 20 books which all went on the *New York Times* bestseller list.
4. I admire you because of your work, ideas, and mind-blowing books.

Anael Ashkenazi, Grade 7

———————————

ROSA PARKS

1. We share the belief for black people's rights.
2. I know how we are different because I am alive and you're dead.
3. You have accomplished black rights.
4. I admire you for standing up for what you believed was right.

Kaiya Ramirez, Grade 7

———————————

DEAR JUAN SEGUIN

1. We both live/lived in Texas.
2. You were a politician and I'm a cellist.
3. You've impacted Texas with your feats of the Alamo and beyond.
4. I love to read/watch movies/study you and the things you accomplished.

Noah Hernandez, Grade 7

WRITER TO WRITER—MRS. BERNABEI

1. One belief that we share is our love for writing.
2. One way that we are different is that you have kids and I don't.
3. What you've accomplished is being a successful writer.
4. A way that I admire you is what new ways of writing that you've invented and how you travel across and all over the country teaching teachers new ways of writing.

Matheu Shiver, Grade 6

———————————

WAYNE ROONEY

1. You and I think soccer takes brains.
2. I think Messi is good and you don't.
3. You made the soccer team Man United.
4. I admire you by buying gear and watching your games.

Joshua Levin, Grade 6

PLANNING PAGE

Name:

TITLE OF YOUR PIECE

TEXT STRUCTURE

Fighting Unfairness with Logic

| What I want to communicate | If this is true | And if this is also true | then this must be true | a ridiculous question (twisting the 3rd box) |

Susan B. Anthony

KERNEL ESSAY

1. _____

2. _____

3. _____

4. _____

5. _____

_____

SUGGESTIONS FOR QUICK LIST:

When you think about unfairness in the world, you can think of ways to solve many problems
- human rights
- waste
- overtesting
- animal cruelty
- unfair rules or practices

MY QUICK LIST OF TOPICS:

1. ....

2. ....

3. ....

4. ....

5. ....

"Women's Rights to the Suffrage" Speech

Susan B. Anthony, 1873

Friends and Fellow Citizens: I stand before you tonight under indictment for the alleged crime of having voted at the last presidential election, without having a lawful right to vote. It shall be my work this evening to prove to you that in thus voting, I not only committed no crime, but, instead, simply exercised my citizen's rights, guaranteed to me and all United States citizens by the National Constitution, beyond the power of any State to deny.

The preamble of the Federal Constitution says:

"We, the people of the United States, in order to form a more perfect union, establish justice, insure domestic tranquility, provide for the common defense, promote the general welfare, and secure the blessings of liberty to ourselves and our posterity, do ordain and establish this Constitution for the United States of America."

It was we, the people; not we, the white male citizens; nor yet we, the male citizens; but we, the whole people, who formed the Union. And we formed it, not to give the blessings of liberty, but to secure them; not to the half of ourselves and the half of our posterity, but to the whole people—women as well as men. And it is a downright mockery to talk to women of their enjoyment of the blessings of liberty while they are denied the use of the only means of securing them provided by this democratic-republican government—the ballot.

For any State to make sex a qualification that must ever result in the disfranchisement of one entire half of the people is to pass a bill of attainder, or an ex post facto law, and is therefore a violation of the supreme law of the land. By it the blessings of liberty are forever withheld from women and their female posterity. To them this government has no just powers derived from the consent of the governed. To them this government is not a democracy. It is not a republic. It is an odious aristocracy; a hateful oligarchy of sex; the most hateful aristocracy ever established on the face of the globe; an oligarchy of wealth, where the rich govern the poor. An oligarchy of learning, where the educated govern the ignorant, or even an oligarchy of race, where the Saxon rules the African, might be endured; but this oligarchy of sex, which makes father, brothers, husband, sons, the oligarchs over the mother and sisters, the wife and daughters of every household—which ordains all men sovereigns, all women subjects, carries dissension, discord and rebellion into every home of the nation.

Webster, Worcester and Bouvier all define a citizen to be a person in the United States, entitled to vote and hold office.

The only question left to be settled now is: Are women persons? And I hardly believe any of our opponents will have the hardihood to say they are not. Being persons, then, women are citizens; and no State has a right to make any law, or to enforce any old law, that shall abridge their privileges or immunities. Hence, every discrimination against women in the constitutions and laws of the several States is today null and void, precisely as is every one against Negroes.

COMPLETED PLANNING PAGE
Fighting Unfairness With Logic

Name: Dante Valencia

TITLE OF YOUR PIECE

Hostages

TEXT STRUCTURE

Fighting Unfairness with Logic

| What I want to communicate | If this is true | And if this is also true | then this must be true | a ridiculous question (twisting the 3rd box) |

Susan B. Anthony

KERNEL ESSAY

1. I think taking hostages to get something you want is unreasonable.

2. It's true that taking people as hostages gets people's attention.

3. It's also true that we give the hostage takers what they want.

4. People who do bad things seem to always get what they want.

5. With this information, shouldn't that mean we should all threaten to get what we want?

SUGGESTIONS FOR QUICK LIST:

When you think about unfairness in the world, you can think of ways to solve many problems
- human rights
- overtesting
- unfair rules or practices
- waste
- animal cruelty

MY QUICK LIST OF TOPICS:

1. Hostages
2. ISIS
3. Reference
4.
5.

FULL ESSAY
Fighting Unfairness With Logic

HOSTAGES

I think taking hostages to get something you want is unreasonable. People do not have to be threatened and have their life on the line for something that they want, especially when they are innocent.

Yes it's true taking innocents as hostages gets much attention from people. It scares people and then we make a move to stop the disaster.

It's also true that we usually give the hostage takers what they want to stop what they're doing. For example when someone is taken, members of their family try to give money to the takers, but there are only some times that they would take it and give back the hostages. Sometimes they would want something greater than money.

I would say that either most or all the time people who do bad things seem to get what they want. They take innocents to get what they want.

With this information, shouldn't it mean that we should all threaten each other to get what we want?

Dante Valencia, Grade 6

PLANNING PAGE

Name: _____

TITLE OF YOUR PIECE

TEXT STRUCTURE

Valuable Advice

| Why I'm giving you this advice | One rule and how it works | another rule and how it works | another rule and how it works | another rule and how it works | If you follow these, then... |

Mark Twain

KERNEL ESSAY

1. _____

2. _____

3. _____

4. _____

5. _____

6. _____

SUGGESTIONS FOR QUICK LIST:

What rules would you need to teach someone else in order to...
- get along with siblings
- get high grades
- get a date
- get ahead
- be popular

MY QUICK LIST OF TOPICS:

1. _____

2. _____

3. _____

4. _____

5. _____

"Advice to Youth" Speech

Being told I would be expected to talk here, I inquired what sort of talk I ought to make. They said it should be something suitable to youth—something didactic, instructive, or something in the nature of good advice. Very well. I have a few things in my mind which I have often longed to say for the instruction of the young; for it is in one's tender early years that such things will best take root and be most enduring and most valuable. First, then. I will say to you my young friends—and I say it beseechingly, urgently—

Always obey your parents, when they are present. This is the best policy in the long run, because if you don't, they will make you. Most parents think they know better than you do, and you can generally make more by humoring that superstition than you can by acting on your own better judgment.

Be respectful to your superiors, if you have any, also to strangers, and sometimes to others. If a person offends you, and you are in doubt as to whether it was intentional or not, do not resort to extreme measures; simply watch your chance and hit him with a brick. That will be sufficient. If you shall find that he had not intended any offense, come out frankly and confess yourself in the wrong when you struck him; acknowledge it like a man and say you didn't mean to. Yes, always avoid violence; in this age of charity and kindliness, the time has gone by for such things. Leave dynamite to the low and unrefined.

Go to bed early, get up early—this is wise. Some authorities say get up with the sun; some say get up with one thing, others with another. But a lark is really the best thing to get up with. It gives you a splendid reputation with everybody to know that you get up with the lark; and if you get the right kind of lark, and work at him right, you can easily train him to get up at half past nine, every time—it's no trick at all.

Now as to the matter of lying. You want to be very careful about lying; otherwise you are nearly sure to get caught. Once caught, you can never again be in the eyes to the good and the pure, what you were before. Many a young person has injured himself permanently through a single clumsy and ill finished lie, the result of carelessness born of incomplete training. Some authorities hold that the young ought not to lie at all. That of course, is putting it rather stronger than necessary; still while I cannot go quite so far as that, I do maintain, and I believe I am right, that the young ought to be temperate in the use of this great art until practice and experience shall give them that confidence, elegance, and precision which alone can make the accomplishment graceful and profitable. Patience, diligence, painstaking attention to detail—these are requirements; these in time, will make the student perfect; upon these only, may he rely as the sure foundation for future eminence. Think what tedious years of study, thought, practice, experience, went to the equipment of that peerless old master who was able to impose upon the whole world the lofty and sounding maxim that "Truth is mighty and will prevail"—the most majestic compound fracture of fact which any of woman born has yet achieved. For the history of our race, and each individual's experience, are sewn thick with evidences that a truth is not hard to kill, and that a lie well told is immortal. There is in Boston a monument of the man who discovered anesthesia; many people are aware, in these latter days, that

(continued) . . .

"Advice to Youth" Speech (Continued)   Mark Twain, 1882

that man didn't discover it at all, but stole the discovery from another man. Is this truth mighty, and will it prevail? Ah no, my hearers, the monument is made of hardy material, but the lie it tells will outlast it a million years. An awkward, feeble, leaky lie is a thing which you ought to make it your unceasing study to avoid; such a lie as that has no more real permanence than an average truth. Why, you might as well tell the truth at once and be done with it. A feeble, stupid, preposterous lie will not live two years—except it be a slander upon somebody. It is indestructible, then of course, but that is no merit of yours. A final word: begin your practice of this gracious and beautiful art early—begin now. If I had begun earlier, I could have learned how.

Never handle firearms carelessly. The sorrow and suffering that have been caused through the innocent but heedless handling of firearms by the young! Only four days ago, right in the next farm house to the one where I am spending the summer, a grandmother, old and gray and sweet, one of the loveliest spirits in the land, was sitting at her work, when her young grandson crept in and got down an old, battered, rusty gun which had not been touched for many years and was supposed not to be loaded, and pointed it at her, laughing and threatening to shoot. In her fright she ran screaming and pleading toward the door on the other side of the room; but as she passed him he placed the gun almost against her very breast and pulled the trigger! He had supposed it was not loaded. And he was right—it wasn't. So there wasn't any harm done. It is the only case of that kind I ever heard of. Therefore, just the same, don't you meddle with old unloaded firearms; they are the most deadly and unerring things that have ever been created by man. You don't have to take any pains at all with them; you don't have to have a rest, you don't have to have any sights on the gun, you don't have to take aim, even. No, you just pick out a relative and bang away, and you are sure to get him. A youth who can't hit a cathedral at thirty yards with a Gatling gun in three quarters of an hour, can take up an old empty musket and bag his grandmother every time, at a hundred. Think what Waterloo would have been if one of the armies had been boys armed with old muskets supposed not to be loaded, and the other army had been composed of their female relations. The very thought of it make one shudder.

There are many sorts of books; but good ones are the sort for the young to read. Remember that. They are a great, an inestimable, and unspeakable means of improvement. Therefore be careful in your selection, my young friends; be very careful; confine yourselves exclusively to Robertson's Sermons, Baxter's Saints' Rest, The Innocents Abroad, and works of that kind.

But I have said enough. I hope you will treasure up the instructions which I have given you, and make them a guide to your feet and a light to your understanding. Build your character thoughtfully and painstakingly upon these precepts, and by and by, when you have got it built, you will be surprised and gratified to see how nicely and sharply it resembles everybody else's.

PLANNING PAGE + ESSAY
Valuable Advice

HIGH SCHOOL SURVIVAL GUIDE

High school. An exciting and scary place for incoming freshmen. A place where you make the greatest memories. However, a lot of people go in not knowing what to expect or how to make it through. As a senior only one month away from graduation, I can truly say that I have been there, done that. Trust me on this. I know exactly how it is. If you happen to be an incoming freshman and reading this, buckle down and get ready. I'm going to give you some tips and advice to help you survive the next four years of your high school career.

First things first. Keep your circle small. This means that you should only be close to a small group of people. Trusting too many people can be one of the deadliest mistakes you can make. A lot of people don't know how to keep secrets. One of the pros to keeping your circle small is when you and your small circle of people try to get into the parties that we both know you won't be able to get into, you're not as embarrassed as you would be if you had a big circle of friends. By the time you become a senior, your circle will be small anyway so you may as well start it off that way.

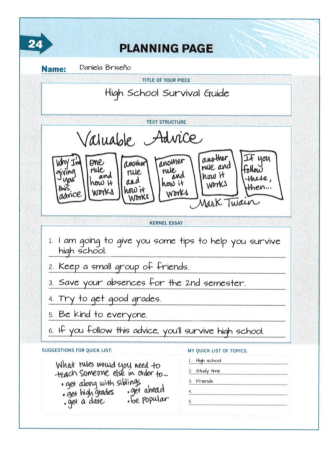

The next important thing is absences. Please, please, please save your absences for the second semester. Trust me on this one. Skipping during the first semester is so fun, don't get me wrong. But if you're absent during the first semester, then you'll have to make up those hours in the second semester which also takes away from you being able to skip during the second semester. So remember to save your absences for the second semester. By then you'll barely be able to find the motivation to go to school but have the wonderful pleasure of knowing that you have absences to be used up.

Ah, grades. Every parent's dream during their children's high school career is for them to get good grades. Freshman year is the year that grades really matter. Try to get the best grades that you possibly can. That way, you don't lower your parents' standards even lower than they already are. Oh and so that your rank and record won't start off so bad, of course.

Last but not least, kindness. This one is so important. Be kind to everyone. Be kind so that you can copy anyone's homework when you didn't do yours because you had better things to do like staying up on social media and watching your favorite shows. Be kind so that when that one crazy kid comes to school with a weapon, he won't target you. Be kind so that teachers will have your back on make-up hours and give you food and candy. Also be kind for good morals, I guess.

Well sadly, the High School Survival Guide has come to an end. If you follow what you have just read, then you should have no problem surviving the terrible yet wonderful experience that the world calls high school.

Daniela Briseño, Grade 12

PLANNING PAGE

Name: _____

TITLE OF YOUR PIECE

TEXT STRUCTURE

Comforting a Friend in Pain

| I know you're suffering | A thought about life's ups and downs | Advice: use the bad feeling; don't be used by it | What all you should do or not do | you will prevail |

Henry James

KERNEL ESSAY

1. _____

2. _____

3. _____

4. _____

5. _____

_____

SUGGESTIONS FOR QUICK LIST:

If you've ever had a friend or loved one who felt down, depressed, distraught, and you wanted to "talk them off the ledge" and help...

MY QUICK LIST OF TOPICS:

1. _____
2. _____
3. _____
4. _____
5. _____

Letter to a Friend

Henry James, 1883

131 Mount Vernon St.
Boston
July 28th

My dear Grace,

Before the sufferings of others I am always utterly powerless, and the letter you gave me reveals such depths of suffering that I hardly know what to say to you. This indeed is not my last word—but it must be my first. You are not isolated, verily, in such states of feeling as this—that is, in the sense that you appear to make all the misery of all mankind your own; only I have a terrible sense that you give all and receive nothing—that there is no reciprocity in your sympathy—that you have all the affliction of it and none of the returns. However—I am determined not to speak to you except with the voice of stoicism.

I don't know why we live—the gift of life comes to us from I don't know what source or for what purpose; but I believe we can go on living for the reason that (always of course up to a certain point) life is the most valuable thing we know anything about and it is therefore presumptively a great mistake to surrender it while there is any yet left in the cup. In other words consciousness is an illimitable power, and though at times it may seem to be all consciousness of misery, yet in the way it propagates itself from wave to wave, so that we never cease to feel, though at moments we appear to, try to, pray to, there is something that holds one in one's place, makes it a standpoint in the universe which it is probably good not to forsake. You are right in your consciousness that we are all echoes and reverberations of the *same*, and you are noble when your interest and pity as to everything that surrounds you, appears to have a sustaining and harmonizing power. Only don't, I beseech you, *generalize* too much in these sympathies and tendernesses—remember that every life is a special problem which is not yours but another's, and content yourself with the terrible algebra of your own. Don't melt too much into the universe, but be as solid and dense and fixed as you can. We all live together, and those of us who love and know, live so most. We help each other—even unconsciously, each in our own effort, we lighten the effort of others, we contribute to the sum of success, make it possible for others to live. Sorrow comes in great waves—no one can know that better than you—but it rolls over us, and though it may almost smother us it leaves us on the spot and we know that if it is strong we are stronger, inasmuch as it passes and we remain. It wears us, uses us, but we wear it and use it in return; and it is blind, whereas we after a manner see.

My dear Grace, you are passing through a darkness in which I myself in my ignorance see nothing but that you have been made wretchedly ill by it; but it is only a darkness, it is not an end, or *the* end. Don't think, don't feel, any more than you can help, don't conclude or decide—don't do anything but *wait*. Everything will pass, and serenity and *accepted* mysteries and disillusionments, and the tenderness of a few good people, and new opportunities and ever so much of life, in a word, will remain. You will do all sorts of things yet, and I will help you. The only thing is not to *melt* in the meanwhile. I insist upon the necessity of a sort of mechanical condensation—so that however fast the horse may run away there will, when he pulls up, be a somewhat agitated but perfectly identical G. N. left in the saddle. Try not to be ill—that is all; for in that there is a future. You are marked out for success, and you must not fail. You have my tenderest affection and all my confidence.

Ever your faithful friend,
Henry James

COMPLETED PLANNING PAGE
Comforting a Friend in Pain

Name: Alejandra Trillo

TITLE OF YOUR PIECE

Moving Away

TEXT STRUCTURE

Comforting a Friend in Pain

| I know you're suffering | A thought about life's ups and downs | Advice: use the bad feeling; don't be used by it | What all you should do or not do | You will prevail |

Henry James

KERNEL ESSAY

1. I know you are very upset about moving away.
2. The funny thing about life is that you never know what it's going to throw at you.
3. Take this opportunity to start over.
4. You should not let this bring you down.
5. You will make new friends and have an amazing time in high school.

SUGGESTIONS FOR QUICK LIST:

If you've ever had a friend or loved one who felt down, depressed, distraught, and you wanted to "talk them off the ledge" and help...

MY QUICK LIST OF TOPICS:

1. Moving away
2. Breaking up
3. Lost phone
4. Overwhelmed
5. Because of HW

FULL ESSAY
Comforting a Friend in Pain

Dear Ale,

I know you're upset about moving away. I usually don't know what to say when someone else is upset, but this time it's you. So I'm writing this because I probably couldn't get through this out loud without crying and embarrassing myself, so I hope you understand.

Think about life. It has chapters, full of beginnings and endings. When any chapter begins, there might be excitement or there might be fear. There might even be both. Of course we know this in our heads, but when you're experiencing it, it's different. It's harder to deal with when your heart is involved. But still, it's a chapter beginning for you. Right now you're probably not thinking about the new chapter because you don't want to let go of the old one. It's sad to leave everything familiar, to leave the places you know and the faces you see every day. It feels like something is ripping away, doesn't it?

But that sadness isn't weakness in you. Instead of being swallowed up by the sadness, I think you should face that sadness and let it be one of your strengths. It is, you know. If you weren't able to love others, to stay open to others, you wouldn't feel sad at all. So even though it hurts, know that it's because you have the power to love, and let that sadness move you forward. It's not weakness—it's fuel.

One thing that might help is if you think about the benefits of starting over. When you move to a new place and nobody knows you, you get to decide everything about what they see. You can dress however you want, cut your hair however you want, wear whatever style you like, and nobody will think, "Oh, what's up with her?" They won't know it's a change. If you tried that here, you know how people just have to make comments. Remember what happened when you dyed your eyebrows?

So don't cry, don't sit alone in sadness, and don't make any stupid moves about last nights out. Most of all, though, don't let this bring you down. I'll miss you so much, so we both have to take this advice.

You will make new friends. As much as it hurts to say, you will make a new best friend too. And you will go to games, to dances, to classes, and to graduation.

I'll see you on FB, and who knows . . . maybe we'll go to the same college.

Your BFF,
Bebe

Bebe Alexander, Grade 8

PLANNING PAGE

Name: _____

TITLE OF YOUR PIECE

[blank box]

TEXT STRUCTURE

I Want More (While I Have the Chance)

| We recently did this | We got this | So that makes me want this | Because in the future, it will be too late |

William G. Hornaday

KERNEL ESSAY

1. _____

2. _____

3. _____

4. _____

_____

_____

SUGGESTIONS FOR QUICK LIST:

When you feel an urge to grab more of something
- food
- a whole collection
- the last of something

MY QUICK LIST OF TOPICS:

1. _____
2. _____
3. _____
4. _____
5. _____

June 1st, 1886
Camp on Little Dry Creek, Montana

Professor S.F. Baird:

Dear Sir:

Mr. Hadley and I with a Cheyenne Indian, White Dog, have just returned to camp from a five days scout through the bad lands, during which we camped beside our horses whenever night overtook us,—and we got an old bull buffalo day before yesterday. There were only two buffalo in that land (!), and we got the largest and finest one.

Since seeing the buffalo on this native heath I am more than ever impressed with our wants in the way of good mountable skins of fine specimens, and still more of the imperative duty which devolves upon some institution to collect a store of skins to meet the demands of the future, when the bones of the last American bison shall lie bleaching on the prairie.

Wm G. Hornaday

Source: Smithsonian Institution: Division of Correspondence, June 7, 1886. 54468.

PLANNING PAGE + ESSAY
I Want More (While I Have the Chance)

EMAIL TO GEORGE STEPHENSON

Dear George Stephenson,

Today my class took a test on the history of steam engines, on trains, steamboats, and all famous people who contributed. There was a question about who created the steam engine. I got this one wrong, and in paragraph 2 you'll find out why.

We had lots of questions about who created the steam engine. Because you're known as the "Father of the Railroad," I thought that must mean you created the steam engine . . . but I got it wrong. So why are you called the "Father of the Railroad"? If you didn't invent the steam engine, then who did?

I want to know this for three reasons. Number one, I want to be an engineer, but I almost failed this test. The second reason is that I want to study his work. Third, I want to be a teacher to engineers someday, and I can't find the answer.

In the future, I want to be an expert in your work, but also the work of your colleagues.

Alex Melchor, Grade 8

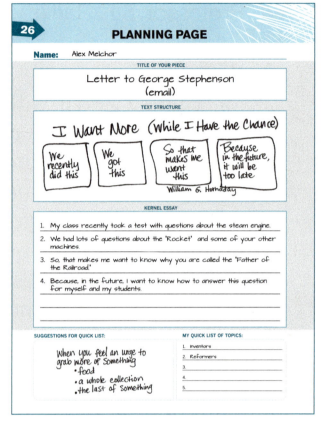

KERNEL ESSAYS BY STUDENTS
I Want More (While I Have the Chance)

MORE PIZZA!

1. We went to Julian's for Italian food.
2. I had some delicious appetizers and a salad, and my friend had pizza.
3. Now I want to go back there at least once a week.
4. They might close, and then we couldn't get any more of that exact food.

Robert Gray, Grade 9

_____

1. Robert's mom took us to an Italian restaurant.
2. I had pizza. Too much pizza.
3. Now I need some water or something for my stomach . . . ugh.
4. If I die of stomach ache, it will be too late to feel better.

Fernando Lopez, Grade 9

_____

1. The Schwann man came by our house.
2. We bought lots of ice cream and put it in the freezer.
3. Now I can't stop thinking about ice cream, and I want to go get some and put chocolate chips on it.
4. If I even blink my eyes, that ice cream will be all gone. That's how our family is.

Lilly Keyes, Grade 5

1. We were watching tv and saw an infomercial for diamonds.
2. We didn't pick up the phone and order one.
3. I sort of wanted to order one then, and I keep thinking about them.
4. Pretty soon, all the diamond mines will be empty, and then we'll only be able to buy fake ones.

Midge Erbach, Grade 10

_____

SPEAKING AS SOPHIA FROM
THE SCHOOL FOR GOOD AND EVIL

1. We had a ball for Evil.
2. We got some success when we tricked the Good Prince Tedros, and he got angry at Agatha.
3. So that makes me want to do something else to make him even more angry at Agatha.
4. I need to hurry to break them up before it's too late.

Anael Ashkenazi, Grade 7

_____

1. My mom, dad and I went to Schlitterbahn this summer.
2. We forgot to put on sunscreen, so we got bad sunburn.
3. So that makes me want to never forget to put on sunscreen again.
4. We need sunscreen because if you are outside too long, you can harm your skin badly or even get skin cancer.

Kennedy Cantu, Grade 7

PLANNING PAGE

Name: _____

TITLE OF YOUR PIECE

TEXT STRUCTURE

First Earnings

| job description | how I looked doing the job | my hours and wages | how I spent it |

Bertha Miller

KERNEL ESSAY

1. _____

2. _____

3. _____

4. _____

_____

_____

SUGGESTIONS FOR QUICK LIST:

What jobs have you held?
What have you been paid for?
- babysitting
- Summer jobs
- yard work
- any jobs
- fundraising

MY QUICK LIST OF TOPICS:

1. _____
2. _____
3. _____
4. _____
5. _____

I was 11 years old when I went to work at the mill. They learnt me to knit. Well, I was so little that they had to build me a box to get up on to put the sock on the machine. I worked in the hosiery mill for a long time and, well, then we finally moved back to the country. But me and my sister Molly finally went back up there in 1910 and I went to work in the silk mill. Molly went to work in the hosiery mill . . . we worked 12 hours a day for 50 cents. When paydays come around, I drawed three dollars. That was for six days, 72 hours. I remember I lacked 50 cents having enough to pay my board.

Bertha Miller
Thomasville, NC

Source: Victoria Byerly, *Hard Times Cotton Mill Girls* (Educational Resource Materials, Levine Museum of the New South, 2003, www.museumofthenewsouth.org)

COMPLETED PLANNING PAGE
First Earnings

Name: Franchesca Gallardo

TITLE OF YOUR PIECE

Henry Ford's First Job

TEXT STRUCTURE

First Earnings

| job description | how I looked doing the job | my hours and wages | how I spent it |

Bertha Miller

KERNEL ESSAY

1. I was a machinist at the Flower & Brothers machine shop.

2. I wore a helmet and protective jumpsuit.

3. I worked five days a week, for $2.50 a week.

4. I spent it on food, shelter, and my own engineering supplies.

SUGGESTIONS FOR QUICK LIST:

What jobs have you held?
What have you been paid for?
- babysitting
- Summer jobs
- yard work
- any jobs
- fundraising

MY QUICK LIST OF TOPICS:

1. Henry Ford
2. Waitressing
3. Babysitting
4. Edison
5. President

FULL ESSAY
First Earnings

FRANCHESCA GALLARDO, SPEAKING AS HENRY FORD

January 19, 1879

Dear Father,

How is everyone? Lately I have been thinking about home and how I miss it. I miss mother's cooking, your jokes, and of course playing hide-and-seek with all my younger siblings. I am planning on visiting everyone soon.

I found a job in Detroit called the Flower & Brothers Machine Shop. This job is just what I have been looking for. Watching how certain things are made just amazes me. While doing my job we have to wear special clothing that helps protect us. This special clothing consists of a rubber jumpsuit that's fireproof and helmet to protect your head. The jumpsuit is quite heavy but has been tested to protect anyone who wears it.

I work for five days a week and receive $2.50 each week. I don't make a lot of money but it will have to do for now. With the money I buy food, pay for my shelter, and other expenses I might need. Thinking about everyone home makes me miss being there, so I am saving up to come back and visit soon.

Write back to me as soon as possible. I would love to hear how things are going back home.

Love,
Henry Ford

Franchesca Gallardo, Grade 8

PLANNING PAGE

Name: _____

TITLE OF YOUR PIECE

TEXT STRUCTURE

My Symbol

I feel _____ (how) | ...about this symbol... | ...and what the symbol represents in my life ... | ...which is important to me because...

Pledge of Allegiance

KERNEL ESSAY

1. _____

2. _____

3. _____

4. _____

_____

_____

SUGGESTIONS FOR QUICK LIST:

If you had a charm bracelet with objects from your life, these would be symbols of important parts of you.

MY QUICK LIST OF TOPICS:

1. _____

2. _____

3. _____

4. _____

5. _____

I pledge allegiance to the Flag

of the United States of America,

and to the Republic for which it stands,

one Nation under God, indivisible,

with liberty and justice for all.

KERNEL ESSAYS BY STUDENTS
My Symbol

TOPIC: ALBERT EINSTEIN'S DIPLOMA

I am glad, as I get this diploma, that I can formally conclude all my years of college, through which I hope to be a professional scientist. This diploma represents my promise that I have made to the school, to get my work done, to study, to understand, with little or no sleep each night.

Nina De La Torre, Grade 8

MUSICAL NOTES

I have great passion about musical notes.

They represent the vast amounts of combinations that these can be used for.

This is important to me because I want variety when I'm playing my piano or listening to music.

Jessica Logan, Grade 4

HORSESHOES

I feel longing when I look at a horseshoe and remember mornings from my childhood spent in the stable, breathing in the horses, the most strong, knowing, and magical creatures.

Gretchen Bernabei, Adult

THE TREE OF LIFE

I cherish the tree of life symbol and the personal growth for which it stands, my own learning, full of roots and branches, constantly keeping me focused.

Jennifer Koppe, Adult

DOG TAGS (SPEAKING AS HIS DOG)

I feel honored wearing my dog tag, which means I have an owner who takes care of me. If I get lost, someone will call her and she will find me.

Jack Shepard, Grade 11

MY GUITAR

I feel alive when I see my guitar. In my life, it's my friend, my voice. It brings me freedom to connect with other people or to be completely alone.

Matilde Bernabei, Grade 11

THE NAZI SWASTIKA

I feel enraged when I see the Nazi swastika, and the horrors that it represents for humanity, and the horrible mistakes made by mankind.

David Martinez, Grade 10

KERNEL ESSAYS BY STUDENTS
My Symbol

SUMMER CLOTHES

I feel joy about summer clothes, Avengers graphic tees with shorts and a pair of white Converse. The colors of summer, pastels, soft or neon, allowing you to dress in anything from a tank top and Nike shorts to a cherry crop top with high waist shorts and still look good.

Maggie Davis, Grade 8

THE BALD EAGLE

I feel strong when I think about the bald eagle, and about the freedom and peace it represents, which means that we will never be imprisoned.

Ramsey Miller, Grade 8

OMAHA BEACH

I get a lump in my throat when I picture Omaha Beach, and the unspeakable courage and sacrifice made by so many of my countrymen, soldiers who knew what was right and did not stop.

Bert Norman, Adult

CAMPFIRES

I feel comforted when I see a campfire burning. This represents the outdoors, tired muscles, good food, and refreshing sounds.

Jennifer Koppe, Adult

ARROWS

When I see arrows, I think about courage and the ability to take a risk, which keeps me on track.

Julie Grauer, Grade 11

LIBRARIES

I feel nostalgic whenever I enter a library, remembering the excitement I felt on my earliest visits to our small town library and the neighborhood bookmobile. I couldn't believe that they let you take the books home for free—and remarkably, they still do.

Jillian Kristof, Adult

PLANNING PAGE

Name: _____

TITLE OF YOUR PIECE

TEXT STRUCTURE

Narrative : Just the Facts

| what happened first | what happened next | what happened last |

Ida B. Wells-Barnett

KERNEL ESSAY

1. _____

2. _____

3. _____

_____

_____

_____

SUGGESTIONS FOR QUICK LIST:

When only the facts are required :
- a police report • an incident report
- a news story • an eyewitness account

MY QUICK LIST OF TOPICS:

1. _____
2. _____
3. _____
4. _____
5. _____

On Lynchings (Excerpt)

Ida B. Wells-Barnett, 1895

While this was going on a small crowd was busy starting a fire in the middle of the street. The material was handy. Some bundles of staves were taken from the adjoining lumber yard for kindling. Heavier wood was obtained from the same source, and coal oil from a neighboring grocery. Then the cries of "Burn him! Burn him!" were redoubled.

Half a dozen men seized the naked body. The crowd cheered. They marched to the fire, and giving the body a swing, it was landed in the middle of the fire. There was a cry for more wood, as the fire had begun to die owing to the long delay. Willing hands procured the wood, and it was piled up on the Negro, almost, for a time, obscuring him from view. The head was in plain view, as also were the limbs, and one arm which stood out high above the body, the elbow crooked, held in that position by a stick of wood. In a few moments the hands began to swell, then came great blisters over all the exposed parts of the body; then in places the flesh was burned away and the bones began to show through. It was a horrible sight, one which, perhaps, none there had ever witnessed before. It proved too much for a large part of the crowd and the majority of the mob left very shortly after the burning began.

But a large number stayed, and were not a bit set back by the sight of a human body being burned to ashes. Two or three white women, accompanied by their escorts, pushed to the front to obtain an unobstructed view, and looked on with astonishing coolness and nonchalance. One man and woman brought a little girl, not over 12 years old, apparently their daughter, to view a scene which was calculated to drive sleep from the child's eyes for many nights, if not to produce a permanent injury to her nervous system. The comments of the crowd were varied. Some remarked on the efficacy of this style of cure for rapists, others rejoiced that men's wives and daughters were now safe from this wretch. Some laughed as the flesh cracked and blistered, and while a large number pronounced the burning of a dead body as a useless episode, not in all that throng was a word of sympathy heard for the wretch himself.

The rope that was used to hang the Negro, and also that which was used to lead him from the jail, were eagerly sought by relic hunters. They almost fought for a chance to cut off a piece of rope, and in an incredibly short time both ropes had disappeared and were scattered in the pockets of the crowd in sections of from an inch to six inches long. Others of the relic hunters remained until the ashes cooled to obtain such ghastly relics as the teeth, nails, and bits of charred skull of the immolated victim of his own lust. After burning the body the mob tied a rope around the charred trunk and dragged it down Main Street to the court house, where it was hanged to a center pole. The rope broke and the corpse dropped with a thud, but it was again hoisted, the charred legs barely touching the ground. The teeth were knocked out and the fingernails cut off as souvenirs. The crowd made so much noise that the police interfered. Undertaker Walsh was telephoned for who took charge of the body and carried it to his establishment, where it will be prepared for burial in the potter's field today.

PLANNING PAGE + ESSAY
Narrative: Just the Facts

NASHVILLE

Only a guitar and an old backpack

A train roars by on an old rough track

Only desert my eyes do see

Here I come ol' Nashville Tennessee

Country songs playing

Glasses clinking

Cheers to Nashville

Cheers to drinking

One down, two down

Three down, four

Girls in boots

Fly through the door

She's a blue eyed

Blond hair

Two-beer pretty

Can't find her in any old city

We danced all night

And drank all day

Hey ol' Nashville

I'm here to stay

Alejandra Trillo, Grade 8

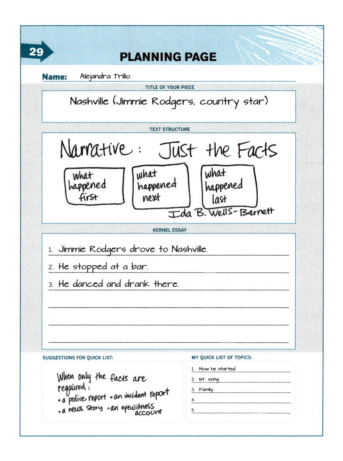

KERNEL ESSAYS BY STUDENTS
Narrative: Just the Facts

TOPIC: SACAJAWEA

1. In my years of experience, Sacajawea is a wonderful person. She knows her way around the creatures, and she can speak more than one language.
2. I've noticed that she is focused in what she is doing, wants to get the job done, is always concerned about other people, and is always ready to help.
3. I feel that she will be able to help you in what you need and help you get around in the places you need to go, like in the woods, rivers, and forests.

Genesis Thomas, Grade 8

1. I got on my bike.
2. I went through the stop sign.
3. A bus nearly ran over me.

Taylor Wright, Grade 4

1. We stood in line for the roller coaster.
2. We got on the roller coaster.
3. We got off the roller coaster.

Frankie Moore, Grade 4

1. I walked in the door.
2. I tripped over the dog.
3. I broke my phone.

Billy Joe Wyatt, Grade 4

1. The United States made a treaty with the American Indians.
2. American Indians left their homeland and journeyed on foot thousands of miles.
3. Gold was discovered and the American Indians were given different land.

Anya Singh, Grade 5

Name: _____

TITLE OF YOUR PIECE

[ ]

TEXT STRUCTURE

Letter of Recommendation

my years of experience with this person/ group

What I've noticed about this person/group

what I feel about this person/group

Clara Barton

KERNEL ESSAY

1. _____

2. _____

3. _____

_____

_____

SUGGESTIONS FOR QUICK LIST:

What do you admire in others?
Persons
• friends • relatives
• classmates
• fictional characters
• historical characters

Groups
• age groups
• job groups
• fan groups

MY QUICK LIST OF TOPICS:

1. _____
2. _____
3. _____
4. _____
5. _____

Letter to Jessie Gladden

Clara Barton, 1898

Clara Barton, the founder of the American Red Cross, worked tirelessly during the Civil War to support and care for sick and wounded soldiers. For her valiant efforts, she was known as the "Angel of the Battlefield." In this letter, she expresses her utmost respect and admiration for the American Soldier.

Washington, D.C., Nov. 7, 1898
Jessie L. Gladden,
P. O. Box 528,
Pueblo, Col.

Dear Madame,

I am in receipt of your request for a brief expression "relative to the noble work of our soldiers and sailors." I was with our boys constantly during the four years of our Civil War, and during the entire time of the late Spanish-American War; and being thoroughly American myself, it is needless for me to say I love and admire the American soldier, and think him equal, if not the superior, of any warrior of any time. He is not only brave but he is generous; and when he has fought for a principle and won, he has no desire to crush his foe, but is eager to abide by the old Latin maxim of "live and let live;" and he forgets and forgives, and lends a helping hand when a disposition to do the right thing is shown. The soldiers of this country know me and my feelings for them too well to need any extended assurance of my faithfulness to them; and they know that as long as I live there will be no truer friend to them than,

Yours sincerely,
Clara Barton

Note: Most often, letters of recommendation are about one individual. In this letter, however, Clara Barton describes the character of an entire group. Because of her extensive experience behind the lines with injured soldiers, her characterization is unlike any other description. It's a stellar example of an observation of positive traits of a group. In this classroom exercise, students are asked to use the foundational structure of Clara's letter—its focus on how long she has known the subjects of the letter, what she has noticed about them, and how she feels about them—to craft their own "letters of recommendation" that describe either individuals or groups.

PLANNING PAGE + ESSAY
Letter of Recommendation

MY RECOMMENDATION TO YOU (WRITTEN BY GENESIS THOMAS IN THE VOICE OF MERIWETHER LEWIS)

I have a wonderful person that I've worked with for 20 years. Her name is Sacajawea and she has helped me in so many ways. She can speak multiple languages so you could ask her to help talk to the other Native Americans. She knows most of the creatures and the plants. She can also help you navigate through rivers, forest, or woods. One thing that she also did was help Lewis and Clark on the expedition and that was a nice start for her to show what big things she could do.

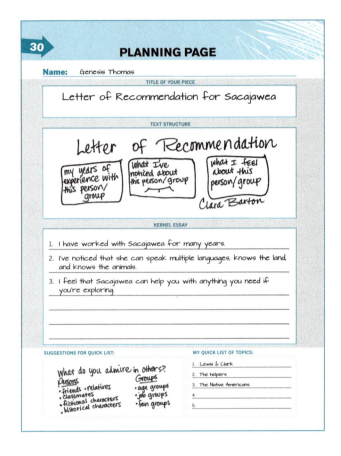

I have noticed that she always wants to get the job done, she is always concerned about other people, she's a hard worker, and she is always ready to help no matter how hard the task is. She is a wonderful person to depend on at all times.

I feel that Sacajawea will be able to help you in what you need if it's to speak with other Native Americans or just to know your way around the river. She will always be there to help you whenever you need it. That's why if you need a guide or just someone you could count on I recommend Sacajawea for you.

Sincerely,
Meriwether Lewis

Genesis Thomas, Grade 8

PLANNING PAGE + ESSAY
Letter of Recommendation

SPURS

I have been watching the Spurs games since I was in diapers, before I could walk, and even before I could talk. The reason I fell in love with the Spurs was because of my papa's passion with sports, but most of all for the Spurs. I watched some players come and go, but my favorite players have always been Tony Parker, Manu Ginobili, and Tim Duncan.

Something I have noticed about the Spurs is they are a team, a very humble team. We are not like LeBron James, Kobe Bryant, or Kevin Durant. A lot of teams have players who have their own shoes, clothing lines, and make everyone think they are the best. I truly think the Spurs are different. Popovich who is the coach of the team is the reason why we have such a humble team. I also think our team is the best in the NBA. We are the best because of our players, their teamwork, and of course our coach. Every time I watch the Spurs games I feel very proud of my team because they always play their best.

I feel like the San Antonio Spurs will never let me down, because they never have. Some nights we don't win which makes me sad but never disappointed. Win or lose the Spurs will always be my favorite team. I think we can be back to back champions this year!

Franchesca Gallardo, Grade 8

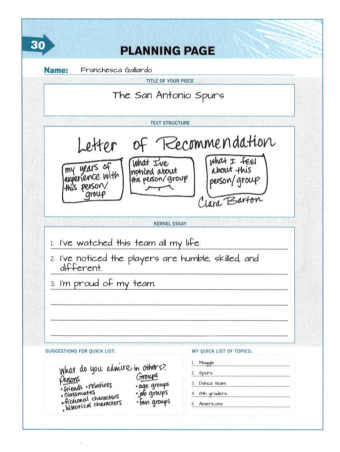

PLANNING PAGE

30

Name: Franchesca Gallardo

TITLE OF YOUR PIECE

The San Antonio Spurs

TEXT STRUCTURE

Letter of Recommendation

my years of experience with this person/group

What I've noticed about this person/group

what I feel about this person/group

Clara Barton

KERNEL ESSAY

1. I've watched this team all my life.
2. I've noticed the players are humble, skilled, and different.
3. I'm proud of my team

SUGGESTIONS FOR QUICK LIST:

What do you admire in others?
Persons
• friends • relatives
• classmates
• fictional characters
• historical characters

Groups
• age groups
• job groups
• fan groups

MY QUICK LIST OF TOPICS:

1. Maggie
2. Spurs
3. Dance team
4. 8th graders
5. Americans

PLANNING PAGE

Name:

TITLE OF YOUR PIECE

TEXT STRUCTURE

Why Something Goes Viral

| one effect these have on people | my example of one that went viral | another version of it | what makes people stop, notice, and share |

Jane Addams

KERNEL ESSAY

1. _____

2. _____

3. _____

4. _____

_____

_____

SUGGESTIONS FOR QUICK LIST:

What goes viral these days?
• videos • songs • pictures • messages
What went viral before computers?
• stories • tales • fables • ghost stories
List some examples.

MY QUICK LIST OF TOPICS:

1. ....
2. ....
3. ....
4. ....
5. ....

"A Modern Day Devil Baby"
(American Journal of Sociology, 20(1), 117–118)

Jane Addams, 1914

There is a theory that women first evolved and used the fairy story, that combination of wisdom and romance, in an effort to tame her mate and to make him a better father to her children. The stories finally became a rude creed, or rather rule of conduct, which softened the treatment men accorded to women.

These first pitiful efforts of women became so widespread and so powerful that we have not yet escaped their influence. We had remarkable experience at Hull House this year of the persistence of one of these tales which has doubtless had its taming effects through the centuries upon recalcitrant husbands and fathers. It burst upon us one day in the persons of three Italian women who, with excited rush into Hull House, demanded to see the devil-baby. No amount of denial convinced them that it was not there for they knew exactly what it was like, with its cloven hoofs, its pointed ears, and its diminutive tail. It had been able to speak as soon as it was born and was most shockingly profane. For six weeks the messages, the streams of visitors from every part of the city and suburbs to this mythical baby, poured all day long and so far into the night that the regular activities were almost swamped. The Italian version, with a hundred variations, dealt with a pious Italian girl married to an atheist who vehemently tore a holy picture from the bedroom wall, saying that he would quite as soon have a devil in the house as that, whereupon the devil incarnated himself in the child. As soon as the devil-baby was born, it ran about the table shaking its finger in deep reproach at its father, who finally caught it and in fear and trembling brought it into Hull House. When the residents there, in spite of the baby's shocking appearance, in order to save its soul took him to church for a baptism, they found the shawl was empty, and the devil-baby, fleeing from the water, ran lightly over the backs of the pews.

The Jewish version, again with variations, was to the effect that the father of six daughters said before the birth of the seventh child that he would rather have a devil than another girl, whereupon the devil-baby promptly appeared. The story was not only used to tame restless husbands, but mothers threatened their daughters that if they went to dance halls or out to walk with strange young men they would be eternally disgraced by devil-babies. Simple, round-eyed girls came to Hull House to see if this were true, many of them quite innocent of the implications in the warning. Save for a red automobile which occasionally figured in the story, and a stray cigar, the tale was mediaeval and unrelieved as if it had been fashioned a thousand years ago in response to the imperative need of anxious wives and mothers. It had fastened itself to a poor little deformed creature, born in an obscure street, destined in its one breath of life to demonstrate the power of an old wives' tale among thousands of people in modern society who are living in a corner of their own, their vision fixed, their intelligence held by some iron chain of silent habit. Or did the incident rather make clear that the love of the marvelous will not die, and that romance springs unexpectedly from the most uncongenial soil?

COMPLETED PLANNING PAGE
Why Something Goes Viral

Name: Efrayim Rios

TITLE OF YOUR PIECE

Almost Had It

TEXT STRUCTURE

Why Something Goes Viral

| one effect these have on people | my example of one that went viral | another version of it | What makes people Stop, notice, and Share |

Jane Addams

KERNEL ESSAY

1. When card extraordinaires get and show new cards people get energized about buying the new cards.

2. When the Pikachu Full Art Promo card came out people went crazy.

3. Another version of the card is rare and worth a lot of money.

4. So when YouTube opened the promo with the unlisted leaf, my favorite card, I wanted it even more.

SUGGESTIONS FOR QUICK LIST:

What goes viral these days?
•videos •songs •pictures •messages
What went viral before computers?
•stories •tales •fables •ghost stories
List some examples.

MY QUICK LIST OF TOPICS:

1. Trading card info
2. Funny pictures
3. Funny videos
4. Funny people
5.

FULL ESSAY
Why Something Goes Viral

ALMOST HAD IT

I was lying on the bed browsing YouTube and there it was. No . . . it couldn't be. It, it, it was Pikachu Promo Full Art Yaw Squid. It was an unlisted leaf, my all time favorite Poker tuber had a pre-release on the one, the only, the Pikachu Prom Full Art Box! I decided to pick that video instead of the other great videos. When Ando (the unlisted leaf's name) opened the box, he was screaming in happiness. Ahhhhhhhh. Then all of the sudden, he started jumping for joy! After the video, I looked on eBay to try and get the card, but it was $750. Another version came when that happened. Yikes!! "That's past our budget Effie," my mom griped. "Okay, mom!"

In conclusion, the card was a viral sensation! What made me stop, and other people, too, was the unlisted leaf, of course!

Efrayim Rios, Grade 5

PLANNING PAGE

Name:

TITLE OF YOUR PIECE

TEXT STRUCTURE

Understanding the Scars of Our Elders

| my curious question to someone | their answer (a memory) | what that leads me to promise | how I will keep (or have kept) this promise |

Tonea Stewart

KERNEL ESSAY

1. _____

2. _____

3. _____

4. _____

_____

SUGGESTIONS FOR QUICK LIST:

When talking to our older family members, we can ask them to tell us about their early lives by asking them to explain their injuries, scars, or any damage or losses.

MY QUICK LIST OF TOPICS:

1. ....
2. ....
3. ....
4. ....
5. ....

"Remembering Slavery" (Excerpt) Tonea Stewart, 1930

[Excerpt from Smithsonian Productions and the Institute of Language and Culture: Remembering Slavery: Those who survived tell their stories]

[music]

My name in Tonea Stewart. When I was a little girl about five or six years old, I used to sit on the garret, the front porch. In the Mississippi Delta the front porch is called the garret. I listened to my Papa Dallas. He was blind and had these ugly scars around his eyes. One day, I asked Papa Dallas what happened to his eyes.

"Well daughter," he answered, "when I was mighty young, just about your age, I used to steal away under a big oak tree and I tried to learn my alphabets so I could learn to read my Bible. But one day the overseer caught me and he drug me out on the plantation and he called out for all the field hands. And he turned to 'em and said, 'Let this be a lesson to all of you darkies. You ain't got no right to learn to read!' And then daughter, he whooped me, and he whooped me, and he whooped me. And daughter, as if that wasn't enough, he turned around and he burned my eyes out!"

At the instant, I began to cry. The tears were streaming down my cheeks, meeting under my chin. But he cautioned, "Don't you cry for me now, daughter. Now you listen to me. I want you to promise me one thing. Promise me that you gonna pick up every book you can and you gonna read it from cover to cover. You see, today daughter, ain't nobody gonna whip you or burn your eyes out because you want to learn to read. Promise me that you gonna go all the way through school, as far as you can. And one more thing, I want you to promise me that you gonna tell all the children my story."

Papa Dallas survived slavery and I, I kept my promise. I'm now a university professor, a Ph.D., and an actress. He and many others deserve to have their story told.

PLANNING PAGE + ESSAY
Understanding the Scars of Our Elders

BABOONS AT MIDNIGHT

Brilliantly vibrant smells of rich, strong coffee filled my nostrils as I entered the renowned Starbucks coffee shop. Outside, temperature is below freezing and wind is howling at unimaginable speeds. With the line out the door, I struggled to make my way to a small table tucked in a corner of the cozy building. Then I spot him; tall and lean, wearing a Scottish cap, dressed in a suit and tie. I shake his hand and he brings me into a breath-sucking bear hug. We greet and exchange small talk for a few minutes, as we order our drinks.

After getting settled into the especially comfortable chairs, I gather my loose paper and pluck my pen from my ear. "Pa," I ask, "What was one of your most memorable experiences?" He pauses, dwelling on my question. Looking at me through soft, blue eyes, he replies, "I have gone through many good things in life, and also many bad things. But by far, one of my experiences that has really stuck, happened when I was much younger. Are you ready?" he asks with a glint in his eyes and a smile on his face. "Go on! Please!" I reply hastily.

"Well, it was back when I was still part of the South African Army. After many months of training, my platoon and I (a group of about 16 men or so) were finally ready for our first patrol. Everybody hated patrols, especially those that take place in middle of the night. Shouldering our guns, we headed down the trail. After about an hour or so of brisk walking, the guy at the front of the line stopped. We all looked around very, very carefully . . . and there it was!

"Someone about ten feet in front of me first saw it, but it didn't take long for everybody to dash behind some sort of shrub, with our guns raised. Out of the night came a menacing-looking creature. With an ugly, pink, warty face, it strode on all fours as it led eleven other baboons out of the brush. Then all of the sudden, a high-pitched blood-curdling scream echoed through the jungle. We all froze, sweat trickling down our necks.

"Shuffling quietly, we slowly inched forward after two minutes of constant earsplitting monkey laughter had come to an end. Then one by one, the baboons retreated back where they'd come from.

We ran as fast as we could back to the observation tower. Too scared to speak, we tried to explain ourselves as best we could. Once I caught my breath, I rushed to wake my friend from his bunk and spread the news of our survival."

Pa grinned at me with a childish look on his face. "It was one of the best adventures I ever had, Noah. I hope you have many, many memorable experiences just as I did. And promise me: never go into a jungle in the middle of the night," he said kindly.

As my mom pulls up to take me home, I whisper in his ear "I promise never to go into any jungle at night, and I will always avoid baboons."

"That's my boy," he replies with a smile. We hug goodbye as I hop into my mom's gleaming silver SUV.

"How was it?" she asked.

"Slightly frightening, but amazing!" I reply. To this day I've never broken my promise, and I don't plan to.

Noah Hernandez, Grade 7

PLANNING PAGE + ESSAY
Understanding the Scars of Our Elders

TEETH AND CROWBARS

My name is Jessicalynn Jackson. When I was only about seven years old I was sitting down watching TV. My dad came home later that day after a long hard day at work. I then saw my dad's two front teeth were yellow and I said, "How come your front teeth are yellow?" He said, "They're not mine." I said, "Whose are they?" He said, "They're fake." "What happened?" I said to my dad.

"Well," he said, "when I was about your age, seven or eight, I was outside playing with my friend and my friend was swinging around a crowbar, this hard silver metal crowbar,

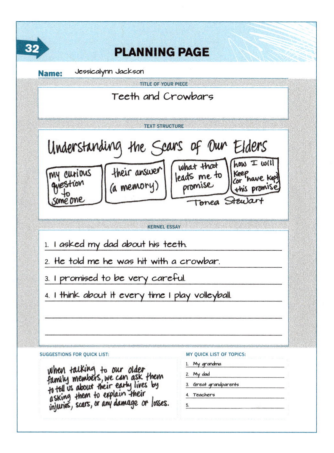

and boom! It hits me in the front of my mouth taking off my two front teeth!" I said, "That is something unexpected."

My dad later said, "Let me tell you something; when you are swinging bats, crowbars, or even food, just promise me you will be very careful when you are playing or hanging out with a friend."

I told my dad I will promise to not swing and play like that with my friends in the near future. My dad then said, "Thank you for respecting me because you know I am your father and I know best for you." My dad also said, "Oh you can also tell your friends about it." I then said, "What happened to your eye, dad?" and he said "That's another story for later."

I am now a 13 year old volleyball player, keeping the story about the crowbar that my dad told me about in my head every time I play volleyball.

Jessicalynn Jackson, Grade 7

PLANNING PAGE

Name: _____

TITLE OF YOUR PIECE

TEXT STRUCTURE

KERNEL ESSAY

1. _____

2. _____

3. _____

4. _____

_____

SUGGESTIONS FOR QUICK LIST:

Sometimes our possessions bring us happiness.
• Collections • clothes • tools
• cards • sports equipment
• craft supplies

MY QUICK LIST OF TOPICS:

1. _____

2. _____

3. _____

4. _____

5. _____

The habit of reading is one of the greatest resources of mankind; and we enjoy reading books that belong to us much more than if they are borrowed. A borrowed book is like a guest in the house; it must be treated with punctiliousness, with a certain considerate formality. You must see that it sustains no damage; it must not suffer while under your roof. You cannot leave it carelessly, you cannot mark it, you cannot turn down the pages, you cannot use it familiarly. And then, some day, although this is seldom done, you really ought to return it.

But your own books belong to you; you treat them with that affectionate intimacy that annihilates formality. Books are for use, not for show; you should own no book that you are afraid to mark up, or afraid to place on the table, wide open and face down. A good reason for marking favorite passages in books is that this practice enables you to remember more easily the significant sayings, to refer to them quickly, and then in later years, it is like visiting a forest where you once blazed a trail. You have the pleasure of going over the old ground, and recalling both the intellectual scenery and your own earlier self.

Everyone should begin collecting a private library in youth; the instinct of private property, which is fundamental in human beings, can here be cultivated with every advantage and no evils. One should have one's own bookshelves, which should not have doors, glass windows, or keys; they should be free and accessible to the hand as well as to the eye. The best of mural decorations is books; they are more varied in color and appearance than any wallpaper, they are more attractive in design, and they have the prime advantage of being separate personalities, so that if you sit alone in the room in the firelight, you are surrounded with intimate friends. The knowledge that they are there in plain view is both stimulating and refreshing. You do not have to read them all. Most of my indoor life is spent in a room containing six thousand books; and I have a stock answer to the invariable question that comes from strangers. "Have you read all of these books?"

"Some of them twice." This reply is both true and unexpected.

There are of course no friends like living, breathing, corporeal men and women; my devotion to reading has never made me a recluse. How could it? Books are of the people, by the people, for the people. Literature is the immortal part of history; it is the best and most enduring part of personality. But book-friends have this advantage over living friends; you can enjoy the most truly aristocratic society in the world whenever you want it. The great dead are beyond our physical reach, and the great living are usually almost as inaccessible; as for our personal friends and acquaintances, we cannot always see them. Perchance they are asleep, or away on a journey. But in a private library, you can at any moment converse with Socrates or Shakespeare or Carlyle or Dumas or Dickens or Shaw or Barrie or Galsworthy. And there is no doubt that in these books you see these men at their best. They wrote for you. They "laid themselves out," they did their ultimate best to entertain you, to make a favorable impression. You are necessary to them as an audience is to an actor; only instead of seeing them masked, you look into their innermost heart of heart.

COMPLETED PLANNING PAGE
Objects of Affection

Name: Lindsay Weingart

TITLE OF YOUR PIECE

Combat Boots

TEXT STRUCTURE

Objects of Affection

- One Kind
- the best Kind
- ways to make a place for this object
- how this object connects you to other people

William Lyon Phelps

KERNEL ESSAY

1. There is only one kind of shoe that dominates the shoe industry.

2. It is the best kind of shoe, the combat boots.

3. You must place them on a very high shelf lined with fur.

4. This object makes me feel powerful and confident.

SUGGESTIONS FOR QUICK LIST:

Sometimes our possessions bring us happiness.
- Collections
- clothes
- tools
- cards
- sports equipment
- craft supplies

MY QUICK LIST OF TOPICS:

1. Boots
2. Medals
3. Ribbons
4. Gifts
5.

FULL ESSAY
Objects of Affection

POWER, CONFIDENCE, AND COMBAT BOOTS

There is only one kind of shoe that dominates the shoe industry. Combat boots. "Why combat boots?" you ask. If you're asking this question you have obviously never had those powerful, pitch black, shoes of wonder on your feet. Combat boots give you a feeling of empowerment; they make you feel like you can do anything, anything. I can promise you that as soon as you put that leathery, tough, mysterious combat boot on your foot, you will feel it, too. No other shoe can compare to the combat boot. Not only do they give you a feeling of empowerment, but they are also all the rage this year.

It is the best kind of shoe, the combat boot. No words can describe the pure awesomeness that is the combat boot. Wearing them makes you taller so you can glare coolly at your enemies while staying sharp at the same time. You can gain confidence just by sitting in a room with combat boots, but be warned, because these shoes are the BEST shoes, anyone else wearing them will immediately steal the power of confidence that the all-mighty combat boot had previously bestowed upon you. Because of this you should never take them off. Does any other type of shoe have the power to give you these feelings of empowerment and confidentiality? I didn't think so.

The flabbergastingly fabulousness of these shoes sadly requires very high maintenance care. These shoes are to be placed in an empty room with maroon walls lined with alpaca fur. The floor must be hard wood made soft with bear-skin rugs every five feet, and a gold framed picture of your boots shall carefully be placed in the front of the room to be gazed at lovingly at least five hours of the day. Your shoes must be placed on a marble altar surrounded with freshly picked red roses. The ceiling must be painting with a mural of multiple baby cupids floating on fluffy white, cotton clouds, on a sunny day with a baby blue sky. A chandelier will be placed in the center of the mural to give the combat boots the proper lighting they need to show their full potential. Your room must maintain a 65 degree temperature to ensure that the quality of your glorious foot wear stays in royally mint condition.

I know that all of this seems insane, enough to give you insomnia in fact, but it's worth it, believe me. I wear my combats every weekend, all weekend, they give me a sense of confidence that other shoes just don't. I don't know what I would do if I didn't have my combat boots. They have become a part of me that I will never be able to shake off, no matter how hard I try. They may be impractical, uncomfortable, and even out of date, but I wouldn't trade them for anything else in the world. They make a rebel out of me and anyone else who dares to try them on at the footwear warehouse. If you are low on confidence or really just need a boost, these shoes won't let you down. They are the best, most fantastic shoe ever, and I don't think my feet could live without them. I'll tell you one thing, I don't plan to find out.

Lindsay Weingart, Grade 7

PLANNING PAGE

Name: _____

TITLE OF YOUR PIECE

[blank box]

TEXT STRUCTURE

True or False?   Neither

Question: Is ___ true or false?	Answer: This part is not true	but I don't know everything	and this part is true	So my definition is different from yours

Albert Einstein

KERNEL ESSAY

1. _____

2. _____

3. _____

4. _____

5. _____

SUGGESTIONS FOR QUICK LIST:

Some questions don't have simple answers because of:
- opposing beliefs
- contradictory behaviors
- reality vs. hope
- contrasts

MY QUICK LIST OF TOPICS:

1. _____
2. _____
3. _____
4. _____
5. _____

Letter From Phyllis

Albert Einstein, 1936

The Riverside Church

January 19, 1936

My dear Dr. Einstein,

We have brought up the question: Do scientists pray? in our Sunday school class. It began by asking whether we could believe in both science and religion. We are writing to scientists and other important men, to try and have our own question answered.

We will feel greatly honored if you will answer our question: Do scientists pray, and what do they pray for?

We are in the sixth grade, Miss Ellis's class.

Respectfully yours,

Phyllis

Einstein answered:

January 24, 1936

Dear Phyllis,

I will attempt to reply to your question as simply as I can. Here is my answer:

Scientists believe that every occurrence, including the affairs of human beings, is due to the laws of nature. Therefore a scientist cannot be inclined to believe that the course of events can be influenced by prayer, that is, by a supernaturally manifested wish.

However, we must concede that our actual knowledge of these forces is imperfect, so that in the end the belief in the existence of a final, ultimate spirit rests on a kind of faith. Such belief remains widespread even with the current achievements in science.

But also, everyone who is seriously involved in the pursuit of science becomes convinced that some spirit is manifest in the laws of the universe, one that is vastly superior to that of man. In this way the pursuit of science leads to a religious feeling of a special sort, which is surely quite different from the religiosity of someone more naive.

With cordial greetings,

your A. Einstein

Note: Albert Einstein is the unquestionable, quintessential scientist. So hearing his voice when he responds to a curious child shows us just how capable he is of connecting to someone with such innocence. The child's question is simplistic; Einstein's answer is nuanced, thoughtful, and complete. Furthermore, in giving her a complex answer, he shows her ultimate respect. This passage makes it clear to all of us that we have the power to be very thorough with how we use our writing to explain things. In this classroom exercise, students are asked to use the foundational structure of Einstein's response—its focus on the exploration of the answer to a complex question and the eventual concession that there may be no real straightforward answer—to craft their own "True or False? Neither" essays.

COMPLETED PLANNING PAGE
True or False? Neither

Name: Rory Gaudette

TITLE OF YOUR PIECE

Letter From Candice by Rory

TEXT STRUCTURE

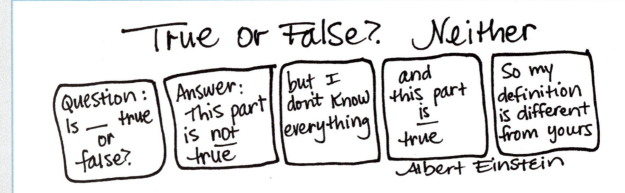

True or False? Neither

| Question: Is ___ true or false? | Answer: This part is not true | but I don't know everything | and this part is true | So my definition is different from yours |

—Albert Einstein

KERNEL ESSAY

1. Is America the best country in the world?

2. America has a lot of problems.

3. But I know some things.

4. Americans have led the world in humane assistance to others.

5. So, it depends on how you define the best country.

SUGGESTIONS FOR QUICK LIST:

Some questions don't have simple answers because of:
- opposing beliefs
- contradictory behaviors
- reality vs. hope
- contrasts

MY QUICK LIST OF TOPICS:

1. Divorce?
2. Good vs. evil
3. Grading policies
4. Altruism or independence
5.

FULL ESSAY
True or False? Neither

Carmel High School

February 18, 2013

Dear Senator Donelly,

A question has come up in my American History class: Is America the best country in the world? Our teacher thinks so, but we looked up statistics on things like health and education, which show America as near the top, but certainly not the best. What do you think? We are in tenth grade, Mr. Jackson's class.

Sincerely,
Candice Weatherby

February 26, 2013

Dear Candice,

I have considered your question for several days, and will do my best to answer it.

America is ranked fifth in the world by the Human Development Index. It is ranked thirty-seventh by the World Health Organization's ranking of the world's healthcare systems. It is ranked fourteenth in an index of cognitive skills and educational attainment.

However, there are Americans like Bill Gates, who will have saved over 11 million lives by 2020 through his foundation to deliver vaccines to Africa. There are brave American men and women who made sacrifices to accomplish things like liberating 60,000 prisoners from Nazi concentration camps. There are the acts of kindness Americans make, like welcoming 3 million refugees into our country. There are the hardworking Americans who are the reason the United States has the highest average income in the world, at $45,482.

My answer to you, Candice, is that there is no way to define what makes the best country in the world. Our system may not be the greatest, but it is the Americans, the people who lay down their lives and give away their fortunes and open up their homes who make American the great nation that it is.

Yours,
Senator Joseph Donelly

Rory Gaudette, Grade 9

PLANNING PAGE

Name: _____

TITLE OF YOUR PIECE

[ ]

TEXT STRUCTURE

How An Experience Changed Me

| what I was like before this experience | why I went (or did it) | how I improved | what one person said to me that helped me the most | how it changed me | who gave me this opportunity |

Robert L. Miller

KERNEL ESSAY

1. _____

2. _____

3. _____

4. _____

5. _____

6. _____

SUGGESTIONS FOR QUICK LIST:

What experiences have helped you become the person you are?
- a team sport
- creating something
- going somewhere
- performing in something
- working on something

MY QUICK LIST OF TOPICS:

1. _____
2. _____
3. _____
4. _____
5. _____

It's a Great Life

Robert L. Miller, 1937

There is no need to mention much of my life before I enrolled in the Civilian Conservation Corps. It is sufficient to say that the six months previous to my enlistment were most unsatisfactory, from both a financial and mental standpoint. I was often hungry, and almost constantly broke.

When I finally enrolled in this great enterprise at Sacramento, California, in October, 1933, I was conscious of just one thing—I would be fed, clothed and sheltered during the coming winter. Also I would receive enough actual cash each month to provide the few luxuries I desired.

The two weeks I had to wait between the time I enrolled and the day we were to leave for camp were given over to much thinking. I began to wonder what kind of a life I was going to live for the next six months. Several questions flashed through my mind. Would I make friends with my fellow members? What kind of work would I be doing? Would I be able to "take it"? This last question was by far the most important to me.

Let me pause for a moment to give you a short character analysis of myself. For years I had been conscious of an inferiority complex that had a firm grip on me. I had tried to hide this complex beneath an outer coating of egotism. To a certain extent I had been successful—I had fooled nearly everyone but myself. Try as I may, I could not overcome the feeling that I was just a little inferior to my fellow men. I did not credit myself with the quality of a leader among men, but how I longed for that virtue. I had always been content to sit back and let someone else get ahead while I wished I were in his boots. It was in this frame of mind that I joined seventy other young men on the morning of October 26, to leave for our camp in the Sierra Nevada Mountains.

Our arrival at camp that same evening was an event that I shall never forget. I was pleasantly surprised at the feeling of genuine hospitality and good cheer that existed among the older members of the company, and reached out to greet we new comers. I had expected a much different atmosphere, and I am ashamed to admit I arrived in camp with a chip on my shoulder. This feeling was soon lost in my pleasant surrounding.

Some of my self-imposed questions were answered in the first two weeks of camp life. Yes, I could make friends with my fellows, and quite easily too. Most of the friendships that I made early in my enlistment have lasted to this day.

The second question to be answered early in the game was, could I take it? I found that I could and liked it. I could work with these boys, play with them, argue with them and hold up my end. They seemed to like me, and I knew I was fond of them.

This new life had a grip on me, and for the first time in months I was really happy. Good food, plenty of sleep, interesting work and genial companions had created quite a change—my mind was at peace.

One night I went to bed rather early after a hard day's work. Something was wrong, and I didn't fall asleep right away as was my usual custom. My thoughts, when simmered down, were something like this—Here is my big chance to see if I'm going to go ahead in this world, or be just one of the crowd the rest of my life. I'm just one man in a group of two hundred young fellows, and I have just as good a chance as any of the others. So here goes, from now on I'm going to try for advancement—and I'm going to succeed. Such were my thoughts that night, for the first time I realized I had the same chance as the rest to make good.

Next morning in the light of day, things did not look so promising as I had pictured them during the night. But I now had the determination. All I needed was a starting point. In a few days I was to have my start, but it was a queer beginning.

At various times in my life I had done a bit of wrestling, and once or twice had engaged in bouts at camp. I was asked to wrestle a boy in our camp. I agreed, not knowing who my opponent was to be. He was not selected until the day of the fight, and when I heard his name I wanted to back out. Pride alone kept me from calling off the bout. My opponent was a huge fellow, weighing twenty-two pounds more than I, and a good three inches taller. No matter how I looked at it, I could picture only a massacre with myself on the losing end. It wasn't fear that made me want to back out, but I dreaded the thought of defeat in front of three or four hundred people.

I climbed into the ring that night a very doubtful, but determined young man. At least I would put up a good fight. When the bout was over and I emerged the victor, I knew immediately that I had made my start. I was terribly stiff and sore, but very proud and happy. Sleep did not come easily that night. I was too excited. I kept saying to myself, "I've done it, I'm on my way." Why a physical victory should put me mentally at ease I do not know, but it did.

At sometime or other, most of us have a friend that has enough interest in our well-being to try to bring us back on the right path after we have gone astray. So it was in my case. There resides in Oakland a young lady whom I have known for several years. As

It's a Great Life (Continued)

it was only a short distance from camp to Oakland, I was frequently a weekend visitor at her home.

One Sunday afternoon, this young lady and I sat talking in the living room of her home. As we had always been very outspoken with each other, I was not surprised when she said she was going to tell me a few things. By the time she had finished I'm afraid my face was a trifle red. She told me that in the last month I had changed from a quiet, unassuming young man to a conceited, self-centered prude. She topped it off by saying she could get along very nicely without my company until I recovered from my attack of pig-headedness. That night I slept very little, spending most of the night trying to get things straight in my mind. Out of the chaos of thoughts that came to me I realized two things. First, the young lady was indeed a friend and she had spoken harshly to try to bring me to my senses. Secondly, I realized that my newfound success had gone to my head, and I was making a perfect fool of myself.

For several days I pondered over my problem with no tangible result. It appeared to me that my job was to strike a happy medium between my old self and this new person that had taken possession of me. I didn't want to go back to the old way, and it was evident that I couldn't continue as I had been doing. The only solution was for me to find an average.

Unconsciously I must have succeeded. Three weeks later when I again visited the young lady for the weekend, she complimented me on my success. She claimed that I was an entirely new person, and she was very pleased. That Sunday night I returned to camp a very happy young man.

A short time later, our Educational Advisor arrived in camp, and that evening I was told I had been appointed his assistant. Out of a group of two hundred young men I had been chosen for a position of real importance.

In a little less than six months I had literally found myself. For twenty-two years I had doubted my right to call myself a man. My fight had been a long one, and here, in six short months I had proved to myself that I was really a man. A great deal of my success I owe to this certain young lady who brought me back on the right path. But if I had not joined the Civilian Conservation Corps I never would have made a start.

I shall try to convey to you Just what the Civilian Conservation Corps has meant to me. There are a great many things of which I could tell, but I shall write of only the most important. The rest I shall keep, deep down in my heart. First of all, by enrolling in President Roosevelt's peace time army! I managed to retain my self respect. I did not have to become either a parasite, living off my relatives, or a professional bum. In other words, it gave me a chance to stand on my own two feet and make my own way in the world.

Then it gave me the opportunity to make friendships that will live forever. Nine months of living in close contact with young men of my own age could hardly pass without at least a few lasting friendships.

I had an excellent chance to develop myself physically. Many months of work in the sun have put layers of muscle on my body and turned my skin a dark tan.

But my memories, those golden thoughts that I shall keep forever, are my most valued and treasured keepsake. My album is full of pictures, each one serving as only a starting point for a long journey into the land of happy days. Days of work in the woods, nights around the fire in the barracks, a trick played on an innocent chap, an all day hike with some of my friends, a fishing trip with one of my pals, the rush for the mess hall when the gong sounds, all of these thoughts are dear to me, and I feel sure that the next few months will bring countless more treasures with each passing day.

These things I have mentioned are benefits derived by every young man who has been a member of the Civilian Conservation Corps. But my personal achievement is the one glorious gift I have received from my association with the young men of the Civilian Conservation Corps.

I enrolled as a boy, unsteady, groping, unsure. I wanted something, but could not describe it or discover a means for attaining it. Then I discovered what it was I was seeking—it was the right to call myself a man. My life at camp has given me that right, and I shall be ever grateful to President Roosevelt and the C.C.C. Now that I am a man, with my feet firmly planted on the steps of life, I feel sure of a reasonable amount of success.

If, in my humble way I have made you realize what the Civilian Conservation Corps has done for me, I am very happy. I do not claim any honor for the change that occurred in me, it just had to be. I'm only deeply thankful that I had the change to get acquainted with the real me.

So in parting I say "Thank God for President Roosevelt and his C.C.C. I shall never forget you."

Source: *It's a Great Life* by Robert L. Miller, Company 999 C.C.C., Pine Grove, California. New Deal Network website: http://newdeal.feri.org/ccc/ccc009.htm

KERNEL ESSAYS BY STUDENTS
How an Experience Changed Me

MY BASKETBALL CAMP

1. I was bad at dribbling, bad at shooting, and slow.
2. I went to the basketball camp so I could get better at shooting and dribbling, etc.
3. I got better at my whole game, even my speed.
4. The coach there said to me, "Work hard and you will get far."
5. This made me work even harder.
6. My parents gave me this opportunity.

Zachary Prescott, Grade 7

JAMES ADAMS, NARRATOR OF CHERUB BOOK SERIES, TELLS HOW HE JOINED CHERUB

1. James was a trouble-making kid with no future.
2. James saw that he can't start over.
3. James started to be taught better at the Cherub Camp.
4. Amy, his lifeguard, talked to him about his new life.
5. James then worked hard on his 100 day basic training.
6. Earlier, James befriended a kid named Kyle who showed him Cherub.

Evan Katzman, Grade 7

BUTTER FINGERS

1. When I was about 10, I would complain a lot that I had cuts and bruises or scabs.
2. One day I was late for a dance practice.
3. My mom would tell me that I had butter fingers and butter feet.
4. When it happened, from that day on, when I would get cuts, bruises and scabs I would talk to myself.
5. This gave me the opportunity change myself.

Kassandra B. Martinez, Grade 6

CAMP RODFEI

1. Before I went to Camp Rodfei, I kept my clothing modest, as a Jewish girl, but I didn't like it.
2. I went to Camp Rodfei because I wanted something to do in the summer.
3. I improved myself by being proud of being modest.
4. One of the counselors suggested that I should be proud of myself for being modest.
5. This changed me by not worrying so much about modesty with my clothes.
6. My dad gave me this opportunity to go to camp and be with other Jewish girls.

Sylvia Geller, Grade 6

THE FATHER OF THE RAILROAD (IN ALEX MELCHOR'S VOICE AS GEORGE STEPHENSON)

1. I started as a coal miner and became an average engineer, but now I'm called the "Father of the Railroad."
2. The reason I started this is because I was curious about whose locomotive model was the best one.
3. My curiosity ended up helping me further develop my vision.
4. My son helped me with all my projects, especially the "Rocket."
5. Now, I was much more confident in my locomotive ideas.
6. I wouldn't have had this opportunity if my colleagues wouldn't have made a bet with me and raced against me.

Alex Melchor, Grade 8

MORE DEMON THAN ANGEL

1. Before I started reading about them, I didn't know what demons were.
2. I learned more about demons in the books.
3. I thought and thought and I realized that I had more demon than angel in me.
4. No one said anything . . . I kind of debated this one myself.
5. I gave myself the opportunity to explore.

Zoe Falk, Grade 6

PLANNING PAGE

Name:

TITLE OF YOUR PIECE

TEXT STRUCTURE

A Bad Situation A Lot Of Us Are In

| a description of how bad we have it | what we wish we could do for ourselves | how many of us there are | the worst part | what we can do to make things better |

Lester Hunter

KERNEL ESSAY

1. _____

2. _____

3. _____

4. _____

5. _____

_____

SUGGESTIONS FOR QUICK LIST:

When a population or group goes through a hard time
- war
- poverty
- trouble
- natural disasters
- civil upheaval
- illness outbreaks

MY QUICK LIST OF TOPICS:

1. ....
2. ....
3. ....
4. ....
5. ....

"I'd Rather Not Be on Relief"

Lester Hunter Song, 1938

We go around all dressed in rags

While the rest of the world goes neat.

And we have to be satisfied

With half enough to eat.

We have to live in lean-tos,

Or else we live in a tent,

For when we buy our bread and beans

There's nothing left for rent.

I'd rather not be on the rolls of relief,

Or work on the W.P.A.

We'd rather work for the farmer

If the farmer could raise the pay;

Then the farmer could plant more cotton

And he'd get more money for spuds,

Instead of wearing patches,

We'd dress up in new duds.

From the east and west and north and south

Like a swarm of bees we come;

The migratory workers

Are worse off than a bum.

We go to Mr. Farmer

And ask him what he'll pay;

He says, "Yon gypsy workers

Can live on a buck a day."

I'd rather not be on the rolls of relief,

Or work on the W.P.A.

We'd rather work for the farmer

If the farmer could raise the pay;

Then the farmer could plant more cotton

And he'd get more money for spuds,

Instead of wearing patches,

We'd dress up in new duds.

We don't ask for luxuries

Or even a feather bed,

But we're bound to raise the dickens

While our families are underfed.

Now the winter is on us

And the cotton picking is done,

What are we going to live on

While we're waiting for spuds to come?

Now if you will excuse me

I'll bring my song to an end.

I've got to go and chuck a crack

Where the howling wind comes in.

The times are going to better

And I guess you'd like to know

I'll tell you all about it

I've joined the C.I.O.

PLANNING PAGE + ESSAY
A Bad Situation a Lot of Us Are In

I'D RATHER NOT BE YOUNG AND IGNORED

We stumble around in confusion

While everyone else knows what to do.

And we try to conquer high school

Without a single clue.

We have to be mature,

Yet we are treated like young kids;

For when we try to express ourselves

Dominant authority forbids.

I'd rather not be young and ignored

Or constantly misunderstood.

We'd rather suppress the troubles

If we could fast forward to the good;

Then our lives would be blissful

And our young suffering would be complete

Instead of drowning,

We'd finally be on our feet.

From crowded hallways to compact classrooms

Like animals trapped in a cage;

The distraught teens

Are confined by hopeless age.

We go to adults

And plead for some advice;

They simply say, "I survived

So you'll suffice."

I'd rather not be young and ignored

Or constantly misunderstood.

We'd rather suppress the troubles

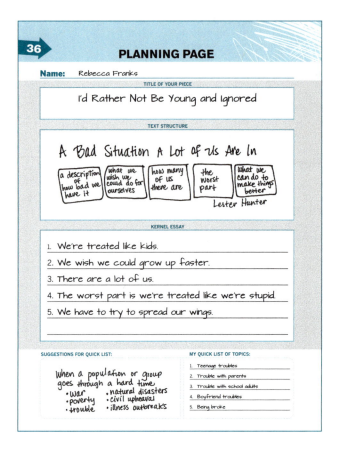

If we could fast forward to the good;

Then our lives would be blissful

And our young suffering would be complete

Instead of drowning,

We'd finally be on our feet.

We don't ask for special treatment

Or even bland excuses,

But we're bound to raise havoc

While we're treated like ignoramuses.

Now our parents reprimand us

And our teachers exhibit doubt,

How are we supposed to be independent

When we're prohibited from branching out?

Rebecca Franks, Grade 9

KERNEL ESSAYS BY STUDENTS
A Bad Situation a Lot of Us Are In

GETTING CAR STUCK IN THE SNOW WHILE DRIVING IN RHODE ISLAND

1. My dad was driving and our car jerked back!
2. We tried to give the car gas, but nothing happened.
3. There were 6 of us in the car and probably other families were in the same situation.
4. We got out of the car and while some of us were pushing the car my dad was giving it gas.
5. We just had to keep trying until we finally got it.

Dylan Totten, Grade 6

A BUS FENDER BENDER

1. None of us can leave the bus and we can't move the bus.
2. We wish we could just walk away and never look back.
3. We are a bus full of middle schoolers.
4. The worst part is none of us can do anything but stay quiet and wait.
5. Waiting is all we can do.

Kaitlyn Postell, Grade 6

THE EBOLA OUTBREAK

1. Africa is affected with a terrible Ebola virus and people are sick and dying everywhere and there aren't enough doctors.
2. People in Africa wish they could have more doctors, hospitals, and medicine.
3. Large parts of Africa and thousands of people are affected or sick.
4. The worst parts are the fact they're so poor they can do very little about it, and the sickness is bad, once you catch it, it's sickness, organ failure, and ultimately death.
5. They can make things better by using all means possible to prevent it from spreading to other parts of the world, and the world can help by sending people to assist.

Iris Hernandez, Grade 6

16 YEAR OLDS AT PAINTBALL

1. I can't even move I'm so scared.
2. I wish I could be made of metal.
3. It was Jack and I and 16 year old twins.
4. The worst part is we can't get away without being shot.
5. We can try to make a run for it or shoot first.

Joshua Levin, Grade 6

MY WORLD CAME CRASHING DOWN

1. It got so bad that my mom, my sister, and I had to leave.
2. We wished that we could have helped ourselves by not having to listen to the arguing.
3. There were three of us, my mom, my little sister, and me.
4. The worst part was that everyone felt pain.
5. What we did to make things better was make new memories to replace the bad ones.

Matheu Shiver, Grade 6

I'M IN A BAD SITUATION AND SO ARE A LOT OF US

1. I can't stick up for myself!
2. I want to stand up for myself.
3. There are a lot of us.
4. I can't talk to anyone I like without sputtering.
5. I will stand up for myself.

Gino Ameri, Grade 7

THE TEST I HATE

1. Nope. I hate it so much. This situation is all bad, it's all about the bad test.
2. What we wish we could do is stop it. We wish we had power.
3. This affects every student in Texas. We're all part of it, every student grades 3–12 in this state.
4. The worst part is voters have a say in it but no one uses their voices and test makers think no problem.
5. We can make things better with protests and knowing more people want to stop this testing.

Ilan Haas, Grade 6

Name: _____

TITLE OF YOUR PIECE

TEXT STRUCTURE

Picking up the Pieces

| what happened | why I didn't see it coming | the damage it has caused | what we will do about it |

Franklin D. Roosevelt

KERNEL ESSAY

1. _____

2. _____

3. _____

4. _____

_____

_____

SUGGESTIONS FOR QUICK LIST:

the upsets in life
- terrible news
- injuries
- crimes
- a loss
- unexpected illnesses

MY QUICK LIST OF TOPICS:

1. _____
2. _____
3. _____
4. _____
5. _____

Pearl Harbor Address to the Nation

Franklin Delano Roosevelt, 1941

December 8, 1941, Washington, D.C.

Mr. Vice President, Mr. Speaker, Members of the Senate, and of the House of Representatives:

Yesterday, December 7th, 1941—a date which will live in infamy—the United States of America was suddenly and deliberately attacked by naval and air forces of the Empire of Japan.

The United States was at peace with that nation and, at the solicitation of Japan, was still in conversation with its government and its emperor looking toward the maintenance of peace in the Pacific.

Indeed, one hour after Japanese air squadrons had commenced bombing in the American island of Oahu, the Japanese ambassador to the United States and his colleague delivered to our Secretary of State a formal reply to a recent American message. And while this reply stated that it seemed useless to continue the existing diplomatic negotiations, it contained no threat or hint of war or of armed attack.

It will be recorded that the distance of Hawaii from Japan makes it obvious that the attack was deliberately planned many days or even weeks ago. During the intervening time, the Japanese government has deliberately sought to deceive the United States by false statements and expressions of hope for continued peace.

The attack yesterday on the Hawaiian Islands has caused severe damage to American naval and military forces. I regret to tell you that very many American lives have been lost. In addition, American ships have been reported torpedoed on the high seas between San Francisco and Honolulu.

Yesterday, the Japanese government also launched an attack against Malaya.

Last night, Japanese forces attacked Hong Kong.

Last night, Japanese forces attacked Guam.

Last night, Japanese forces attacked the Philippine Islands.

Last night, the Japanese attacked Wake Island.

And this morning, the Japanese attacked Midway Island.

Japan has, therefore, undertaken a surprise offensive extending throughout the Pacific area. The facts of yesterday and today speak for themselves. The people of the United States have already formed their opinions and well understand the implications to the very life and safety of our nation.

As Commander in Chief of the Army and Navy, I have directed that all measures be taken for our defense. But always will our whole nation remember the character of the onslaught against us.

No matter how long it may take us to overcome this premeditated invasion, the American people in their righteous might will win through to absolute victory.

I believe that I interpret the will of the Congress and of the people when I assert that we will not only defend ourselves to the uttermost, but will make it very certain that this form of treachery shall never again endanger us.

Hostilities exist. There is no blinking at the fact that our people, our territory, and our interests are in grave danger.

With confidence in our armed forces, with the unbounding determination of our people, we will gain the inevitable triumph—so help us God.

I ask that the Congress declare that since the unprovoked and dastardly attack by Japan on Sunday, December 7th, 1941, a state of war has existed between the United States and the Japanese empire.

PLANNING PAGE + ESSAY
Picking Up the Pieces

A SINGLE GOODBYE EMAIL

On September 11th, 2011, my father's base was under attack. Baghdad is a battlefield and attacks are expected; however, on this day, a day of mourning, the enemy attacked with unexpected force. Alarms blaring, my father wrote a single goodbye email and sent it to my mother.

My family waited, watching the phone intensely. It was not until 24 hours later that we received an email that wrote "I am OK!" However, when my father arrived home three months later, he was far from "OK."

The battle had taken a toll on my father in a way we could not fix. My father, along with hundreds of others, is plagued with nightmares and has intense fear reactions. His view of the world is shaded with the tragedies that have occurred around him. He is riddled with the scars of war both emotionally and physically.

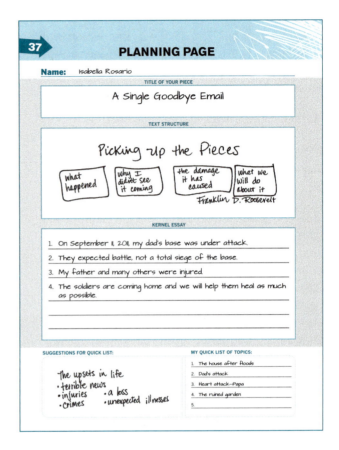

My father was diagnosed with Post Traumatic Stress Disorder (PTSD). This disease is very common among soldiers due to the horrors they witness overseas. There is no simple cure for this disease. Each case is unique and needs to be treated as such. My father is a very honorable man and refuses therapy; however he treats his disorder by speaking openly about his experiences with trusted friends and family and works through his traumas slowly and steadily.

Many others, however, cannot get through their symptoms through simply talking through it. A majority of cases involve deep therapy and at many times medications. The problem with this is that only around half of Americans truly know and understand PTSD's toll on a person. People everywhere see people like the man who shot Chris Kyle and write them off as an insane person, lost to the world who cannot be helped. This is not true! There are treatments and ways of managing their symptoms. The citizens of the United States need to understand this and work along with us to help our nation's heroes. I believe that there are many cases out there that progressed to such a devastating place just due to a lack of understanding from those around them. We should work together to stop this.

Isabella Rosario, Grade 10

KERNEL ESSAYS BY STUDENTS
Picking Up the Pieces

STOLEN PURSE

1. My mom's purse was stolen.
2. Her purse has never been stolen before.
3. Our car window has been shattered and her credit and debit cards were in that purse.
4. We are going to cancel the checks and all the cards that were in that purse.

Nina De La Torre, Grade 8

UNCLE ANDREW'S ACCIDENT

1. Uncle Andrew fell off his bike going 60 mph down a hill (without a helmet) and hit his head.
2. I didn't see it coming because when Uncle Andrew was 21 he was a professional mountain biker and always wore a helmet.
3. As a result, it shocked our family and scared us.
4. We prayed for him through his long recovery.

Jacob Fiero, Grade 8

THE GLOBE IS WARMING

1. In the beginning of time, we admired the beauty of the world and the commodities it possessed.
2. We wanted to be able to live off the land and experience the world in a lively way.
3. What we got was pollution from cars and overproduction in factories.
4. Scientists warn that if we don't address climate change, we can expect heat waves, wildfires, floods and droughts.
5. I still hope that we can reverse the destruction of global warming and bring back the beauty and cleanliness the world beholds.

Destin Pate, Grade 10

SCOLIOSIS

1. My family and I found out that my scoliosis had gotten bad.
2. I felt fine before my back never hurt, I never knew what scoliosis was, and going to my chiropractor had always been like a trip to the park so I didn't see this coming.
3. Now my back is crooked, my internal organs could be crushed, and under certain circumstances I might never give birth.
4. We are going to get a back brace for me so my spine won't get a bigger curve.

Nina De La Torre, Grade 8

THE DIAGNOSIS

1. Our friend was diagnosed with leiomyosarcoma.
2. She had had no symptoms.
3. It had attacked her soft tissues and her morale.
4. We will triumph over this disease.

Nitesh Kartha, Grade 9

1. There was a devastating flood last week.
2. We didn't see it coming because the Blanco River has never risen 40 feet before.
3. The flood wiped out most of the town and killed several families, and my car was totaled while it just sat in an auto repair shop in Wimberly.
4. We will all have to mourn the lost, pitch in with the cleanup, and I'll have to save up money for another car.

Katy Shoopman, Grade 11

PLANNING PAGE

Name: _____

TITLE OF YOUR PIECE

TEXT STRUCTURE

Heads Up from Your Wingman

| I just heard this... | Which upset these people... | and here is what I think you should do or say | Why you should handle it with care |

Eleanor Roosevelt

KERNEL ESSAY

1. _____

2. _____

3. _____

4. _____

_____

_____

SUGGESTIONS FOR QUICK LIST:

Who are your buds? Who watches your back? When you see trouble ahead for someone else, what do you tell them?
- teammates   • siblings
- friends   • teachers

MY QUICK LIST OF TOPICS:

1. _____

2. _____

3. _____

4. _____

5. _____

Letter to Her Husband   **Eleanor Roosevelt, circa WWII**

I have just heard that no meeting was ever held between colored leaders like Walter White, Mr. Hill and Mr. Randolph, with the secretary of War and Navy on the subject of how the colored people can participate in the services.

There is growing feeling amongst the colored people, and they are creating a feeling among many white people. They feel they should be allowed to participate in any training that is going on, in the aviation, army, navy, and have opportunities for service.

I would suggest that a conference be held with the attitude of the gentlemen: these are our difficulties, how do you suggest that we make a beginning to change the situation?

There is no use of going into a conference unless they have the intention of doing something. This is going to be very bad politically, besides being intrinsically wrong, and I think you should ask that a meeting be held and if you cannot be present yourself, you should ask them to give you a report and it might be well to have General Watson present.

E. R.

Note: It's important to look out for others. This letter from Eleanor Roosevelt is a perfect example of a message that was written to do just that. Eleanor positions herself as her husband's "wingman," in a sense, calling him to take decisive action in a charged situation. In this classroom exercise, students are asked to use the foundational structure of Eleanor's letter—its focus on her recollection of something she heard, her description of how it made others feel, and her suggestions about how and why the situation should be addressed—to craft their own "Heads Up From Your Wingman" essays.

KERNEL ESSAYS BY STUDENTS
Heads Up From Your Wingman

TINKERBELL TO PETER PAN

1. I just saw Captain Hook poison your medicine.
2. If you drink it you'll die.
3. Don't drink it; let me drink it.
4. It will poison you if you ingest it.

Kaitlyn Postell, Grade 6

_____

MERLIN TO KING ARTHUR

1. I found out that Morgana is going to make you go crazy.
2. This would make you go mad and not get your spot on the throne.
3. You should capture Morgana and her contact.
4. If all goes bad Morgana will make Camelot miserable.

Evalenna Elam, Grade 6

_____

GLORY TO CLAY: WINGS OF FIRE (*THE DRAGONET PROPHESY #1*)

1. Clay, the Skywing guards are circling the area.
2. They just set the Mudwings on alert and told them to look for us.
3. We need to roll in the mud to blend in.
4. Try and fit in to pass by and I'll be right behind you.

Iris Hernandez, Grade 6

_____

TAMARA TO KATY PERRY

1. I just saw one of the pieces of floor broke.
2. This will hurt if you fall, Katy.
3. For that not to happen, you need to delay the show to fix it.
4. We need to do it quickly so you don't hurt yourself like that last time when the swing almost fell.

Sylvia Geller, Grade 6

GUS GUS TO CINDERELLA

1. "Hey, hey, Cinderella, I just saw your step mum holding an invitation to the ball tomorrow night!"
2. "Thanks, Gus Gus, but my step mum and two step sisters wouldn't like it."
3. "Hey, hey, let's gather people to make Cinderella happy. Let's make a dress!"
4. "Hey, hey, don't let your mum see or your step sisters too or else your sisters will rip your dress to tatters!"

Kassandra B. Martinez, Grade 6

_____

TAKE A SHOWER! (DAVID BEN GURION WAS ALBERT EINSTEIN'S FRIEND AND THIS IS WHAT DAVID MIGHT SAY TO ALBERT)

1. I recently heard that your smell has not been pleasant.
2. The President of the U.S. doesn't like bad smells.
3. Every day take at least 30 minutes to groom yourself.
4. People won't want to talk to you if you smell like a dog.

Nina De La Torre, Grade 8

KERNEL ESSAYS BY STUDENTS
Heads Up From Your Wingman

FROM A SISTER TO A BROTHER

1. Psst! You forgot Mother's Day.
2. Mom's going to have hurt feelings.
3. You should write a card for Mom.
4. Moms don't forget!

Lisa Duncan, Grade 5

FROM A PASSENGER TO A DRIVER

1. I just noticed that there's a fire in the back of your truck.
2. Your truck might explode if you don't do something to put out the fire.
3. Maybe we should pull over.
4. Fires aren't such a good idea in a moving vehicle.

Maurice Phelps, Grade 5

FROM A PASSENGER TO A DRIVER

1. I think you're speeding.
2. The police will give you another ticket if they see you.
3. Maybe you should slow down just a little.
4. You don't want another ticket on your record.

Julian Ponce, Grade 4

1. Ms. Bernabei, is your shirt on inside out?
2. It doesn't bother me if it doesn't bother you.
3. You might want to change it.
4. The students will notice right away.

Gail Markson, Fellow Teacher

---

1. I was watching TV and I heard Mika talking with her new braces and she lisped.
2. This made some Joe Scarborough and a couple of others laugh uncontrollably.
3. I think they should get control of themselves.
4. It makes people feel bad to be laughed at.

Carmen Gonzales, Grade 4

ANNA TO ELSA FROM *FROZEN*

1. I know you're upset, but the whole town is frozen.
2. Everyone in the town is frightened.
3. Can you please unfreeze everything?
4. The whole town depends on you to take care of this.

Karel Molinar, Grade 4

PLANNING PAGE

Name: _____

TITLE OF YOUR PIECE

```
┌─────────────────────────────────────────────────┐
│                                                   │
│                                                   │
│                                                   │
└─────────────────────────────────────────────────┘
```

TEXT STRUCTURE

What Do I Mean? Well...

| You asked me to explain " ～～～. " | Part of it means this... | Another part of it does <u>not</u> mean... | What the whole thing really means... |

— Ayn Rand

KERNEL ESSAY

1. _____

2. _____

3. _____

4. _____

_____

_____

SUGGESTIONS FOR QUICK LIST:

Think of things you've said. Imagine another person asking you, "What do you mean by that?"
- Good morning
- Talk to the hand
- Time to go!
- I miss you.

MY QUICK LIST OF TOPICS:

1. _____
2. _____
3. _____
4. _____
5. _____

"I Love You" Letter — Ayn Rand, 1948

May 22, 1948

Dear Ms. Rondeau:

You asked me to explain the meaning of my sentence in *The Fountainhead:* "To say 'I love you' one must know first how to say the 'I.'"

The meaning of that sentence is contained in the whole of *The Fountainhead.* And it is stated right in the speech on page 400 from which you took that sentence. The meaning of the "I" is an independent, self-sufficient entity that *does not* exist for the sake of any other person.

A person who exists only for the sake of his loved one is not an independent entity, but a spiritual parasite. The love of a parasite is worth nothing.

The usual (and very vicious) nonsense preached on the subject of love claims that love is self-sacrifice. A man's self is his spirit. If one sacrifices his spirit, who or what is left to feel the love? True love is profoundly *selfish,* in the noblest meaning of the word—it is an expression of one's *self,* of one's highest values. When a person is in love, he seeks his own happiness—and *not* his sacrifice to the loved one. And the loved one would be a monster if she wanted or expected sacrifice.

Any person who wants to live *for* others—for one sweetheart or for the whole of mankind— is a selfless nonentity. An independent "I" is a person who exists for his own sake. Such a person does not make any vicious pretense of self-sacrifice and does not demand it from the person he loves. Which is the only way to be in love and the only form of a self-respecting relationship between two people.

Note: One of the biggest problems in our culture comes into play when we misunderstand each other's messages, both verbal and nonverbal. Usually when we are then asked, "What did you mean?" we simply repeat our message verbatim, without giving it much thought. Ayn Rand's letter gives us a structure that promises to help us come to a place of clarity in countless moments such as these. She parses her message, showing the reader exactly how to decode what she means. In this classroom exercise, students are asked to use the foundational structure of Ayn's letter—its focus on her calculated explanation of what her words mean, what they do not mean, and on what she is trying to convey overall—to craft their own "What Do I Mean? Well . . ." essays.

PLANNING PAGE + ESSAY
What Do I Mean? Well . . .

"I HATE YOU"

Phrases rely heavily on the connotation rather than the denotation. They rely on how something is said and more importantly, who is saying it. Just because I say "I hate you" doesn't mean I do.

Allow me to break down the phrase. The word "I" is obviously referring to me. Specifically how I feel about "you." However, when I use the word "hate" I am not referring to a "feeling of passionate or intense dislike."

When I say "I hate you" I am exclaiming how much I care about you even though you don't deserve it. Even though I don't want to. Caring about you gives you the power to hurt me. A power you abuse often. And yet, despite this, when I say the words "I hate you," I don't.

Abbey Murgatroyd, Grade 9

KERNEL ESSAYS BY STUDENTS
What Do I Mean? Well . . .

TOPIC: BEING LEFT OUT

1. You asked me to explain what it means to be left out.
2. It's that feeling inside you when nobody is talking to you.
3. It means when people don't recognize you and your feelings.
4. It mainly means you feel like you're missing out on this or that.

Evalenna Elam, Grade 6

GOAL

1. You asked me to explain "Goal."
2. Part of it means an objective to do something.
3. Another part of it has to do with confidence.
4. What the whole thing really means is to finish what you have started and get where you planned.

Dylan Totten, Grade 6

MEMORIAL DAY

1. You asked me to explain Memorial Day.
2. Part of it means a three-day weekend.
3. Another part of it means a day to remember the soldiers that have died fighting for our country.
4. What the whole thing really means is remember everyone who is gone during this three-day weekend.

Matheu Shiver, Grade 6

PEACE

1. You asked me to explain peace.
2. Part of it means no fear.
3. Peace doesn't mean freedom, freedom is rights for all. There can be two peaceful countries without freedom.
4. Peace means no one should fear one another.

Norman Davis, Grade 6

WHAT DO I MEAN WHEN I SAY "THAT KILLS ME"

1. You asked me to explain "that kills me."
2. Part of it means you're doing or saying something completely ridiculous.
3. Another part of it does not mean it's actually killing me but it would if it could.
4. The whole thing really means you need to stop acting like you're an uneducated phony.

Victoria Rodriguez, Grade 10

TOO NICE

1. I finally understand, "sometimes people can be too nice."
2. Being too nice can lead to being taken advantage of.
3. It doesn't mean you're a weak or naïve person.
4. Being too nice means liking someone so much and going to the ends of the earth for them, but at the same time, you're blinded by their true motives and manipulating tricks.

Kathy Le, Grade 7

TO DO THINGS FOR THE WORLD

1. You asked me to explain, "I want to do great things with my life."
2. I want to use my life to help others and benefit the world.
3. I do not want to use my life to my own advantage.
4. It means that someone who strives to do well for the good will succeed more than the man who chooses to pamper his profit.

Lily Shenoy, Grade 7

PLANNING PAGE

Name: _____

TITLE OF YOUR PIECE

```
┌─────────────────────────────────────────┐
│                                           │
│                                           │
└─────────────────────────────────────────┘
```

TEXT STRUCTURE

My Advice About Your Strong Feeling

| I see that you feel ___. | Two Kinds of ___ that feeling (good and bad) | What you should do about those feelings | How I think you should show those feelings | Parting thought |

John Steinbeck

KERNEL ESSAY

1. _____

2. _____

3. _____

4. _____

5. _____

_____

SUGGESTIONS FOR QUICK LIST:

Any kind of very strong feeling you've seen someone else have
- panic
- rage
- love
- excitement
- heartbreak
- frustration

MY QUICK LIST OF TOPICS:

1. _____
2. _____
3. _____
4. _____
5. _____

Letter to His Son Thom

John Steinbeck, 1958

John Steinbeck's son Thom was 14 when he wrote to his father from boarding school— confessing that he felt he might be in love for the first time. This letter is his father's response.

November 10, 1958

Dear Thom,

We had your letter this morning. I will answer it from my point of view and of course Elaine will from hers.

First—if you are in love—that's a good thing—that's about the best thing that can happen to anyone. Don't let anyone make it small or light to you.

Second—There are several kinds of love. One is a selfish, mean, grasping, egotistical thing which uses love for self-importance. This is the ugly and crippling kind. The other is an outpouring of everything good in you—of kindness and consideration and respect—not only the social respect of manners but the greater respect which is recognition of another person as unique and valuable. The first kind can make you sick and small and weak but the second can release in you strength, and courage and goodness and even wisdom you didn't know you had.

You say this is not puppy love. If you feel so deeply—of course it isn't puppy love.

But I don't think you were asking me what you feel. You know that better than anyone. What you wanted me to help you with is what to do about it—and that I can tell you.

Glory in it for one thing and be very glad and grateful for it.

The object of love is the best and most beautiful. Try to live up to it.

If you love someone—there is no possible harm in saying so—only you must remember that some people are very shy and sometimes the saying must take that shyness into consideration.

Girls have a way of knowing or feeling what you feel, but they usually like to hear it also.

It sometimes happens that what you feel is not returned for one reason or another—but that does not make your feeling less valuable and good.

Lastly, I know your feeling because I have it and I am glad you have it.

We will be glad to meet Susan. She will be very welcome. But Elaine will make all such arrangements because that is her province and she will be very glad to. She knows about love too and maybe she can give you more help than I can.

And don't worry about losing. If it is right, it happens—The main thing is not to hurry. Nothing good gets away.

Love

Fa

Note: Everybody has moments when their feelings are inflamed, and it's important that we recognize and observe them in ourselves and in others. Even when emotions are running high, a compassionate observer can step in to help facilitate mature conversation. Who better than John Steinbeck to advise a loved one in this regard? In this classroom exercise, students are asked to use the foundational structure of Steinbeck's letter—its focus on bringing an emotion to light, explaining the different manifestations of the emotion, describing what should be done about it, suggesting how it should be made apparent, and providing final reflective thoughts—to craft their own essays in the form of "My Advice About Your Strong Feeling."

PLANNING PAGE + ESSAY
My Advice About Your Strong Feeling

SELF-TALK SWITCHBACK DRIVING

Dear Me,

You just drove up the mountain, and Berthoud Pass truly frightened you. Your knuckles turned white, your palms got sweaty, and you had trouble breathing. You felt like you were driving on a leaning ledge, suspended over sheer space. You were surprised to experience terror because you are usually so strong and unafraid of anything. In a few days, when your vacation time on the mountain is over, you're going to be driving back down. You're terrified. Instead of going to sleep, you're lying there, obsessing over it. You've googled Berthoud Pass, looking for alternate routes, comments from others, help in any form.

PLANNING PAGE — 40

Name: Gretchen Bernabei

TITLE OF YOUR PIECE: Self-Talk Switchback Driving

TEXT STRUCTURE: My Advice About Your Strong Feeling

I see that you feel ___. | Two Kinds of that feeling (good and bad) | What you should do about those feelings | How I think you should show those feelings | Parting thought

John Steinbeck

KERNEL ESSAY:
1. I see you're scared to drive down the mountain.
2. Fear can protect you or cripple you.
3. Get a grip and let terror guide you.
4. Laugh. Research. Make a plan.
5. You have what you need to get through this.

SUGGESTIONS FOR QUICK LIST:
Any kind of very strong feeling you've seen someone else have:
• panic • excitement
• rage • heartbreak
• love • frustration

MY QUICK LIST OF TOPICS:
1. Keith and the gingerbread
2. Chickens in the garden
3. Losing Beauty's Foal
4. Up Berthoud pass
5. Seeing T in Secret Garden

Let me tell you, self . . . there are two kinds of fear. Fear that stops you from living a full life, and fear that helps you live a full life. If your fear is keeping you safe, then maybe it's not such a bad thing. If it's ruining your quality of life, then it's unhealthy.

Look for an alternate route, and if there is one, take it. If there's a way to learn not to be afraid of it, learn it. Take the shuttle with some other driver, and learn the way he thinks about those curves. Watch. Don't be afraid to close your eyes if you need to.

Ask questions of others at the top of the mountain. Make jokes about your sweaty palms. Go ahead and refuse to drive back down until you feel calm about it.

Don't forget, you're resourceful and strong. And you've got a great team around you who will help you any time. Enjoy this surprising new experience, terror. It'll give you something to write about.

Your friend forever,
Me

Gretchen Bernabei

KERNEL ESSAYS BY STUDENTS
My Advice About Your Strong Feeling

FROM DEMETRIUS TO HELENA (BEFORE THEY RUN AWAY) FROM *A MIDSUMMER NIGHT'S DREAM*

1. I see that you're in love with me.
2. There are good types of love and there are bad types.
3. You should hide these nonmutual feelings that you have.
4. Have a nice life. See you at my wedding to Hermia.

Alejandra Trillo, Grade 8

_____

1. I know you really, really want a dog.
2. There are two kinds of pet-owners: those that really take care of their dogs, and those that only want to see them once in a while and forget about them the rest of the time.
3. Maybe you should volunteer at the animal shelter to see which kind of feelings you really do have.
4. Then if you still want a dog, you could put it on your Christmas list. If you mention it to your parents every day, they will know you are serious.
5. Nagging sometimes is your best approach.

Scott Porter, Grade 11

_____

BEAUTY TO THE BEAST

1. Your growling tells me that you don't want anybody in your castle.
2. There are two kinds of beasts: ones that are mean on the outside, and ones that are mean on the inside.
3. You should send me home if you hate me being here so much.
4. Growling isn't the way to show your feelings; you could speak plainly . . . you know, use your words.
5. A haircut would be good.

Tamara Wartsbaugh, Grade 5

THE NURSE TO JULIET

1. I know you love Romeo and you already married him.
2. But there are two kinds of marriages: passionate ones and business ones.
3. You should take those passionate feelings you have for banished Romeo and realize that it's never going to work, so move on. Remember the good times but move on.
4. You might write a little note to Romeo to tell him goodbye, and let your father know you're going to obey him now.
5. And by the way . . . Friar Lawrence sent over this cute little bottle for you.

Delores Morley, Grade 7

_____

LYSANDER TALKING TO DEMETRIUS ABOUT HERMIA (FROM *A MIDSUMMER NIGHT'S DREAM*)

1. I see that you feel in love with Hermia.
2. Two kinds of love (1) she loves me (2) she will never love you.
3. You should just get over her and move on.
4. I think you should show those feelings with another girl.
5. Good luck winning her heart cuz you never will!

Genesis Thomas, Grade 8

_____

1. I know you like Dylan.
2. There are two kinds of liking: from a distance and in-your-face.
3. If you want the distance kind, don't do anything. Just watch him and have fun being a secret admirer.
4. But I think you should tell him. Write him a note, or just walk up and tell him.
5. No pain, no gain!

Jamie Hull, Grade 8

Name: _____

TITLE OF YOUR PIECE

TEXT STRUCTURE

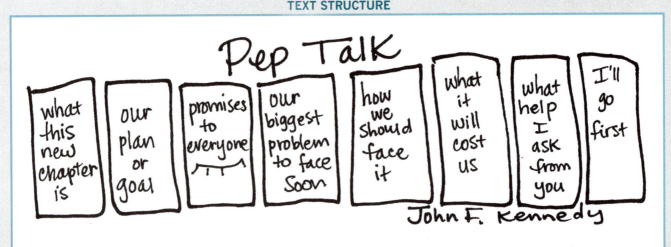

Pep Talk

| what this new chapter is | our plan or goal | promises to everyone | our biggest problem to face soon | how we should face it | what it will cost us | what help I ask from you | I'll go first |

John F. Kennedy

KERNEL ESSAY

1. _____
2. _____
3. _____
4. _____
5. _____
6. _____
7. _____
8. _____

SUGGESTIONS FOR QUICK LIST:

Think about things we launch
- plans • jobs • programs
- new school year
- new relationships
- new seasons of any kind

MY QUICK LIST OF TOPICS:

1. _____
2. _____
3. _____
4. _____
5. _____

Inaugural Address   John F. Kennedy, 1961

Vice President Johnson, Mr. Speaker, Mr. Chief Justice, President Eisenhower, Vice President Nixon, President Truman, reverend clergy, fellow citizens:

We observe today not a victory of party, but a celebration of freedom—symbolizing an end, as well as a beginning—signifying renewal, as well as change. For I have sworn before you and Almighty God the same solemn oath our forebears prescribed nearly a century and three-quarters ago.

The world is very different now. For man holds in his mortal hands the power to abolish all forms of human poverty and all forms of human life. And yet the same revolutionary beliefs for which our forebears fought are still at issue around the globe—the belief that the rights of man come not from the generosity of the state, but from the hand of God.

We dare not forget today that we are the heirs of that first revolution. Let the word go forth from this time and place, to friend and foe alike, that the torch has been passed to a new generation of Americans—born in this century, tempered by war, disciplined by a hard and bitter peace, proud of our ancient heritage, and unwilling to witness or permit the slow undoing of those human rights to which this nation has always been committed, and to which we are committed today at home and around the world.

Let every nation know, whether it wishes us well or ill, that we shall pay any price, bear any burden, meet any hardship, support any friend, oppose any foe, to assure the survival and the success of liberty.

This much we pledge—and more.

To those old allies whose cultural and spiritual origins we share, we pledge the loyalty of faithful friends. United there is little we cannot do in a host of cooperative ventures. Divided there is little we can do—for we dare not meet a powerful challenge at odds and split asunder.

To those new states whom we welcome to the ranks of the free, we pledge our word that one form of colonial control shall not have passed away merely to be replaced by a far more iron tyranny. We shall not always expect to find them supporting our view. But we shall always hope to find

them strongly supporting their own freedom—and to remember that, in the past, those who foolishly sought power by riding the back of the tiger ended up inside.

To those people in the huts and villages of half the globe struggling to break the bonds of mass misery, we pledge our best efforts to help them help themselves, for whatever period is required—not because the Communists may be doing it, not because we seek their votes, but because it is right. If a free society cannot help the many who are poor, it cannot save the few who are rich.

To our sister republics south of our border, we offer a special pledge: to convert our good words into good deeds, in a new alliance for progress, to assist free men and free governments in casting off the chains of poverty. But this peaceful revolution of hope cannot become the prey of hostile powers. Let all our neighbors know that we shall join with them to oppose aggression or subversion anywhere in the Americas. And let every other power know that this hemisphere intends to remain the master of its own house.

To that world assembly of sovereign states, the United Nations, our last best hope in an age where the instruments of war have far outpaced the instruments of peace, we renew our pledge of support—to prevent it from becoming merely a forum for invective, to strengthen its shield of the new and the weak, and to enlarge the area in which its writ may run.

Finally, to those nations who would make themselves our adversary, we offer not a pledge but a request: that both sides begin anew the quest for peace, before the dark powers of destruction unleashed by science engulf all humanity in planned or accidental self-destruction. We dare not tempt them with weakness. For only when our arms are sufficient beyond doubt can we be certain beyond doubt that they will never be employed.

But neither can two great and powerful groups of nations take comfort from our present course—both sides overburdened by the cost of modern weapons, both rightly alarmed by the steady spread of the deadly atom, yet both racing to alter that uncertain balance of terror that stays the hand of mankind's final war.

(continued)...

Inaugural Address (Continued) John F. Kennedy, 1961

So let us begin anew—remembering on both sides that civility is not a sign of weakness, and sincerity is always subject to proof. Let us never negotiate out of fear, but let us never fear to negotiate.

Let both sides explore what problems unite us instead of belaboring those problems which divide us.

Let both sides, for the first time, formulate serious and precise proposals for the inspection and control of arms, and bring the absolute power to destroy other nations under the absolute control of all nations.

Let both sides seek to invoke the wonders of science instead of its terrors. Together let us explore the stars, conquer the deserts, eradicate disease, tap the ocean depths, and encourage the arts and commerce.

Let both sides unite to heed, in all corners of the earth, the command of Isaiah—to "undo the heavy burdens, and [to] let the oppressed go free."

And, if a beachhead of cooperation may push back the jungle of suspicion, let both sides join in creating a new endeavor—not a new balance of power, but a new world of law—where the strong are just, and the weak secure, and the peace preserved.

All this will not be finished in the first one hundred days. Nor will it be finished in the first one thousand days; nor in the life of this Administration; nor even perhaps in our lifetime on this planet. But let us begin.

In your hands, my fellow citizens, more than mine, will rest the final success or failure of our course. Since this country was founded, each generation of Americans has been summoned to give testimony to its national loyalty. The graves of young Americans who answered the call to service surround the globe.

Now the trumpet summons us again—not as a call to bear arms, though arms we need—not as a call to battle, though embattled we are—but a call to bear the burden of a long twilight struggle, year in and year out, "rejoicing in hope; patient in tribulation"— a struggle against the common enemies of man: tyranny, poverty, disease, and war itself.

Can we forge against these enemies a grand and global alliance, North and South, East and West, that can assure a more fruitful life for all mankind? Will you join in that historic effort?

In the long history of the world, only a few generations have been granted the role of defending freedom in its hour of maximum danger. I do not shrink from this responsibility—I welcome it. I do not believe that any of us would exchange places with any other people or any other generation. The energy, the faith, the devotion which we bring to this endeavor will light our country and all who serve it. And the glow from that fire can truly light the world.

And so, my fellow Americans, ask not what your country can do for you; ask what you can do for your country. My fellow citizens of the world, ask not what America will do for you, but what together we can do for the freedom of man.

Finally, whether you are citizens of America or citizens of the world, ask of us here the same high standards of strength and sacrifice which we ask of you. With a good conscience our only sure reward, with history the final judge of our deeds, let us go forth to lead the land we love, asking His blessing and His help, but knowing that here on earth God's work must truly be our own.

KERNEL ESSAYS BY STUDENTS
Pep Talk

BASKETBALL TEAM

1. From now on we are going to become more like a team.
2. Teamwork helps you win and makes you a better person.
3. I promise to work harder with everyone around me and play as a team member.
4. Our biggest problems are not passing the ball to each other, taking bad shots, and fouling unnecessarily.
5. We won't be able to be ball hogs and we'll have to give up our personal time to practice.
6. We will get help from our coaches, parents and each other.
7. We can do this and I'll be the first to start!

Franchesca Gallardo, Grade 8

CHEER COMPETITION

1. We are going to a cheer competition.
2. Our plan is to win.
3. I promise that I, your captain, will do my very best for this team.
4. Our biggest problems are the other teams.
5. We should face them all smiles and no bad sportsmanship.
6. It will cost a lot of hard work.
7. I am asking for everyone's hardest work.
8. Let's go. I'll go first.

Alejandra Trillo, Grade 8

BECOMING FOREST PEOPLE

1. We're going to become forest people.
2. Our goal is to become friends with all wild life.
3. I promise that you will be happy, and you won't die.
4. Our biggest problem is parasites.
5. This could cost us our lives!
6. Please help gather any necessary materials.
7. Let's go! I'll go first!

Lauren Messer, Grade 7

1. I've just been cast in the play, *The Secret Garden!*
2. My goal is to play my part well.
3. I promise the director to give my attention and all my heart and soul to this work.
4. My biggest problem is moving like a ghost in a huge dress.
5. I will face it by rehearsing with the fabric.
6. This will take hours of rehearsal and lots of compromise with cast members who wish they had my role.
7. I ask that my director give me plenty of feedback and know that I can take it.
8. I'm on it.

Lilly Rosewood, Grade 11

1. I've just signed up for the Army.
2. I plan to become all that I can be.
3. I promise I will make my drill sergeant happy and my parents proud.
4. Soon I will be facing strenuous boot camp.
5. I will not whine or wimp out, and I will push myself beyond my limit every day.
6. My muscles will burn and I may spend some time frustrated.
7. I will be there for my platoon, and I will ask that they be there for me.
8. I'm ready.

Brent Lockamy, Grade 10

PLANNING PAGE

Name: _____

TITLE OF YOUR PIECE

```
┌─────────────────────────────────────────────────────────────┐
│                                                               │
│                                                               │
│                                                               │
└─────────────────────────────────────────────────────────────┘
```

TEXT STRUCTURE

Memory Reflection

where I was	what happened first	what happened next	what happened last	what I learned or noticed

John Howard Griffin

KERNEL ESSAY

1. _____

2. _____

3. _____

4. _____

5. _____

SUGGESTIONS FOR QUICK LIST:

Moments when you noticed something that surprised you; moments when you saw something from a new perspective

MY QUICK LIST OF TOPICS:

1. ....

2. ....

3. ....

4. ....

5. ....

Black Like Me (Excerpt) John Howard Griffin, 1961

When I left him I caught the bus into town, choosing a seat halfway to the rear. As we neared Canal, the car began to fill with whites. Unless they could find a place to themselves or beside another white, they stood in the aisle.

A middle-aged woman with stringy gray hair stood near my seat. She wore a clean but faded print house dress that was hoisted to one side as she clung to an overhead pendant support. Her face looked tired and I felt uncomfortable. As she staggered with the bus's movement my lack of gallantry tormented me. I half rose from my seat to give it to her, but Negroes behind me frowned disapproval. I realized I was "going against the race" and the subtle tug-of-war became instantly clear. If the whites would not sit with us, let them stand. When they became tired enough or uncomfortable enough, they would eventually take seats beside us and soon see that it was not so poisonous after all. But to give them your seat was to let them win. I slumped back under the intensity of their stares.

But my movement had attracted the white woman's attention. For an instant our eyes met. I felt sympathy for her, and thought I detected sympathy in her glance. The exchange blurred the barriers of race (so new to me) long enough for me to smile and vaguely indicate the empty seat beside me, letting her know she was welcome to accept it.

Her blue eyes, so pale before, sharpened and she spat out, "What're you looking at me like *that* for?"

I felt myself flush. Other white passengers craned to look at me. The silent onrush of hostility frightened me.

"I'm sorry," I said, staring at my knees. "I'm not from here." The pattern of her skirt turned abruptly as she faced the front.

"They're getting sassier every day," she said loudly. Another woman agreed and the two fell into conversation.

My flesh prickled with shame, for I knew the Negroes rightly resented me for attracting such unfavorable attention. I sat the way I had seen them do, sphynxlike, pretending unawareness. Gradually people lost interest. Hostility drained to boredom. The poor woman chattered on, reluctant apparently to lose the spotlight.

Note: In Black Like Me, *the white author travels through the segregated South disguised as a black man. This excerpt recounts one specific moment in this journey. The text structure accompanying this piece is a narrative, of which there are plenty of examples; this example demonstrates the power of one kind of retelling, moving the reader from a cerebral understanding to a visceral experience. Everyone knows "it's painful to experience prejudice," but until reading this author's experience, the general American understanding of racism does not include the nuances, undercurrent, and magnitude of black life in racially divided America. This excerpt demonstrates how a simple narrative can do the work of the most powerfully written informational and persuasive texts.*

PLANNING PAGE + ESSAY
Memory Reflection

JOURNAL OF A NO-NAME SLAVE (WRITTEN BY ALEJANDRA TRILLO, SPEAKING IN THE VOICE OF AN AMERICAN SLAVE)

July 6, 1804.

It was a hot Texas summer day, around 12pm. The sun was becoming blistering hot on our sore and beat up skin. Try to imagine lying down on a hot piece of metal with grease on your back, that's what the sun felt like. On most summer days it was more than 100 degrees outside. Today was supposed to be just like any other day, working from sunrise to sunset with tears in our eyes, hoping one day this would end. Sadly most of us slaves died before we could ever see that day. You might have noticed that I haven't mentioned my name. When I was born, my mother didn't want to give me a name until I was older, just in case the plague got to me, but before I turned 10, she was sold among other slaves for teaching me how to read and write. Long story short, I was never given a name.

This particular morning was different. First we heard distant screaming. Most of us didn't even bother to turn our heads. We thought it was someone hallucinating again, which happens a lot when we are dehydrated and suffering from too much sun. Then, it eventually became more dramatic in a matter of minutes. Louder and louder until we heard a shotgun fired, then it stopped. There was complete silence. Later that day some of us ended up seeing some white men carrying out a woman's body, and we all made assumptions. "She was punished for not doing her work," someone said. "I heard she tried to injure one of the masters of the house," said another.

Why didn't we just ask what had happened? Why couldn't one of us just go up and talk to the keepers of the plantations? The thing was that if we even looked at them the wrong way, it meant severe consequences. So talking to them wasn't ever an option. Work all hours of the day, keep your mouth shut, and only speak when commanded to speak.

Those were the rules. To them we weren't people; we were objects.

It turned out that she was trying to escape when she was caught jumping the rusty, old, barbed wire fence. They demanded that she stop, but anyone knew that if she surrendered, her consequences would be much worse than death. So she started running. When she started screaming, the keepers pulled out a gun and fired. Boom, one shot and then nothing. The whole plantation was silent. No remorse, no tears, no regret from anyone. As if they had no regard for the life they had just ended.

This is just one incident. There were many others. All anyone could think about was that maybe one day there will be remorse. Maybe one day we will get an apology. Maybe one day this will end, but for now, we work, we obey our masters, and the only thing that keeps us going is our hope.

Alejandra Trillo, Grade 8

KERNEL ESSAYS BY STUDENTS
Memory Reflection

A WONDERFUL DAY

1. I was at the Science Expo in College Station, TX.
2. I waited in line.
3. I rode on a Segway!
4. I jogged back and shot a crossbow.
5. I figured that this was the most fun that I'd had all year!

Noah Hernandez, Grade 7

LEARNING ABOUT SLAVERY

1. I was in school.
2. I learned how horrible it used to be in the United States.
3. I realized slaves were a big deal and treated bad.
4. I was shocked.
5. I learned that not all people are treated the same.

Franchesca Gallardo, Grade 8

THE BROTHER

1. I was at my elementary school, making the morning announcements.
2. I finished the announcements and my mom went straight to the hospital.
3. I was picked up from school early and was brought to the hospital.
4. My family and I were waiting, and my dad came to get me from the waiting room.
5. You will always need siblings in your life, no matter what.

Abbi Pullen, Grade 7

OOPS!

1. I was at a restaurant.
2. I thought I hit someone on accident.
3. I said "I'm sorry."
4. She asked why and gave me a weird look.
5. Sometimes you should just leave things alone.

Talia Delambre, Grade 7

FIRST SPEECH

1. I was at school.
2. Ms. Koppe called my name and my heart started to beat out of my chest.
3. I stood up and started my speech.
4. I cried at the end of my speech.
5. I should practice speaking in front of crowds more.

Nina De La Torre, Grade 8

PLAYING TAG INSIDE

1. I was at a hotel.
2. My cousins, my brother, and I wanted to play a game.
3. We decided to play tag.
4. We were running around the hotel playing tag.
5. I learned that you need to make sure no one sees you playing tag inside or you'll get in trouble!

Anael Ashkenazi, Grade 7

PLANNING PAGE

Name:

TITLE OF YOUR PIECE

TEXT STRUCTURE

Parting Advice to Your Replacement

| Character traits *that are most important to you | what * (char. traits) do, teach you, give you, creates in you | who you will serve | how to give them * (char. traits) | what memories you will create | good-bye |

Douglas MacArthur

KERNEL ESSAY

1. _____

2. _____

3. _____

4. _____

5. _____

6. _____

SUGGESTIONS FOR QUICK LIST:

What do you do? What service to others? Who will replace you in this role as you move on?
• next year's class?
• next student leaders?
• next people in your job?

MY QUICK LIST OF TOPICS:

1. _____
2. _____
3. _____
4. _____
5. _____

"Duty, Honor, Country"   General Douglas MacArthur, 1962

No human being could fail to be deeply moved by such a tribute as this [Thayer Award]. Coming from a profession I have served so long and a people I have loved so well, it fills me with an emotion I cannot express. But this award is not intended primarily to honor a personality, but to symbolize a great moral code—a code of conduct and chivalry of those who guard this beloved land of culture and ancient descent. For all hours and for all time, it is an expression of the ethics of the American soldier. That I should be integrated in this way with so noble an ideal arouses a sense of pride, and yet of humility, which will be with me always.

Duty, Honor, Country: Those three hallowed words reverently dictate what you ought to be, what you can be, what you will be. They are your rallying point to build courage when courage seems to fail, to regain faith when there seems to be little cause for faith, to create hope when hope becomes forlorn.

Unhappily, I possess neither that eloquence of diction, that poetry of imagination, nor that brilliance of metaphor to tell you all that they mean.

The unbelievers will say they are but words, but a slogan, but a flamboyant phrase. Every pedant, every demagogue, every cynic, every hypocrite, every troublemaker, and, I am sorry to say, some others of an entirely different character, will try to downgrade them even to the extent of mockery and ridicule.

But these are some of the things they do. They build your basic character. They mold you for your future roles as the custodians of the Nation's defense. They make you strong enough to know when you are weak, and brave enough to face yourself when you are afraid.

What the Words Teach

They teach you to be proud and unbending in honest failure, but humble and gentle in success; not to substitute words for actions, not to seek the path of comfort, but to face the stress and spur of difficulty and challenge; to learn to stand up in the storm, but to have compassion on those who fall; to master yourself before you seek to master others; to have a heart that is clean, a goal that is high; to learn to laugh, yet never forget how to weep; to reach into the future, yet never neglect the past; to be serious, yet never to take yourself too seriously; to be modest so that you will remember the simplicity of true greatness, the open mind of true wisdom, the meekness of true strength.

They give you a temperate will, a quality of the imagination, a vigor of the emotions, a freshness of the deep springs of life, a temperamental predominance of courage over timidity, of an appetite for adventure over love of ease.

They create in your heart the sense of wonder, the unfailing hope of what next, and joy and inspiration of life. They teach you in this way to be an officer and a gentleman.

And what sort of soldiers are those you are to lead? Are they reliable? Are they brave? Are they capable of victory?

Their story is known to all of you. It is the story of the American man-at-arms. My estimate of him was formed on the battlefield many, many years ago, and has never changed. I regarded him then, as I regard him now, as one of the world's noblest figures; not only as one of the finest military characters, but also as one of the most stainless.

His name and fame are the birthright of every American citizen. In his youth and strength, his love and loyalty, he gave all that mortality can give. He needs no eulogy from me; or from any other man. He has written his own history and written it in red on his enemy's breast.

But when I think of his patience in adversity of his courage under fire and of his modesty in victory, I am filled with an emotion of admiration I cannot put into words. He belongs to history as furnishing one of the greatest examples of successful patriotism. He belongs to posterity as the instructor of future generations in the principles of liberty and freedom. He belongs to the present, to us, by his virtues and by his achievements.

Witness to the Fortitude

In 20 campaigns, on a hundred battlefields, around a thousand camp fires, I have witnessed that enduring fortitude, that patriotic self-abnegation, and that invincible determination which have carved his statue in the hearts of his people.

From one end of the world to the other, he has drained deep the chalice of courage. As I listened to those songs [of the glee club], in memory's eye I could see those staggering columns of the first World War, bending under soggy packs on many a weary march, from dripping dusk to drizzling dawn,

"Duty, Honor, Country" (Continued)

slogging ankle deep through the mire of shell-pocked roads to form grimly for the attack, blue-lipped, covered with sludge and mud, chilled by the wind and rain, driving home to their objective, and for many to the judgment seat of God.

I do not know the dignity of their birth, but I do know the glory of their death. They died, unquestioning, uncomplaining, with faith in their hearts, and on their lips the hope that we would go on to victory.

Always for them: Duty, honor, country. Always their blood, and sweat, and tears, as we sought the way and the light and the truth. And 20 years after, on the other side of the globe, again the filth of murky foxholes, the stench of ghostly trenches, the slime of dripping dugouts, those boiling suns of relentless heat, those torrential rains of devastating storms, the loneliness and utter desolation of jungle trails, the bitterness of long separation from those they loved and cherished, the deadly pestilence of tropical disease, the horror of stricken areas of war.

Swift and Sure Attack

Their resolute and determined defense, their swift and sure attack, their indomitable purpose, their complete and decisive victory—always victory, always through the bloody haze of their last reverberating shot, the vision of gaunt, ghastly men, reverently following your password of duty, honor, country.

You now face a new world, a world of change. The thrust into outer space of the satellite, spheres, and missiles marks a beginning of another epoch in the long story of mankind. In the five or more billions of years the scientists tell us it has taken to form the earth, in the three or more billion years of development of the human race, there has never been a more abrupt or staggering evolution.

We deal now, not with things of this world alone, but with the illimitable distances and as yet unfathomed mysteries of the universe. We are reaching out for a new and boundless frontier. We speak in strange terms of harnessing the cosmic energy, of making winds and tides work for us, of creating unheard of synthetic materials to supplement or even replace our old standard basics; to purify sea water for our drink; of mining ocean floors for new fields of wealth and food; of disease preventatives to expand life into the hundred of years; of controlling the weather for a more equitable distribution of heat and cold, of rain and shine; of spaceships to the moon; of the primary target in war, no longer limited to the armed forces of an enemy, but instead to include his civil populations; of ultimate conflict between a united human race and the sinister forces of some other planetary galaxy; of such dreams and fantasies as to make life the most exciting of all times.

And through all this welter of change and development your mission remains fixed, determined, inviolable. It is to win our wars. Everything else in your professional career is but corollary to this vital dedication. All other public purposes, all other public projects, all other public needs, great or small, will find others for their accomplishment; but you are the ones who are trained to fight.

You are the leaven which binds together the entire fabric of our national system of defense. From your ranks come the great captains who hold the Nation's destiny in their hands the moment the war tocsin sounds.

The long, gray line has never failed us. Were you to do so, a million ghosts in olive drab, in brown khaki, in blue and gray, would rise from their white crosses, thundering those magic words: Duty, honor, country.

Prays for Peace

This does not mean that you are warmongers. On the contrary, the soldier above all other people prays for peace, for he must suffer and bear the deepest wounds and scars of war. But always in our ears ring the ominous words of Plato, that wisest of all philosophers: "Only the dead have seen the end of war."

The shadows are lengthening for me. The twilight is here. My days of old have vanished, tone and tint. They have gone glimmering through the dreams of things that were. Their memory is one of wondrous beauty, watered by tears and coaxed and caressed by the smiles of yesterday. I listen vainly, but with thirsty ear, for the witching melody of faint bugles blowing reveille, of far drums beating the long roll.

In my dreams I hear again the crash of guns, the rattle of musketry, the strange, mournful mutter of the battlefield. But in the evening of my memory always I come back to West Point. Always there echoes and re-echoes: *Duty, honor, country.*

Today marks my final roll call with you. But I want you to know that when I cross the river, my last conscious thoughts will be of the corps, and the corps, and the corps.

I bid you farewell.

PLANNING PAGE + ESSAY
Parting Advice to Your Replacement

PUNCTUAL, HARD WORKING, CARING

These three qualities are the most important to have while becoming a student trainer. Practices will be very long and hard. Practices will have a start and end time; as trainers we have to be punctual. The head trainers will expect punctuality from the moment you step on the field to the moment you step off. Hard work and dedication will be the motto; there is no time for slacking off and being lazy. As student trainers being sharp is a must, so whether it is giving them water or tending to the athletes' injuries, we must always be there. No matter what sport we are at; soccer, baseball, or a football game, student trainers should always show sympathy towards the players. When an athlete gets hurt the first thing running through their mind is that they may not be able to go back on that field.

What the Words Teach

These three words have the ability to teach anyone the basics of all jobs. Remember to work hard in all aspects of life. If there is no representation of hard work, then why even do it? Always show compassion towards the players. Caring is one of the best qualities for a student trainer. These three things will fill you with a beautiful mindset.

How to Give Them

There is no way to enforce hard work, punctuality, or the ability to care. You can pave a path for them to follow, but you cannot make them walk it. When trying to work hard all that has to be done is to give 100% all the time. Your 100% may not always be at the same level all the time, and that is okay as long as 100% is being given at that point in time. Having a set schedule will make being on time a piece of cake. A schedule will help make a sense of structure in your time. Caring is basically just finding it in the bottom of your heart to show love to the people that surround you.

Memories Made

Making long lasting memories as a student trainer will become so easy. Everyone starts to feel like a second family; the players, coaches, and especially the other trainers. The Program will start to feel like a second home. (Literally you never go home!) Making friends with all the seniors is fun, until you realize that they are all going off to school. As the season comes to an end you just want it to start up all over again.

Goodbye!

I hope the best of luck to the incoming student trainers! May you make memories that last a lifetime.

Lizzy Araujo, Grade 9

PLANNING PAGE

Name:

TITLE OF YOUR PIECE

TEXT STRUCTURE

Bon Voyage

| how we share this with you | the most valuable thing you'll get from this experience | I believe in a higher power | I ask that you be protected |

Marion Scott Carpenter

KERNEL ESSAY

1. _____

2. _____

3. _____

4. _____

_____

_____

SUGGESTIONS FOR QUICK LIST:

When someone you love is leaving for an adventure, and you want to send them off with love
• a vacation • a quest   • a mission

MY QUICK LIST OF TOPICS:

1. _____
2. _____
3. _____
4. _____
5. _____

Letter to His Astronaut Son

Scott Carpenter, 1962

M. Scott Carpenter
PO Box 95
PALMER LAKE,
COLORADO

Dear Son,

Just a few words on the eve of your great adventure for which you have trained yourself and anticipated for so long—to let you know that we all share it with you, vicariously.

As I think I remarked to you at the outset of the space program, you are privileged to share in a pioneering project on a grand scale—in fact the grandest scale yet known to man. And I venture to predict that after all the huzzas have been uttered and the public acclaim is but a memory, you will derive the greatest satisfaction from the serene knowledge that you have discovered new truths. You can say to yourself: this I saw, this I experienced, this I know to be the truth. This experience is a precious thing; it is known to all researchers, in whatever field of endeavour, who have ventured into the unknown and have discovered new truths.

You are probably aware that I am not a particularly religious person, at least in the sense of embracing any of the numerous formal doctrines. Yet I cannot conceive of a man endowed with intellect, perceiving the ordered universe about him, the glory of the mountain top, the plumage of a tropical bird, the intricate complexity of a protein molecule, the utter and unchanging perfection of a salt crystal, who can deny the existence of some higher power. Whether he chooses to call it God or Mohammed or Buddha or Turquoise Woman or the Law of Probability matters little. I find myself in my writings frequently calling upon Mother Nature to explain things and citing Her as responsible for the order of the universe. She is a very satisfactory divinity for me. And so I shall call upon Her to watch over you and guard you and, if she so desires, share with you some of Her secrets which She is usually so ready to share with those who have high purpose.

With all my love, Dad

Note: This love letter, from a father to a son, shows the inherent beauty that can be bound up in writing to someone who is going off on an adventure or even just on a vacation. It also reminds us to think about how we value other people. Rather than a simplistic, "Have a good time," this father offers his son a connection, an insight, and a blessing—all in one short piece. In this classroom exercise, students are asked to use the foundational structure of this letter—its focus on sharing common ground, foreseeing the outcome of a future experience, conveying beliefs in a higher power, and asking for protection—to craft their own "Bon Voyage" essays.

COMPLETED PLANNING PAGE
Bon Voyage

Name: Alex Melchor

TITLE OF YOUR PIECE

Monster Hunter's Address

TEXT STRUCTURE

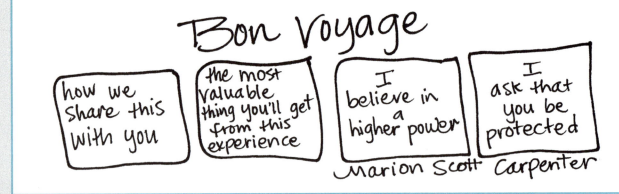

Bon Voyage

| how we share this with you | the most valuable thing you'll get from this experience | I believe in a higher power | I ask that you be protected |

Marion Scott Carpenter

KERNEL ESSAY

1. We are both hunters in the game. When you go through the game, you'll kill the monsters.

2. You'll get much needed parts.

3. Nobody protects you in the game, so you will have to be very careful.

4. Come back safe.

SUGGESTIONS FOR QUICK LIST:

When someone you love is leaving for an adventure, and you want to send them off with love
• a vacation • a quest • a mission

MY QUICK LIST OF TOPICS:

1. Strategic games
2. Monster hunters
3. Attack strategies
4. Movies
5.

FULL ESSAY
Bon Voyage

MONSTER HUNTER'S ADDRESS

We are both hunters in the game. We hunt leviathans, wyverns, both brute and flying, and pelagius. We use weapons like charge blades, the insect glaiv, longswords, lances, and gun lances. We also have bow guns.

When you go through the game, you kill the monsters to get much-needed parts. Just the way that deer hunters kill and keep the antlers as trophies, you keep parts of the monsters for different reasons. You can create weapons or armor from rathalos tails or zinogre shockfur. Even monoblos horns can become weapons or armor.

Nobody protects you in the game, though you could watch out for each other if you play with others. You might give each other potions or rations, atamin pills or might pills for attack, or you could share dash juice for added stamina. If you don't have an internet connection, though, you play alone. If this is the case, you have to be careful. You have to bring more items and fight more strategically.

Go have a good time, and I pray you come back safe! (And if you don't, you start over and they return you back to base camp.)

Alex Melchor, Grade 8

PLANNING PAGE

Name: _____

TITLE OF YOUR PIECE

```
┌─────────────────────────────────────────────────────┐
│                                                       │
│                                                       │
│                                                       │
└─────────────────────────────────────────────────────┘
```

TEXT STRUCTURE

I Feel Your Pain

| our bond (who we are) | wrong ideas other people have about you | What you're dealing with (and why it's bad) | how if it's bad for one person, it's bad for all | Imagine good for all (how that will look) | What we will say when that day comes |

John F. Kennedy

KERNEL ESSAY

1. _____

2. _____

3. _____

4. _____

5. _____

6. _____

SUGGESTIONS FOR QUICK LIST:

Any time you've watched someone you care about, going through a tough time and you wished you could help
- a long sadness
- losing a pet
- suffering punishment

MY QUICK LIST OF TOPICS:

1. _____
2. _____
3. _____
4. _____
5. _____

"Ich bin ein Berliner" Speech

John F. Kennedy, 1963

I am proud to come to this city as the guest of your distinguished Mayor, who has symbolized throughout the world the fighting spirit of West Berlin. And I am proud to visit the Federal Republic with your distinguished Chancellor who for so many years has committed Germany to democracy and freedom and progress, and to come here in the company of my fellow American, General Clay, who has been in this city during its great moments of crisis and will come again if ever needed.

Two thousand years ago the proudest boast was "civis Romanus sum." Today, in the world of freedom, the proudest boast is "Ich bin ein Berliner." I appreciate my interpreter translating my German!

There are many people in the world who really don't understand, or say they don't, what is the great issue between the free world and the Communist world. Let them come to Berlin. There are some who say that communism is the wave of the future. Let them come to Berlin. And there are some who say in Europe and elsewhere we can work with the Communists. Let them come to Berlin. And there are even a few who say that it is true that communism is an evil system, but it permits us to make economic progress. Lass' sie nach Berlin kommen. Let them come to Berlin.

Freedom has many difficulties and democracy is not perfect, but we have never had to put a wall up to keep our people in, to prevent them from leaving us. I want to say, on behalf of my countrymen, who live many miles away on the other side of the Atlantic, who are far distant from you, that they take the greatest pride that they have been able to share with you, even from a distance, the story of the last 18 years. I know of no town, no city, that has been besieged for 18 years that still lives with the vitality and the force, and the hope and the determination of the city of West Berlin. While the wall is the most obvious and vivid demonstration of the failures of the Communist system, for all the world to see, we take no satisfaction in it, for it is, as your Mayor has said, an offense not only against history but an offense against humanity, separating families, dividing husbands and wives and brothers and sisters, and dividing a people who wish to be joined together.

What is true of this city is true of Germany—real, lasting peace in Europe can never be assured as long as one German out of four is denied the elementary right of free men, and that is to make a free choice. In 18 years of peace and good faith, this generation of Germans has earned the right to be free, including the right to unite their families and their nation in lasting peace, with good will to all people. You live in a defended island of freedom, but your life is part of the main. So let me ask you, as I close, to lift your eyes beyond the dangers of today, to the hopes of tomorrow, beyond the freedom merely of this city of Berlin, or your country of Germany, to the advance of freedom everywhere, beyond the wall to the day of peace with justice, beyond yourselves and ourselves to all mankind.

Freedom is indivisible, and when one man is enslaved, all are not free. When all are free, then we can look forward to that day when this city will be joined as one and this country and this great Continent of Europe in a peaceful and hopeful globe. When that day finally comes, as it will, the people of West Berlin can take sober satisfaction in the fact that they were in the front lines for almost two decades.

All free men, wherever they may live, are citizens of Berlin, and, therefore, as a free man, I take pride in the words "Ich bin ein Berliner!"

PLANNING PAGE + ESSAY
I Feel Your Pain

THE RISE OF INDUSTRY (LETTER FROM ONE YOUNG FACTORY WORKER TO ANOTHER WRITTEN BY NINA DE LA TORRE)

My dearest Melinda,

We have been friends since we worked together as youngsters in the country life. Our long summer days had tormented us as we worked for long hours in the hot sun. At that time we worked to support our family with the chores they assigned us. Since then I know that we have drifted apart, but I have recently heard some rumors that you have gone to the city life. I have heard that you have not been taken care of as you should be, and I hope that you can read this on your free hours.

I have read in your past letters that your boss has been working you long hours with just a small wage. He thinks that you and all your fellow coworkers are just complaining and he has no care of any health or fire regulations. I have also heard other people say that all of the workers in the factories are just trying to squeeze all the money out of their boss. I know that these rumors are not true and that you have been mistreated and I hope that everyone will know the truth.

In your job you only get 7 dollars a week and your boss locks the doors so you will never leave. Your child, Mary, only has a wage of 2 dollars a week. All of the employees at your work don't get enough sleep, food, and your little apartment is barely livable.

I know that not only you are suffering, but because of the conditions you have to work through, your family is being poorly fed, not taken care of, and unhealthy. This job is not only bad for you, but bad for your whole family. These poor conditions are also wrong for all the other workers and for their family and for families to come.

When all these hard conditions are over you will be able to wake up when the sun is out and you will be paid much better. I will be able to make your family a big meal and we can catch up on all the things we have missed. You will be able to design clothes of your own just like you have dreamed of in your letters.

When the day of rest comes you can invite me to write letters to your boss saying how better your life is and how he tortured all the women in his factory. You can also rest on your bed and write in your letters of how your new life is and how you enjoy it.

Your friend,
May

Nina De La Torre, Grade 8

PLANNING PAGE + ESSAY
I Feel Your Pain

CHILD LABOR (LETTER FROM ONE FACTORY WORKER TO ANOTHER, 1890, WRITTEN BY MAGGIE DAVIS)

We've known each other forever and now we work together.

It's ridiculous that there are people watching us work fourteen hour days and don't do anything about it. As children, we should be going to get an education, playing with other kids, or helping around the house instead of sitting in a cramped, disgusting room with no breaks, and enough pay in a year to buy something miniscule.

We're worked to death for a majority of the day and what do we get out of it? Fast-spreading illness, little to no breaks, and no food. We basically get locked in a big jail cell with another hundred kids.

Maggie Davis, Grade 8

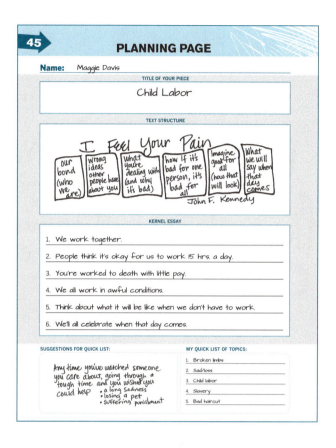

PLANNING PAGE — 45

Name: Maggie Davis

TITLE OF YOUR PIECE
Child Labor

TEXT STRUCTURE

I Feel Your Pain
- our bond (who we are)
- wrong ideas other people have about you
- what you're dealing with (and why it's bad)
- how if it's bad for one person, it's bad for all
- imagine good for all (how that will look)
- What we will say when that day comes

John F. Kennedy

KERNEL ESSAY
1. We work together.
2. People think it's okay for us to work 15 hrs. a day.
3. You're worked to death with little pay.
4. We all work in awful conditions.
5. Think about what it will be like when we don't have to work.
6. We'll all celebrate when that day comes.

SUGGESTIONS FOR QUICK LIST:
Any time you've watched someone you care about, going through a tough time and you wished you could help
- a long sadness
- losing a pet
- suffering punishment

MY QUICK LIST OF TOPICS:
1. Broken limbs
2. Sad/loss
3. Child labor
4. Slavery
5. Bad haircut

PLANNING PAGE

Name: _____

TITLE OF YOUR PIECE

TEXT STRUCTURE

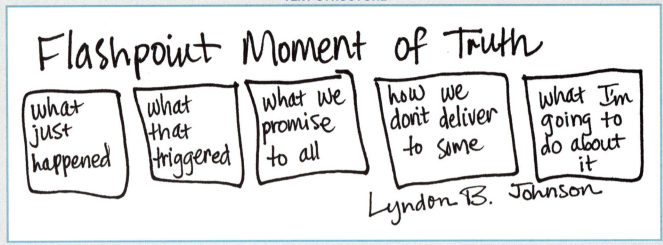

Flashpoint Moment of Truth

| what just happened | what that triggered | what we promise to all | how we don't deliver to some | what I'm going to do about it |

Lyndon B. Johnson

KERNEL ESSAY

1. _____

2. _____

3. _____

4. _____

5. _____

SUGGESTIONS FOR QUICK LIST:

Sometimes something gets our attention and makes us notice that a change is needed <u>now</u>.
- a habit
- a custom
- the way we talk

MY QUICK LIST OF TOPICS:

1. ....

2. ....

3. ....

4. ....

5. ....

"And We Shall Overcome" Special Message to Congress (Excerpt)   Lyndon B. Johnson, 1965

[As delivered in person before a joint session at 9:02 p.m.]

Mr. Speaker, Mr. President, Members of the Congress:

I speak tonight for the dignity of man and the destiny of democracy.

I urge every member of both parties, Americans of all religions and of all colors, from every section of this country, to join me in that cause.

At times history and fate meet at a single time in a single place to shape a turning point in man's unending search for freedom. So it was at Lexington and Concord. So it was a century ago at Appomattox. So it was last week in Selma, Alabama.

There, long-suffering men and women peacefully protested the denial of their rights as Americans. Many were brutally assaulted. One good man, a man of God, was killed.

There is no cause for pride in what has happened in Selma. There is no cause for self-satisfaction in the long denial of equal rights of millions of Americans. But there is cause for hope and for faith in our democracy in what is happening here tonight.

For the cries of pain and the hymns and protests of oppressed people have summoned into convocation all the majesty of this great Government—the Government of the greatest Nation on earth.

Our mission is at once the oldest and the most basic of this country: to right wrong, to do justice, to serve man.

In our time we have come to live with moments of great crisis. Our lives have been marked with debate about great issues; issues of war and peace, issues of prosperity and depression. But rarely in any time does an issue lay bare the secret heart of America itself. Rarely are we met with a challenge, not to our growth or abundance, our welfare or our security, but rather to the values and the purposes and the meaning of our beloved Nation.

The issue of equal rights for American Negroes is such an issue. And should we defeat every enemy, should we double our wealth and conquer the stars, and still be unequal to this issue, then we will have failed as a people and as a nation.

For with a country as with a person, "What is a man profited, if he shall gain the whole world, and lose his own soul?"

There is no Negro problem. There is no Southern problem. There is no Northern problem. There is only an American problem. And we are met here tonight as Americans—not as Democrats or Republicans—we are met here as Americans to solve that problem.

This was the first nation in the history of the world to be founded with a purpose. The great phrases of that purpose still sound in every American heart, North and South: "All men are created equal"— "government by consent of the governed"—"give me liberty or give me death." Well, those are not just clever words, or those are not just empty theories. In their name Americans have fought and died for two centuries, and tonight around the world they stand there as guardians of our liberty, risking their lives.

Those words are a promise to every citizen that he shall share in the dignity of man. This dignity cannot be found in a man's possessions; it cannot be found in his power, or in his position. It really rests on his right to be treated as a man equal in opportunity to all others. It says that he shall share in freedom, he shall choose his leaders, educate his children, and provide for his family according to his ability and his merits as a human being.

To apply any other test—to deny a man his hopes because of his color or race, his religion or the place of his birth—is not only to do injustice, it is to deny America and to dishonor the dead who gave their lives for American freedom . . .

Wednesday I will send to Congress a law designed to eliminate illegal barriers to the right to vote.

The bill that I am presenting to you will be known as a civil rights bill. But, in a larger sense, most of the program I am recommending is a civil rights program. Its object is to open the city of hope to all people of all races.

Because all Americans just must have the right to vote. And we are going to give them that right.

COMPLETED PLANNING PAGE
Flashpoint Moment of Truth

Name: Cara Afaisen

TITLE OF YOUR PIECE

Time for a Change

TEXT STRUCTURE

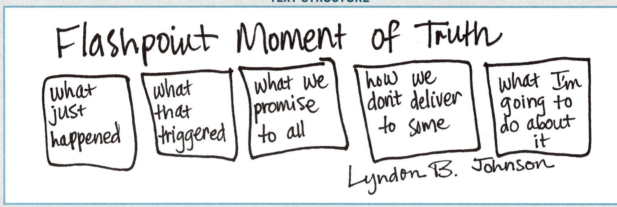

Flashpoint Moment of Truth

| what just happened | what that triggered | what we promise to all | how we don't deliver to some | what I'm going to do about it |

Lyndon B. Johnson

KERNEL ESSAY

1. My privileges were taken away.

2. I realized I was spending too much time online.

3. I promised to spend more time with loved ones.

4. I had been failing myself and others.

5. I now discipline myself and try harder.

SUGGESTIONS FOR QUICK LIST:

Sometimes something gets our attention and makes us notice that a change is needed now.
- a habit
- a custom
- the way we talk

MY QUICK LIST OF TOPICS:

1. Being grounded
2. Getting in an accident
3. Getting sick
4. Too talkative
5. Sent to office

FULL ESSAY
Flashpoint Moment of Truth

LOSING MY ELECTRONIC DEVICES: TIME FOR A CHANGE

I once had many privileges taken away from me. All that I believed I couldn't live without. Computer privileges were taken from me along with my phone. I think most children my age would think that these objects are their life just how I did.

This caused me to notice why it happened: my lack of being social. I'd been spending less time with my family and more time locked in my room. I avoided all contact with my family and everyone I cared for. Most of my time was spent playing games or watching shows or movies. I hardly went outside or even out of my room.

Because of what was taken away from me I decided to do as my parents pleased and spend more time with them. Instead of cowarding to a corner I'd speak up and "socialize." I will keep "family first" in mind and spend less time playing games and whatnot.

If I didn't I'd discipline myself by spending a lot of time away from the thing that separated my family and me. Spending time with family has changed me a lot. I've learned so much about my family members and have fun, more fun than anyone would have playing League of Legends or Skyrim.

I now enjoy and want to spend more time with family.

Cara Afaisen, Grade 9

PLANNING PAGE

Name: _____

TITLE OF YOUR PIECE

[ ]

TEXT STRUCTURE

Walking the Walk to Make a Difference

| whose methods we admire | life lessons we learned from him/ ← her | one social situation in our world that needs change | the story of one example (and proof this is widespread) | what we should do to reverse it |

Cesar Chavez

KERNEL ESSAY

1. _____

2. _____

3. _____

4. _____

5. _____

_____

SUGGESTIONS FOR QUICK LIST:

What in our world should be changed? What living conditions are not right? What working conditions?
What can we do to make things better?

MY QUICK LIST OF TOPICS:

1. _____

2. _____

3. _____

4. _____

5. _____

"Lessons of Dr. Martin Luther King, Jr." Cesar Chavez, 1990

My friends, today we honor a giant among men: today we honor the reverend Martin Luther King, Jr.

Dr. King was a powerful figure of destiny, of courage, of sacrifice, and of vision. Few people in the long history of this nation can rival his accomplishment, his reason, or his selfless dedication to the cause of peace and social justice.

Today we honor a wise teacher, an inspiring leader, and a true visionary, but to truly honor Dr. King we must do more than say words of praise.

We must learn his lessons and put his views into practice, so that we may truly be free at last.

Who was Dr. King?

Many people will tell you of his wonderful qualities and his many accomplishments, but what makes him special to me, the truth many people don't want you to remember, is that Dr. king was a great activist, fighting for radical social change with radical methods.

While other people talked about change, Dr. King used direct action to challenge the system. He welcomed it, and used it wisely.

In his famous letter from the Birmingham jail, Dr. King wrote that "The purpose of direct action is to create a situation so crisis-packed that it will inevitably open the door to negotiation."

Dr. King was also radical in his beliefs about violence. He learned how to successfully fight hatred and violence with the unstoppable power of nonviolence.

He once stopped an armed mob, saying: "We are not advocating violence. We want to love our enemies. I want you to love our enemies. Be good to them. This is what we live by. We must meet hate with love."

Dr. King knew that he very probably wouldn't survive the struggle that he led so well. But he said "If I am stopped, the movement will not stop. If I am stopped, our work will not stop. For what we are doing is right. What we are doing is just, and God is with us."

My friends, as we enter a new decade, it should be clear to all of us that there is an unfinished agenda, that we have miles to go before we reach the promised land.

The men who rule this country today never learned the lessons of Dr. King, they never learned that non-violence is the only way to peace and justice.

Our nation continues to wage war upon its neighbors, and upon itself.

The powers that be rule over a racist society, filled with hatred and ignorance.

Our nation continues to be segregated along racial and economic lines.

My friends, the time for action is upon us. The enemies of justice want you to think of Dr. King as only a civil rights leader, but he had a much broader agenda. He was a tireless crusader for the rights of the poor, for an end to the war in Vietnam long before it was popular to take that stand, and for the rights of workers everywhere.

Many people find it convenient to forget that Martin was murdered while supporting a desperate strike on that tragic day in Memphis, Tennessee. He died while fighting for the rights of sanitation workers.

Dr. King's dedication to the rights of the workers who are so often exploited by the forces of greed has profoundly touched my life and guided my struggle.

Just as Dr. King was a disciple of Ghandi [sic] and Christ, we must now be Dr. King's disciples.

Dr. King challenged us to work for a greater humanity. I only hope that we are worthy of his challenge.

The United Farm Workers are dedicated to carrying on the dream of reverend Martin Luther King, Jr. My friends, I would like to tell you about the struggle of the Farm workers who are waging a desperate struggle for our rights, for our children's rights and for our very lives.

Many decades ago the chemical industry promised the growers that pesticides would bring great wealth and bountiful harvests to the fields.

Just recently, the experts are learning what farm workers, and the truly organized farmers have known for years.

The prestigious National Academy of Sciences recently concluded an exhaustive five-year study which determined that pesticides do not improve profits and do not produce more crops.

What, then, is the effect of pesticides? Pesticides have created a legacy of pain, and misery, and death for farm workers and consumers alike.

The crop which poses the greatest danger, and the focus of our struggle, is the table grape crop. These pesticides soak the fields. Drift with the wind, pollute the water, and are eaten by unwitting consumers.

These poisons are designed to kill, and pose a very real threat to consumers and farm workers alike. The fields are sprayed with pesticides: like Captan, Parathion, Phosdrin, and Methyl Bromide. These poisons cause cancer, DNA mutation, and horrible birth defects.

The Central Valley of California is one of the wealthiest agricultural regions in the world. In its midst are clusters of children dying from cancer.

(continued) . . .

"Lessons of Dr. Martin Luther King, Jr." (Continued)   Cesar Chavez, 1990

The children live in communities surrounded by the grape fields that employ their parents. The children come into contact with the poisons when they play outside, when they drink the water, and when they hug their parents returning from the fields.

And the children are dying.

They are dying slow, painful, cruel deaths in towns called cancer clusters, in cancer clusters like McFarland, where the children cancer rate is 800 percent above normal. A few months ago, the parents of a brave little girl in the agricultural community of Earlimart came to the United Farm Workers to ask for help.

The Ramirez family knew about our protests in nearby McFarland and thought there might be a similar problem in Earlimart. Our union members went door to door in Earlimart, and found that the Ramirez family's worst fears were true.

There are at least four other children suffering from cancer in the little town of Earlimart, a rate 1200 percent above normal.

These same pesticides can be found on the grapes you buy in the stores. My friends, the suffering must end. So many children are dying, so many babies are born without limbs and vital organs, so many workers are dying in the fields.

We have no choice, we must stop the plague of pesticides.

My friends, even those farm workers who do not have to bury their young children are suffering from abuse, neglect, and poverty.

Our workers labor for many hours every day under the hot sun, often without safe drinking water or toilet facilities.

Our workers are constantly subjected to incredible pressures and intimidation to meet excessive quotas.

The women who work in the fields are routinely subjected to sexual harassment and sexual assaults by the grower's thugs. When our workers complain, or try to organize, they are fired, assaulted, and even murdered.

The stench of injustice in California should offend every American.

The growers and their allies have tried to stop us for years with intimidation, with character assassination, with public relations campaigns, with outright lies, and with murder.

But those same tactics did not stop Dr. King, and they will not stop us.

Once social change begins, it cannot be reversed.

You cannot uneducate the person who has learned to read. You cannot humiliate the person who feels pride. And you cannot oppress the people who are not afraid anymore.

In our life and death struggle for justice we have turned to the court of last resort: the American people. And the people are ruling in our favor.

As a result, grape sales keep falling. We have witnessed truckloads of grapes being dumped because no one would stop to buy them. As demand drops, so do prices and profits. The growers are under tremendous economic pressure.

We are winning, but there is still much hard work ahead of us. I hope that you will join our struggle.

The simple act of refusing to buy table grapes laced with pesticides is a powerful statement that the growers understand.

Economic pressure is the only language the growers speak, and they are beginning to listen.

Please, boycott table grapes. For your safety, for the workers, and for the children, we must act together.

My friends, Dr. King realized that the only real wealth comes from helping others.

I challenge you to join the struggle of the United Farm Workers. And if you don't join our cause, then seek out the many organizations seeking peaceful social change.

Seek out the many outstanding leaders who will speak to you this week, and make a difference.

If we fail to learn that each and every person can make a difference, then we will have betrayed Dr. King's life's work. The reverend Martin Luther King, Jr. had more than just a dream, he had the love and the faith to act.

God Bless You.

Note: It's important to get swept up in our passions and, at the same time, to pay close attention to the realities of the world around us. Cesar Chavez did both. In this piece, he weaves his observations about Dr. King and about the working conditions for migrants together with his lofty convictions about making the world a better place. The shape his writing takes is unique, in that it reflects his ability to take a message from one voice and recreate it to make it his own. In this classroom exercise, students gain a model to help them turn their admiration of others into action. Specifically, they are asked to use the foundational structure of this work—its focus on identifying an admirable person and on life lessons we have learned from that person—to craft their own essays on "Walking the Walk to Make a Difference."

PLANNING PAGE + ESSAY
Walking the Walk to Make a Difference

GIRLS' EDUCATION

Dear Society,

We should all admire Malala Yousafzai from Pakistan and her methods. This young, but courageous young woman is a great role model for the young and old. I propose that we all follow in her footsteps.

I've learned not to be afraid to stand up for what I believe in. This is something we can all use in today's world. Today's generation can be, well, skittish and shy.

We need to stand up for girls' rights to education all over the world, among other problems. In the United States, we have a Constitution that guarantees education, but some other parts of the world do not. They deserve the same thing we have and that is freedom to education.

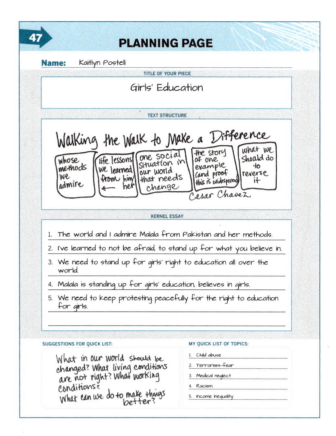

Malala is standing up for girls' education because she believes that girls deserve the same rights to educational rights as the boys. Malala protests peacefully by giving speeches and telling her story. She protests against the law preventing girls the right to an education in Pakistan and could be our inspiration.

We need to keep protesting peacefully for girls' education rights all over the world. Just like Malala, we shouldn't let anything get in our way for "being there" and "standing up for other people" who can't stand up for themselves in their country, like the girls from Pakistan.

In conclusion, I believe we should all stand up and speak up to peacefully protest for all people to receive equal rights to education, like Malala, and not ban education for anyone.

Sincerely,
Kaitlyn Postell, Grade 6

PLANNING PAGE

Name: _____

TITLE OF YOUR PIECE

[blank box]

TEXT STRUCTURE

Using a Story to Make a Point

| a Story | What the parts of the story stand for | life lesson this gives us | alternate ending to the story |

Toni Morrison

KERNEL ESSAY

1. _____

2. _____

3. _____

4. _____

_____

_____

SUGGESTIONS FOR QUICK LIST:

think of any small stories you know:
- fables • children's stories
- parables • family stories
- tales from any culture

MY QUICK LIST OF TOPICS:

1. ....
2. ....
3. ....
4. ....
5. ....

Nobel Lecture (Abridged)

"Once upon a time there was an old woman. Blind but wise." Or was it an old man? A guru, perhaps. Or a griot soothing restless children. I have heard this story, or one exactly like it, in the lore of several cultures.

"Once upon a time there was an old woman. Blind. Wise."

In the version I know the woman is the daughter of slaves, black, American, and lives alone in a small house outside of town. Her reputation for wisdom is without peer and without question. Among her people she is both the law and its transgression. The honor she is paid and the awe in which she is held reach beyond her neighborhood to places far away; to the city where the intelligence of rural prophets is the source of much amusement.

One day the woman is visited by some young people who seem to be bent on disproving her clairvoyance and showing her up for the fraud they believe she is. Their plan is simple: they enter her house and ask the one question the answer to which rides solely on her difference from them, a difference they regard as a profound disability: her blindness. They stand before her, and one of them says, "Old woman, I hold in my hand a bird. Tell me whether it is living or dead."

She does not answer, and the question is repeated. "Is the bird I am holding living or dead?"

Still she doesn't answer. She is blind and cannot see her visitors, let alone what is in their hands. She does not know their color, gender or homeland. She only knows their motive.

The old woman's silence is so long, the young people have trouble holding their laughter.

Finally she speaks and her voice is soft but stern. "I don't know," she says. "I don't know whether the bird you are holding is dead or alive, but what I do know is that it is in your hands. It is in your hands."

Her answer can be taken to mean: if it is dead, you have either found it that way or you have killed it. If it is alive, you can still kill it. Whether it is to stay alive, it is your decision. Whatever the case, it is your responsibility.

For parading their power and her helplessness, the young visitors are reprimanded, told they are responsible not only for the act of mockery but also for the small bundle of life sacrificed to achieve its aims. The blind woman shifts attention away from

assertions of power to the instrument through which that power is exercised.

Speculation on what (other than its own frail body) that bird-in-the-hand might signify has always been attractive to me, but especially so now thinking, as I have been, about the work I do that has brought me to this company. So I choose to read the bird as language and the woman as a practiced writer. She is worried about how the language she dreams in, given to her at birth, is handled, put into service, even withheld from her for certain nefarious purposes.

She would not want to leave her young visitors with the impression that language should be forced to stay alive merely to be. The vitality of language lies in its ability to limn the actual, imagined and possible lives of its speakers, readers, writers. Although its poise is sometimes in displacing experience it is not a substitute for it. It arcs toward the place where meaning may lie. When a President of the United States thought about the graveyard his country had become, and said, "The world will little note nor long remember what we say here. But it will never forget what they did here," his simple words are exhilarating in their life-sustaining properties because they refused to encapsulate the reality of 600,000 dead men in a cataclysmic race war. Refusing to monumentalize, disdaining the "final word," the precise "summing up," acknowledging their "poor power to add or detract," his words signal deference to the uncapturability of the life it mourns. It is the deference that moves her, that recognition that language can never live up to life once and for all. Nor should it. Language can never "pin down" slavery, genocide, war. Nor should it yearn for the arrogance to be able to do so. Its force, its felicity is in its reach toward the ineffable.

Word-work is sublime, she thinks, because it is generative; it makes meaning that secures our difference, our human difference—the way in which we are like no other life.

We die. That may be the meaning of life. But we do language. That may be the measure of our lives.

"Once upon a time, . . ." visitors ask an old woman a question. Who are they, these children? What did they make of that encounter? What did they hear in those final words: "The bird is in your hands"? A sentence that gestures towards possibility or one that drops a latch? Perhaps what the children heard was "It's not my problem. I am old, female, black, blind. What

(continued) . . .

wisdom I have now is in knowing I cannot help you. The future of language is yours."

They stand there. Suppose nothing was in their hands? Suppose the visit was only a ruse, a trick to get to be spoken to, taken seriously as they have not been before? A chance to interrupt, to violate the adult world, its miasma of discourse about them, for them, but never to them? Urgent questions are at stake, including the one they have asked: "Is the bird we hold living or dead?" Perhaps the question meant: "Could someone tell us what is life? What is death?" No trick at all; no silliness. A straightforward question worthy of the attention of a wise one. An old one. And if the old and wise who have lived life and faced death cannot describe either, who can?

But she does not; she keeps her secret; her good opinion of herself; her gnomic pronouncements; her art without commitment. She keeps her distance, enforces it and retreats into the singularity of isolation, in sophisticated, privileged space.

Nothing, no word follows her declaration of transfer. That silence is deep, deeper than the meaning available in the words she has spoken. It shivers, this silence, and the children, annoyed, fill it with language invented on the spot.

"Is there no speech," they ask her, "no words you can give us that help us break through your dossier of failures? Through the education you have just given us that is no education at all because we are paying close attention to what you have done as well as to what you have said? To the barrier you have erected between generosity and wisdom?

"We have no bird in our hands, living or dead. We have only you and our important question. Is the nothing in our hands something you could not bear to contemplate, to even guess? Don't you remember being young when language was magic without meaning?

"Why didn't you reach out, touch us with your soft fingers, delay the sound bite, the lesson, until you knew who we were? Did you so despise our trick, our modus operandi you could not see that we were baffled about how to get your attention?

"You trivialize us and trivialize the bird that is not in our hands. Is there no context for our lives? No song, no literature, no poem full of vitamins, no history connected to experience that you can pass along to help us start strong? You are an adult. The old one, the wise one. Stop thinking about saving your face. Think of our lives and tell us your particularized world. Make up a story. Narrative is radical, creating us at the very moment it is being created. We will not blame you if your reach exceeds your grasp; if love so ignites your words they go down in flames and nothing is left but their scald.

"Tell us about ships turned away from shorelines at Easter, placenta in a field. Tell us about a wagonload of slaves, how they sang so softly their breath was indistinguishable from the falling snow. How they knew from the hunch of the nearest shoulder that the next stop would be their last. How, with hands prayered in their sex, they thought of heat, then sun. Lifting their faces as though it was there for the taking. Turning as though there for the taking. They stop at an inn. The driver and his mate go in with the lamp leaving them humming in the dark. The horse's void steams into the snow beneath its hooves and its hiss and melt are the envy of the freezing slaves.

"The inn door opens: a girl and a boy step away from its light. They climb into the wagon bed. The boy will have a gun in three years, but now he carries a lamp and a jug of warm cider. They pass it from mouth to mouth. The girl offers bread, pieces of meat and something more: a glance into the eyes of the one she serves. One helping for each man, two for each woman. And a look. They look back. The next stop will be their last. But not this one. This one is warmed."

It's quiet again when the children finish speaking, until the woman breaks into the silence.

"Finally," she says, "I trust you now. I trust you with the bird that is not in your hands because you have truly caught it. Look. How lovely it is, this thing we have done—together."

Note: We often analyze literature by looking at a story, then at its parts, and then at the theme. Tony Morrison goes beyond this pattern, though, with a rejection of the predictable, and provides us with an alternate ending to her story. The pattern she uses in this piece leads us to think about how we can make changes in our writing patterns, our stories, and—by extension—our lives. In this classroom exercise, students are asked to use the foundational structure of Morrison's work—her focus on telling a story, explaining what the parts of the story stand for, revealing the life lessons this gives us, and considering an alternate ending—to craft their own essays on "Using a Story to Make a Point."

KERNEL ESSAYS BY STUDENTS
Using a Story to Make a Point

CINDERELLA

1. Cinderella was a maid then got married to a prince.
2. Cinderella was a maid for her stepmother and stepsisters.
3. Always be courageous and kind.
4. Cinderella went to the ball, then the prince fell in love with her and they got married.

Jessicalynn Jackson, Grade 7

FROZEN

1. A girl had powers of snow and ice.
2. Her powers show us we could be independent.
3. It shows us we could do anything.
4. She stays alone and makes friends out of snow.

Anael Ashkenazi, Grade 7

HUMPTY DUMPTY'S GREAT FALL

1. Humpty Dumpty sat on a wall and he fell. He then cracked open and could not be saved.
2. When Humpty fell, everyone tried to save him but couldn't.
3. This shows that sometimes the things we love cannot be saved.
4. Humpty Dumpty fell but then he did a backflip and made the news.

Evan Katzman, Grade 7

OUR WORLD

1. In a place where heartbreaks, deaths, poverty, rage, loss, betrayal, and darkness exist, there was a miller's daughter, who, with the help of Rumpelstiltskin, spun straw into gold and married a king.
2. Rumpelstiltskin's name in the story represents a terrible force, a force strong enough to undo her child's curse.
3. This force is not life itself, and the name is not important.
4. Perhaps reality could be better than a fairy tale. Perhaps R could live happy in the castle

too. In my version, when the princess finds his true name, it shines and broke the chains of lies and they all lived happily ever after.

Deniff Lara, Grade 7

GOLDILOCKS THE PERP

1. Goldilocks broke into a home, ate porridge, sat in (and broke) chairs, slept in beds, and was found there by the returning residents. The perp awoke and fled the scene.
2. The porridge represents those possessions we own that are irreplaceable; the chairs represent the places where we feel comfortable; the beds represent death.
3. This tells us that criminals can take away our possessions and ruin our sense of safety, but they cannot change our fate.
4. If the bears wanted to take back their safety, they would have rebuilt the chair ruined by Goldilocks, and possibly snatched the escaping perp and turned her in to the authorities. Or they could have eaten her instead of the porridge.

Tim Logan, Grade 10

THE ANTS AND THE GRASSHOPPER

1. The ant worked and got ready for winter while the grasshopper sang. When winter came, the ant survived, and the grasshopper suffered.
2. The ant stands for those type-A personalities which plan ahead, succeed with future goals, and have terrible relationships because they condescend to others with a smugness that's repugnant. The grasshopper represents those artistic, communicative free spirits who are warm and friendly, but can end up depending on others for survival.
3. The grasshopper and the ant both have a lot to learn from each other.
4. A better ending for the story would be for the ant to teach the grasshopper to work ahead, while the grasshopper teaches the ant to enjoy life more as he works.

Mary Sue Knight, Grade 10

Name: _____

TITLE OF YOUR PIECE

TEXT STRUCTURE

New Perspectives from a Photo

| a surprising truth that the photo demonstrates | previous action that the photo does <u>not</u> show | what belief this makes us rethink | And what changes this makes us want to make in ourselves |

Carl Sagan

KERNEL ESSAY

1. _____
2. _____
3. _____
4. _____
_____
_____

SUGGESTIONS FOR QUICK LIST:

For this, any compelling photos will do. Google "top photos" or "National Geographic picture of the day" or any similar site.

MY QUICK LIST OF TOPICS:

1.
2.
3.
4.
5.

"Pale Blue Dot" Speech

Carl Sagan, 1996

In this speech, Carl Sagan, a noted astronomer, reflects on the deeper meaning of the image of planet Earth that was captured in a 1990 photograph taken from Voyager 1.

Look again at that dot. That's here. That's home. That's us. On it everyone you love, everyone you know, everyone you ever heard of, every human being who ever was, lived out their lives. The aggregate of our joy and suffering, thousands of confident religions, ideologies, and economic doctrines, every hunter and forager, every hero and coward, every creator and destroyer of civilization, every king and peasant, every young couple in love, every mother and father, hopeful child, inventor and explorer, every teacher of morals, every corrupt politician, every "superstar," every "supreme leader," every saint and sinner in the history of our species lived there—on a mote of dust suspended in a sunbeam.

The Earth is a very small stage in a vast cosmic arena. Think of the rivers of blood spilled by all those generals and emperors so that, in glory and triumph, they could become the momentary masters of a fraction of a dot. Think of the endless cruelties visited by the inhabitants of one corner of this pixel on the scarcely distinguishable inhabitants of some other corner, how frequent their misunderstandings, how eager they are to kill one another, how fervent their hatreds.

Our posturings, our imagined self-importance, the delusion that we have some privileged position in the Universe, are challenged by this point of pale light. Our planet is a lonely speck in the great enveloping cosmic dark. In our obscurity, in all this vastness, there is no hint that help will come from elsewhere to save us from ourselves.

The Earth is the only world known so far to harbor life. There is nowhere else, at least in the near future, to which our species could migrate. Visit, yes. Settle, not yet. Like it or not, for the moment the Earth is where we make our stand.

It has been said that astronomy is a humbling and character-building experience. There is perhaps no better demonstration of the folly of human conceits than this distant image of our tiny world. To me, it underscores our responsibility to deal more kindly with one another, and to preserve and cherish the pale blue dot, the only home we've ever known.

Note: Carl Sagan's research is well known, but this speech gives us an additional gift—a pattern we can use to develop a new way of thinking about the deeper meaning of a photograph. In this piece, it becomes apparent to the reader that Sagan uses his scientist's eye to gaze not only at what is in the picture, but to also imagine what came before the picture. Then, Sagan takes his contemplation a step further, stepping back to consider a belief, and to think about how such a belief can lead to change. In this classroom exercise, students are asked to use the foundational structure of this speech—its focus on finding a truth within a photo, looking back to envision what came before it, and making a related life change—to craft their own essays on "New Perspectives From a Photo."

PLANNING PAGE + ESSAY
New Perspectives From a Photo

THE MOUND

Look again at that mound. Look at those moving specks on top. That mound is home to the specks and those specks are ants. For many of the ants, this mound is the only home they've ever known. Every ant with his own job of either a worker, a builder, or the queen-mother of them all. Every ant living in that mound strives to be the strongest one. This striving for power may cause conflict between them. Yet at the end of the day, all they are is a population of ants living on a pile of dirt surrounded by the rest of the world.

This mound is a very small stage in a vast cosmic area. Think of all the ants who died in the process of building the mound or searching for food to gather for the colony. Think of all the animals who tried to invade their mound. Think of all the people who stepped on it, destroying that fraction of the yard in which they lived.

Every ant takes pride in himself and each believes that he is the most important. Yet what these ants do not understand is that they are just an insignificant dot on the surface of this vast globe.

At their time now, the ants know that there is nowhere else that they have discovered that could sustain them or that they could migrate to. Whether they like it or not, at this moment, the mound is where the ants make their stand.

It has been said that studying ants is a humbling and character-building experience. It shows us about hard work and devotion towards others. It also shows us how responsibility and kindness help them to preserve and cherish their small, brown dot; the only home these ants have ever known.

Nicole Payne, Grade 9

PLANNING PAGE + ESSAY
New Perspectives From a Photo

IT TAKES A LOT TO CHANGE SOMETHING

We are all like one sprinkle on a cupcake. One sprinkle doesn't make the cupcake much better. It takes a lot of sprinkles to make the cupcake better. Our world is like a cupcake. There are about 7 billion of us here on Earth and one out of 7 billion doesn't amount to much. So we all need to change to make the world sweeter.

Right before my picture was taken, I held the sugary, delicious, and sweet sprinkles in my hand. My sister bumped me and they all spilled on to the table. I quickly, hurriedly and swiftly pushed the sprinkles into a pile.

49	**PLANNING PAGE**

Name: Molly Meyer

TITLE OF YOUR PIECE

It Takes a Lot to Change Something

TEXT STRUCTURE

New Perspectives from a Photo

| a surprising truth that the photo demonstrates | previous action that the photo does not show | What belief this makes us rethink | And what changes this makes us want to make in ourselves |

Carl Sagan

KERNEL ESSAY

1. We are all one sprinkle on a cupcake and it takes a lot of us to make it better.
2. The photo doesn't show someone spilling the sprinkles.
3. This makes us rethink that we alone can change the world.
4. Thinking of this, it makes us want to spark a change in the world, earth, and society.

SUGGESTIONS FOR QUICK LIST:

For this, any compelling photos will do. Google "top photos" or "National Geographic picture of the day" or any similar site.

MY QUICK LIST OF TOPICS:

1. Cooking
2. Painting a room
3. Bathing a dog
4. Painting a picture
5. Moving furniture

This makes us rethink that we alone can change the world. Everybody says to be kind and we can change the world, but can we really change much? The answer is no. But let's say the entire U.S.A. starts being kind. The world will be a much better place. We alone can't change the world.

Hearing this it makes us want to change the world. It makes us want to change ourselves and get other people to change, too. If that happens, the world will be a better place. Just like that cupcake with lots of sprinkles.

Molly Meyer, Grade 4

PLANNING PAGE

Name: _____

TITLE OF YOUR PIECE

TEXT STRUCTURE

So You'll Know Me After I'm Gone

| What I wish I knew about my grandparents | What I wished to experience with you | Why I have to go | What made me understand life | What I offer you |

Lt. Col. Mark M. Weber

KERNEL ESSAY

1. _____

2. _____

3. _____

4. _____

5. _____

SUGGESTIONS FOR QUICK LIST:

what details would you want people to know about?
what guides you?
what thoughts?

MY QUICK LIST OF TOPICS:

1. _____

2. _____

3. _____

4. _____

5. _____

Letter to My Sons (Preface)

Lieutenant Colonel Mark Weber, 2012

Dear Matthew, Joshua, and Noah,

I wrote a book for you. I started writing it long before any of you were born, and even before I met your mom, but it was always written for you.

When I was twelve years old, my grandma Weber died of a sudden heart attack. As we helped Grandpa go through her things, we came across a letter he wrote to her in August 1944. His work kept them separated, he was writing to tell her about his job, the weather—no mention of the world war raging across the sea—and how "it seems like it has been a year here without you." He was playful. He drew several doodles in the margins, one of which was a man sticking out his tongue. He closed the note by telling her how much he enjoyed the roast and the cake she made for him, and then he drew two birds—one for each of his sons at the time.

The faded letter looked and felt like an ancient treasure, but what impressed me most was that I had never heard Grandpa talk or act that sweet. He didn't even remember writing it and said it didn't sound like him at all. That bugged me. I wanted to know more about Grandma. And I sure wouldn't want to forget what it was like to write a letter like that.

As I grew older, I found that all three of my remaining grandparents were short on details. Of course they had stories, but not always the details I wanted to know about. They couldn't remember young emotions or reasoning, and they wouldn't talk about their biggest mistakes or regrets. The questions I had didn't match the answers they were willing or able to give. I imagined someday I would have grandkids (yes, grandkids) who might be just as interested in me as I was in my grandparents. And so I started writing a journal, and I kept it brutally honest. Looking back, there's a lot of stuff I'm really not proud of but I figure maybe those ugly things reflect my growth through the years. This book comes from that journal.

Of course, I imagined one day sharing these stories in person, but now I'm dying, and I realize I might not even get to share it with you boys, let alone with any grandkids.

If attitude alone determined survival, I would live another fifty years. Unfortunately, our bodies get a vote, and my forty-year-old frame is giving out way sooner than it should. Despite some breathtaking treatments, I still have cancer, I can't have any more surgeries, and the chemo is failing. I may look invincible in my army uniform or while cutting down trees with a feeding machine strapped over my shoulder, but to suggest that I'm not dying is just dishonest.

So I started thinking about ways to tell you my stories.

There's an eighteen-year-old boy inside of me who sees the three of you quickly approaching the age when I started really thinking about life. That boy stood out on a parade field twenty-three years ago as a day-four enlisted soldier in the army and listened while an unseen narrator passionately recited an adaptation of General Douglas MacArthur's famous 1962 speech to the cadets of West Point. The words and the accompanying music pulled at the hair on my arms and neck, and I felt tears roll down my cheeks. For the first time—and forever after—I understood life was much bigger than the things that were happening around me.

I committed the speech to memory and have recited it with the same passion during countless retirement ceremonies and military holidays over the past twenty years. You three were all just babies when the army recognized me as one of the best company-grade officers of the more than thirty thousand in the army. The honor? The General MacArthur Leadership Award.

The truth is, I'm not a big fan of Douglas MacArthur and never have been. I attended a military high school and have been in an army uniform since age fourteen, so I knew who MacArthur was when I first heard his

(continued) . . .

Letter to My Sons (Preface) (Continued) — Lieutenant Colonel Mark Weber, 2012

words. He always seemed more movie character than actual man, and it struck me then that if you want to be a real-life man, you have to learn from real-life men.

But his speech to those young men is about being a real man. It's about life as a struggle and our need to embrace it, about the contradictions and complexity and confusion, about the courage and search for wisdom required to get through it all, and about coming to it all as honestly as a man can reasonably do.

So when it came time to share with you what I've learned about life, I knew I had to draw on that speech just one more time—with the three of you as my aspiring young "cadets," and each chapter framed in a moral from that speech.

Matthew, when you were twelve, I tried to offer you some advice after a brief discussion on some mundane subject, and you interrupted me. "Dad," you said with an elevated tone to get my attention, "I'll figure it out." You were right then, and you're still right. You had asked the question, gained some context, and then set out on your own course. With such understanding, I have faith that the three of you will indeed figure it out. And so these pages reflect observations and perspective rather than advice or instruction. Though I'll speak with my usual conviction and passion, I know I gained those attributes over a long period of time and in the same manner Matthew expressed. My stories are not examples of the way to live your life; my stories are just examples of an infinite number of paths.

Which one should you take?

With the help of many other people you'll meet in your life, you'll figure it out.

Along the way, I hope you'll consult these pages as often and as casually as you would if I were still here and you could pick up the phone. I hope you'll ask this book different questions at different times in your lives. And I hope you'll find answers or perspectives to match.

I hate writing this letter, but I would hate not writing it even more. Nothing can replace the long talks I hoped to have while fishing or driving to some far-off adventure with you, just as I got to do with my dad. But, thankfully, I've been blessed with enough time to pass along the most compelling experiences of my life. As sad as the reasons are for writing any of this, let's see if we can squeeze some joy out of it before I have to leave.

Love,
Dad

Note: Before Lieutenant Colonel Mark Weber passed away, he left his sons with the gift of his thoughts. In this introduction, he explains why he is writing. The piece takes the reader on a journey, using a structure that we too can make use of when we don't want to regret leaving things unsaid. The structure moves the reader along, from sadness and regret toward understanding and warmth and, in the process, gives us a way to use writing to transform our grief. In this classroom exercise, students are asked to use the foundational structure of Weber's letter—his focus on wishing things were different, realizing that life must come to an end, understanding life, and making an offering to another person—to craft their own "So You'll Know Me After I'm Gone" essays.

Source: Preface from *Tell My Sons: A Father's Last Letters* by Lieutenant Colonel Mark M. Weber

PLANNING PAGE + ESSAY
So You'll Know Me After I'm Gone

TO MY FUTURE DAUGHTERS

My Dearest Daughter(s),

I am writing this letter for you. You still have many years before I even try to bring you into existence, but I am writing this for you because one day I will die, and if that happens before you are old enough to remember me, I want you to know, that without a doubt, that I love you. I love you now, before I've graduated from high school, before I've gotten my license, before I've been kissed, before I've even had a boyfriend. I love you so much.

When I was ten years old, my parents celebrated their 20th anniversary. I was watching them exchange gifts that morning and I remember my dad handing my mom a card and a box. She opened the card, which contained a long, super sentimental message, and I remember she started crying. Then she opened the box and started crying even more. There was a lot of crying that day.

I just now remembered this. And that bugs me because I remember thinking, "Wow. One day I want to teach my kids about love by doing stuff like that for my husband." Well, I don't know how I'm going to do that if I forget it again. While I'm good-ish at many things, remembering important stuff is not something I excel at.

I am 15 years old right now, but I don't know how old I'll be when you are finally old enough to read this. Though I may be perfectly fine right now, I know that age will weaken me as time goes on. If positivity deemed survival I would live to be 570, but unfortunately my body has the final say in whether or not I will be able to tell you these stories while I'm still alive. But I don't think I'll die soon. Nevertheless I'm going to find ways to tell you my stories. I have not been alive for long, but I still feel that it is important to share with you what I have learned.

I have decided that the one most important thing I have to say to you is this: try not to grow up too fast. It will be hard for me to watch you grow as it is. As much I will want to figure out everything for

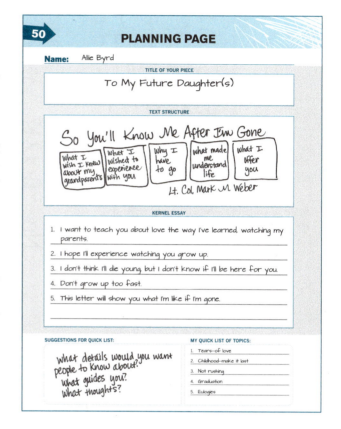

you, I am confident that you are able to set your own course, and that you will be able to find an answer to every question you ask, I am a reference, not a set of directions. Use me, and my stories, as an example of the path I chose, not as a map of your own.

It was hard for me to figure out what to say in this letter, but I believe it was well worth it. Hopefully you will never have to use this as a replacement for me and the long talks we would have had, but I can rest assured knowing this exists for you, should it ever become necessary. I know it is morose for me to think about my death, but you need to know I love you unconditionally. You will do amazing things, my love.

Love,
Allie

Allie Byrd, Grade 9

Complete Collection of 50 Text Structures

Stepping Up to A New Role

- What I will give → to those who came before me
- What I promise not to do in my new work
- my high standards of behavior (what common bad habits you won't see in me)
- Consequences I hope for

— Hippocratic Oath

Humble Request for Help

- Here is my view
- Here is what we have accomplished
- Here are ways we have made progress
- But these things are causing problems
- So here is what I wish you would do
- Humble thanks

— E.W. – Plymouth Plantations

Can't We Just Get Along?
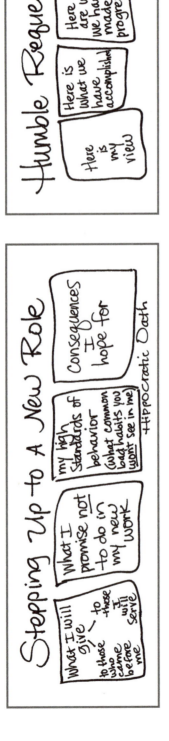

- my reason for speaking up right now
- We offer you cooperation in these ways
- But we fear you because...
- What you must do so that we can live peacefully

— Chief Powhatan

No, Thank You
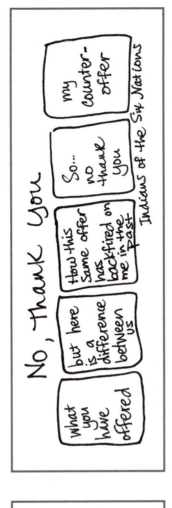

- What you have offered
- but here is a difference between us
- How this same offer has backfired on me in the past
- So... no thank you

— Indians of the Six Nations

Team Promise

- What group we are
- what we are doing
- What we promise to each other
- how we are signing and sealing our promise

— Mayflower Compact

Lighting a Fire Under a Procrastinator
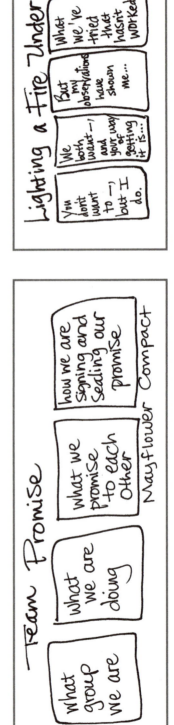

- You don't want to — but I do.
- We both want — and your way of getting it is...
- But my observations have shown me...
- What we've tried that hasn't worked
- Here are our assets/strengths right now...
- What is happening while we do nothing
- Let's go.

— Patrick Henry

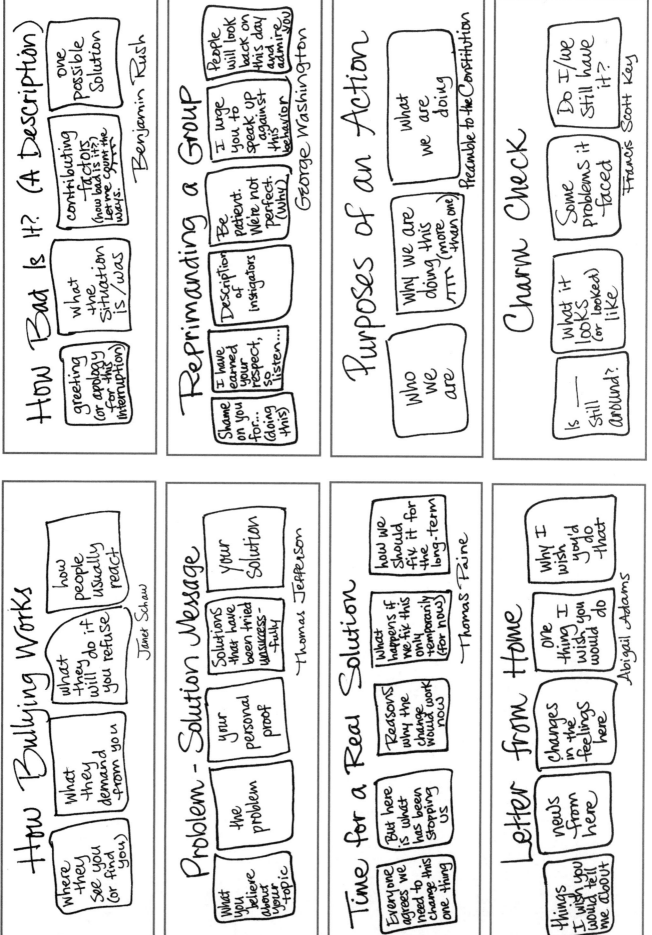

How Bad Is It? (A Description)

greeting (or apology for this interruption) — what the situation is/was — contributing factors (how bad is it? Let me count the ways.) — one possible solution

Benjamin Rush

Reprimanding a Group

Shame on you for... (doing this) — I have earned your respect, so listen... — Description of instigators — Be patient. We're not perfect. (why) — I urge you to speak up against this behavior — People will look back on this day and admire you

George Washington

Purposes of an Action

Who we are — what we are doing — Why we are doing this (more than one)

Preamble to the Constitution

Charm Check

Is ___ still around? — what it looks (or looked) like — Some problems it faced — Do I/we still have it?

Francis Scott Key

How Bullying Works

Where they see you (or find you) — What they demand from you — what they will do it you refuse — how people usually react

Janet Schaw

Problem – Solution Message

What you believe about your topic — the problem — your personal proof — Solutions that have been tried unsuccessfully — your Solution

Thomas Jefferson

Time for a Real Solution

Everyone agrees we need to change this one thing — But here is what has been stopping us — Reasons why the change would work now — What happens if we fix this only temporarily (for now) — how we should fix it for the long-term

Thomas Paine

Letter from Home

things I wish you would tell me about — news from here — changes in the feelings here — one thing I wish you would do — why I wish you'd do that

Abigail Adams

(continued) . . .

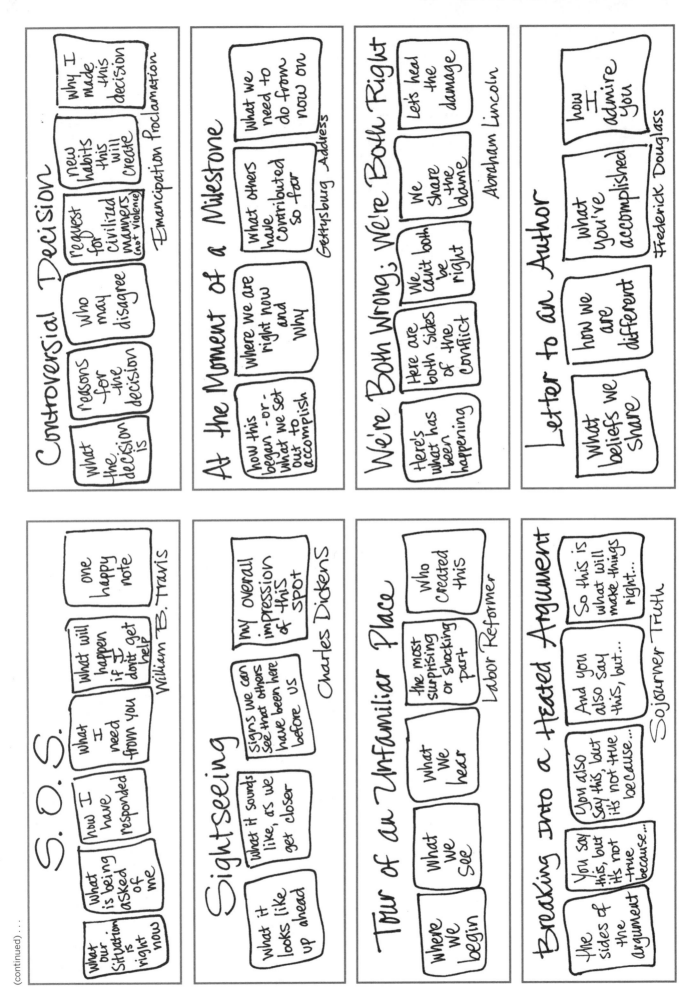

Controversial Decision

What the decision is | reasons for the decision | Who may disagree | request for civilized manners (not violence) | new habits this will create | why I made this decision

— Emancipation Proclamation

At the Moment of a Milestone

how this began — or — what we set out to accomplish | where we are right now and why | what others have contributed so far | what we need to do from now on

— Gettysburg Address

We're Both Wrong; We're Both Right

Here's what has been happening | Here are both sides of the conflict | We can't both be right | We share the blame | Let's heal the damage

— Abraham Lincoln

Letter to an Author

What beliefs we share | how we are different | what you've accomplished | how I admire you

— Frederick Douglass

S.O.S.

What our situation is right now | what is being asked of me | how I have responded | what I need from you | what will happen if I don't get help | one happy note

— William B. Travis

Sightseeing

what it looks like up ahead | what it sounds like, as we get closer | signs we can see that others have been here before us | my overall impression of this spot

— Charles Dickens

Tour of an Unfamiliar Place

Where we begin | What we see | What we hear | the most surprising or shocking part | Who created this

— Labor Reformer

Breaking Into a Heated Argument

The sides of the argument | You say this, but it's not true because... | You also say this, but it's not true because... | And you also say this, but... | So this is what will make things right...

— Sojourner Truth

(continued) . . .

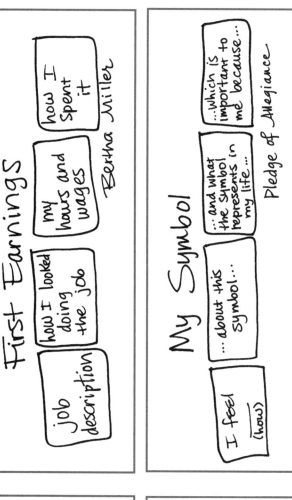

First Earnings

Job description → how I looked doing the job → my hours and wages → how I spent it

— Bertha Miller

My Symbol

I feel (how) → ...about this symbol... → ...and what the symbol represents in my life... → ...which is important to me because...

— Pledge of Allegiance

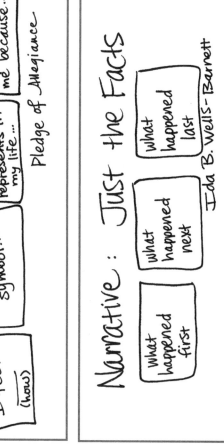

Narrative: Just the Facts

what happened first → what happened next → what happened last

— Ida B. Wells-Barnett

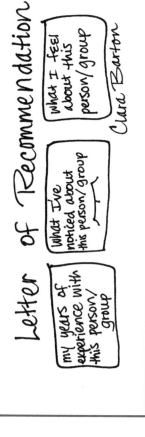

Letter of Recommendation

my years of experience with this person/group → what I've noticed about this person/group → what I feel about this person/group

— Clara Barton

Fighting Unfairness with Logic

What I want to communicate → If this is true → And if this is also true → then this must be true → A ridiculous question (twisting the 3rd box)

— Susan B. Anthony

Valuable Advice

Why I'm giving you this advice → one rule and how it works → another rule and how it works → another rule and how it works → If you follow these, then...

— Mark Twain

Comforting a Friend in Pain

I know you're suffering → A thought about life's ups and downs → advice: use the bad feelings; don't be used by it → what all you should do or not do → you will prevail

— Henry James

I Want More (While I Have the Chance)

We recently did this → We got this → So that makes me want this → Because in the future, it will be too late

— William G. Hornaday

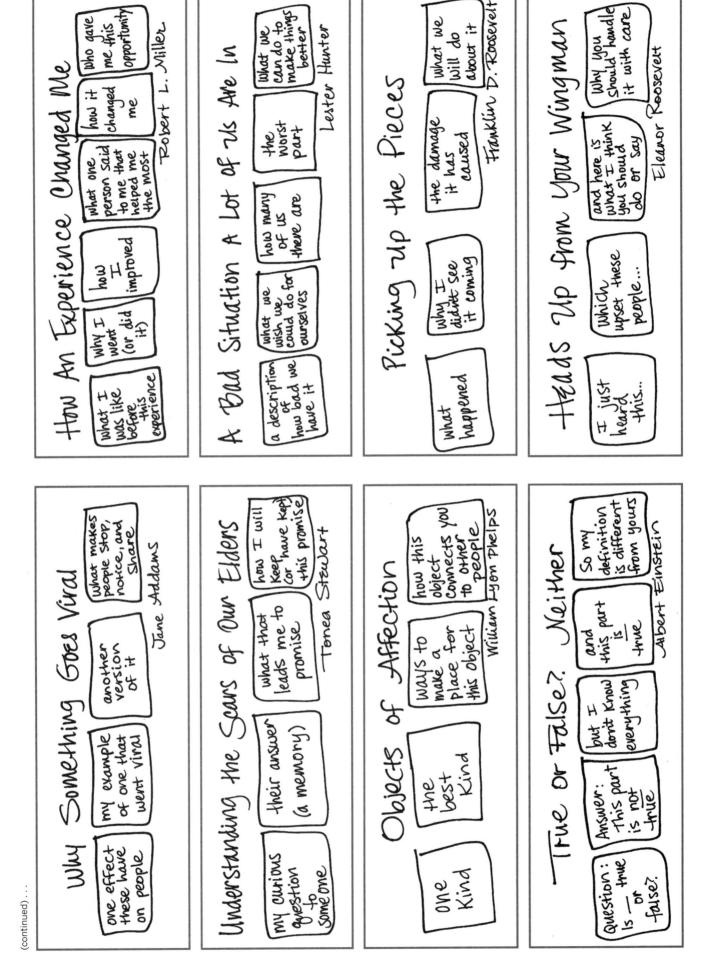

How An Experience Changed Me

what I was like before this experience → Why I went (or did it) → how I improved → what one person said to me that helped me the most → how it changed me → who gave me this opportunity

Robert L. Miller

A Bad Situation A Lot of Us Are In

a description of how bad we have it → what we wish we could do for ourselves → how many of us there are → the worst part → what we can do to make things better

Lester Hunter

Picking up the Pieces

what happened → why I didn't see it coming → the damage it has caused → what we will do about it

Franklin D. Roosevelt

Heads Up From Your Wingman

I just heard this... → which upset these people... → and here is what I think you should do or say → Why you should handle it with care

Eleanor Roosevelt

Why Something Goes Viral

one effect these have on people → my example of one that went viral → another version of it → what makes people stop, notice, and share

Jane Addams

Understanding the Scars of Our Elders

My curious question to someone → their answer (a memory) → what that leads me to promise → how I will keep (or have kept) this promise

Tonea Stewart

Objects of Affection

One Kind → the best Kind → ways to make a place for this object → how this object connects you to other people

William Lyon Phelps

True or False? Neither

Question: Is ___ true or false? → Answer: This part is not true → but I don't know everything → and this part is true → So my definition is different from yours

Albert Einstein

Parting Advice to Your Replacement

Character traits that are most important to you → What (char. traits) do, teach you, give you, creates in you → Who you will serve → how to give them * (char. traits) → What memories you will create → good-bye

— Douglas MacArthur

Bon Voyage

how we share this with you → the most valuable thing you'll get from this experience → I believe in a higher power → I ask that you be protected

— Marion Scott Carpenter

I Feel Your Pain

our bond (who we are) → wrong ideas other people have about you → What you're dealing with (and why it's bad) → how if it's bad for one person, it's bad for all → Imagine good for all (how that will look) → What we will say when that day comes

— John F. Kennedy

Flashpoint Moment of Truth

What just happened → What that triggered → what we promise to all → how we don't deliver to some → What I'm going to do about it

— Lyndon B. Johnson

What Do I Mean? Well...

You asked me to explain " ___ " → Part of it means this... → Another part of it does not mean... → What the whole thing really means...

— Ayn Rand

My Advice About Your Strong Feeling

I see that you feel ___ → Two kinds of that feeling (good and bad) → What you should do about those feelings → How I think you should show those feelings → Parting thought

— John Steinbeck

Pep Talk

what this new chapter is → our plan or goal → promises to everyone → our biggest problem to face soon → how we should face it → what it will cost us → what help I ask from you → I'll go first

— John F. Kennedy

Memory Reflection

where I was → what happened first → what happened next → what happened last → What I learned or noticed

— John Howard Griffin

(continued) . . .

(continued) . . .

New Perspectives from a Photo

| a surprising truth that the photo demonstrates | previous action that the photo does not show | what belief this makes us re-think | And what changes this makes us want to make in ourselves |

Carl Sagan

So You'll Know Me After I'm Gone

| What I wish I knew about my grandparents | What I wished to experience with you | Why I have to go | what made me understand life | what I offer you |

Lt. Col. Mark M. Weber

Walking the Walk to Make a Difference

| whose methods we admire → | life lessons we learned from him/her | one social situation in our world that needs change | the story of one example (and proof this is widespread) | what we should do to reverse it |

Cesar Chavez

Using a Story to Make a Point

| A Story | What the parts of the story stand for | life lesson this gives us | alternate ending to the story |

Toni Morrison

Available for download at **https://resources.corwin.com/textstructures**

Appendix 2

Text Structures Useful as Promises to Others

Understanding the Scars of Our Elders

- My curious question to someone
- their answer (a memory)
- what that leads me to promise
- how I will keep (or have kept) this promise

— Tonea Stewart

Can't We Just Get Along?

- my reason for speaking up right now
- We offer you cooperation in these ways ↗
- But we fear you because...
- What you must do so that we can live peacefully

— Chief Powhatan

Team Promise

- What group we are
- what we are doing
- What we promise to each other
- how we are signing and sealing our promise

— Mayflower Compact

Stepping Up to a New Role

- What I will give — to those who came before me
- to those I will serve
- What I promise not to do in my new work
- my high standards of behavior (what common bad habits you won't see in me)
- Consequences I hope for

— Hippocratic Oath

At the Moment of a Milestone

- how this began - or - what we set out to accomplish
- Where we are right now and why
- What others have contributed so far
- What we need to do from now on

— Gettysburg Address

Available for download at **https://resources.corwin.com/textstructures**

Copyright © 2016 by Corwin. All rights reserved. Reprinted from *Text Structures From the Masters: 50 Lessons and Nonfiction Mentor Texts to Help Students Write Their Way In and Read Their Way Out of Every Single Imaginable Genre, Grades 6–10* by Gretchen Bernabei and Jennifer Koppe. Thousand Oaks, CA: Corwin, www.corwin.com. Reproduction authorized only for the local school site or nonprofit organization that has purchased this book.

Appendix 3

Text Structures of Our Identity

My Symbol

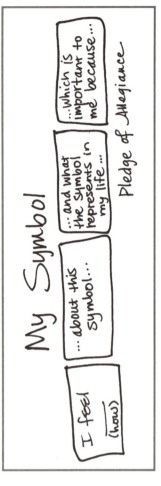

I feel ___ (how) ... about this symbol... ...and what the symbol represents in my life ... ...which is important to me because ...

Pledge of Allegiance

What Do I Mean? Well...

You asked me to explain "___." Part of it means this... Another part of it does not mean... What the whole thing really means...

Ayn Rand

Parting Advice to Your Replacement

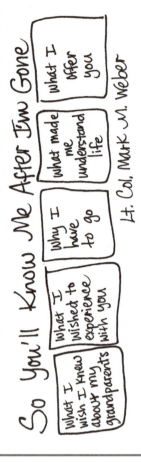

Character traits & ___ that are most important to you What ___ (char. traits) do, teach you, give you, creates in you who you will serve how to give them ___ (char. traits) what memories you will create good-bye

Douglas MacArthur

Charm Check

Is ___ still around? What it looks (or looked) like Some problems it faced Do I/we still have it?

Francis Scott Key

So You'll Know Me After I'm Gone

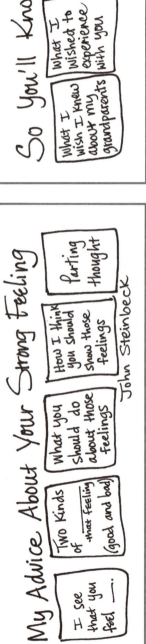

What I wish I knew about my grandparents What I wished to experience with you Why I have to go What made me understand life what I offer you

Lt. Col. Mark M. Weber

My Advice About Your Strong Feeling

I see that you feel ___. Two Kinds of that feeling (good and bad) What you should do about those feelings How I think you should show those feelings Parting thought

John Steinbeck

Appendix 4
Text Structures for Travel

Sightseeing

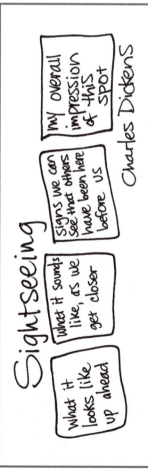

| What it looks like up ahead | What it sounds like, as we get closer | Signs we can see that others have been here before us | My overall impression of this spot |

Charles Dickens

Tour of an Unfamiliar Place

| Where we begin | What we see | What we hear | The most surprising or shocking part | Who created this |

Labor Reformer

Memory Reflection

| Where I was | What happened first | What happened next | What happened last | What I learned or noticed |

John Howard Griffin

Pep Talk

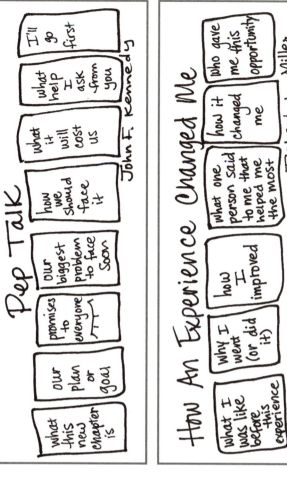

| What this new chapter is | Our plan or goal | Promises to everyone | Our biggest problem to face soon | How we should face it | What it will cost us | What help I ask from you | I'll go first |

John F. Kennedy

How An Experience Changed Me

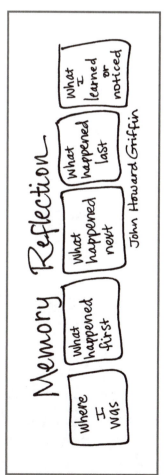
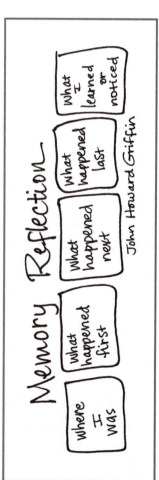

| What I was like before this experience | Why I went (or did it) | How I improved | What one person said to me that helped me the most | How it changed me | Who gave me this opportunity |

Robert L. Miller

Appendix 5

Text Structures for Important Moments

Valuable Advice

| Why I'm giving you this advice | one rule and how it works | another rule and how it works | another rule and how it works | If you follow these, then... |

Mark Twain

Letter from Home

| things I wish you would tell me about | news from here | changes in the feelings here | one thing I wish you would do | Why I wish you'd do that |

Abigail Adams

Bon Voyage

| how we share this with you | the most valuable thing you'll get from this experience | I believe in a higher power | I ask that you be protected |

Marion Scott Carpenter

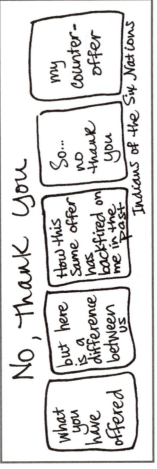

Letter of Recommendation

| my years of experience with this person/group | What I've noticed about this person/group | what I feel about this person/group |

Clara Barton

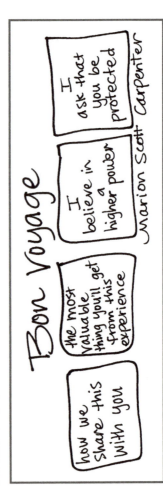

No, Thank You

| what you have offered | but here is a difference between us | How this same offer has backfired on me in the past | So... no thank you | my counter-offer |

Indians of the Six Nations

Appendix 6

Text Structures for Desperation

S.O.S.

| What our situation is right now | How I have responded | What is being asked of me | What I need from you | What will happen if I don't get help | One happy note |

— William B. Travis

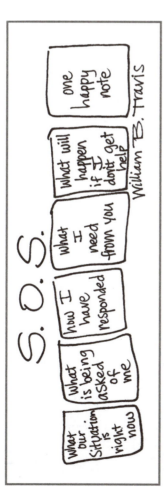

Humble Request for Help

| Here is my view | Here is what we have accomplished | Here are ways we have made progress | But these things are causing problems | So here is what I wish you would do | Humble thanks |

— E.W. — Plymouth Plantations

How Bad Is It? (A Description)

| greeting (or apology for that interruption) | what the situation is/was | contributing factors (how bad is it?) Let me count the ways. | one possible solution |

— Benjamin Rush

A Bad Situation A Lot of Us Are In

| a description of how bad we have it | what we wish we could do for ourselves | how many of us there are | the worst part | What we can do to make things better |

— Lester Hunter

Heads Up from Your Wingman

| I just heard this... | Which upset these people... | and here is what I think you should do or say | Why you should handle it with care |

— Eleanor Roosevelt

Breaking Into a Heated Argument

| the sides of the argument | You say this, but it's not true because... | You also say this, but it's not true because... | And you also say this, but... | So this is what will make things right... |

— Sojourner Truth

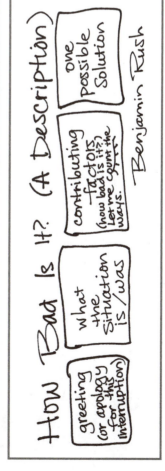

Appendix 7

Text Structures Useful as Persuasion About Some Needed Change

Problem-Solution Message

| What you believe about your topic | your personal proof | Solutions that have been tried unsuccessfully | your Solution |

— Thomas Jefferson

Time for a Real Solution

| Everyone agrees we need to change this one thing | But here is what has been stopping us | Reasons why the change would work now | What happens if we fix this only temporarily (for now) | how we should fix it for the long-term |

— Thomas Paine

Fighting Unfairness with Logic

| What I want to communicate | If this is true | And if this is also true | then this must be true | a ridiculous question (twisting the 3rd box) |

— Susan B. Anthony

Walking the Walk to Make a Difference

| whose methods we admire | life lessons we learned from him/her → | one social situation in our world that needs change | the story of one example (and proof this is widespread) | what we should do to reverse it |

— Cesar Chavez

New Perspectives from a Photo

| a surprising truth that the photo demonstrates | previous action that the photo does not show | what belief this makes us rethink | And what changes this makes us want to make in ourselves |

— Carl Sagan

Available for download at **https://resources.corwin.com/textstructures**

Appendix 8

Text Structures Useful for Bad Times

A Bad Situation A Lot of us Are In

- a description of how bad we have it
- what we wish we could do for ourselves
- how many of us there are
- the worst part
- what we can do to make things better

Lester Hunter

Comforting a Friend in Pain

- I know you're suffering
- A thought about life's ups and downs
- advice: use the bad feeling; don't be used by it
- what all you should do or not do
- you will prevail

Henry James

Valuable Advice

- Why I'm giving you this advice
- one rule and how it works
- Another rule and how it works
- another rule and how it works
- If you follow these, then...

Mark Twain

Picking up the Pieces

- what happened
- Why I didn't see it coming
- the damage it has caused
- what we will do about it

Franklin D. Roosevelt

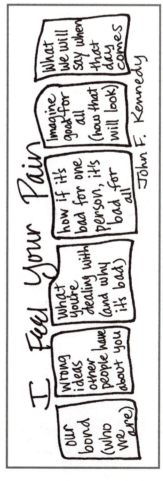

I Feel Your Pain

- our bond (who we are)
- wrong ideas other people have about you
- what you're dealing with (and why it's bad)
- how if it's bad for one person, it's bad for all
- Imagine good for all (how that will look)
- What we will say when that day comes

John F. Kennedy

Appendix 9

Text Structures for Times of Conflict

Lighting a Fire Under a Procrastinator

| You don't want to — but I do. | We both want — and your way of getting it is... | But my observations have shown me... | What we've tried that hasn't worked | Here are our assets/ strengths right now... | What is happening while we do nothing... | Let's go. |

Patrick Henry

Narrative: Just the Facts

| What happened first | what happened next | What happened last |

Ida B. Wells-Barnett

Breaking Into a Heated Argument

| The sides of the argument | You say this, but its not true because... | You also say this, but it's not true because... | And you also say this, but... | So this is what will make things right... |

Sojourner Truth

How Bullying Works

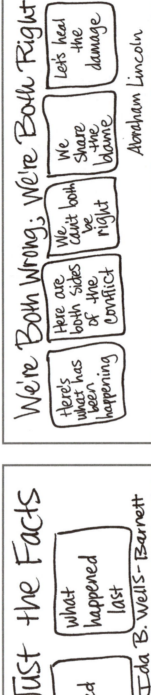

| Where they see you (or find you) | What they demand from you | what they will do if you refuse | how people usually react |

Janet Schaw

We're Both Wrong; We're Both Right

| Here's what has been happening | Here are both sides of the conflict | We can't both be right | We share the blame | Let's heal the damage |

Abraham Lincoln

Appendix 10

More Ways to Use the Lessons in an English Language Arts Classroom

Starting With a Plan Sheet

Change the Structure

1. Revise the structure. Rewrite one (or more) of the boxes to create an adapted text structure. Write a kernel essay afterward to see how it works. If you like it, add the structure to your collection.
2. Rearrange the structure. Rearrange the boxes, and read the resulting structure. If you like it, write a kernel essay.
3. Play with opposites. Add the word *not* to one or more of the boxes or to the structure title and see what happens.

Change the Speaker or Point of View

4. Write as someone else. Start with a structure and ask yourself, "Who might ever need to deliver this message?" Pick a character from fiction (a book or movie) or from the world (history, sports, popular culture, world politics, or business). Write in first person as that person.
5. Write about someone else. Do the same as above, but write in third person about that person.
6. Write in third person about yourself. Imagine how someone else would phrase the sentences.

Mix and Match Kernel Essays

7. Luck of the draw. Using a single kernel essay structure, write the kernel sentences on separate small cards. Put everyone's first sentence in a bag, everyone's second sentence in a bag, and so forth. Have students draw one card from each bag, and see what new crazy kernel they create.
8. Story starter essay. Ask for three volunteers to share their first sentence from a single kernel essay structure, and put these on the board. Let everyone choose one and write their own kernel essay using that beginning sentence.
9. Have students write a kernel essay from a single kernel essay structure. Next, do a read-around, with each student only reading one sentence from his or her kernel. These can be the same sentence to hear the variety in sentence constructions and content or sequential sentences to listen for random connection.

Starting With a Collection of Text Structures

Write a Response to a Book

1. Write a pressing message from a character. Look over the structures, and find one that works for your character. Write a kernel essay first, and then flesh it out with details from the story.

2. Choose one character, use three different structures, and write three different kernel essays. Flesh one out.
3. Choose three different characters, three different structures, and write three different kernel essays.
4. Play "Name That Structure." Students read their kernel essays aloud, and the class figures out which structure it is.
5. Study one character from fiction, and do one of the following projects:

- Make a timeline of the character's life.
- Choose five different important moments from the character's life.
- Use five different text structures, and write five different pieces, one about each of those moments.

(Assignment sheet and tracking sheet follow.)

Write Autobiographically

6. Think of five important moments in your life. Browse the structures, and choose five. Write a kernel essay for each of those specific moments in your life. Flesh out several.
7. Make a list of dramatic memories in your life. Think about other people in your close circle, and choose a structure about a message that you witnessed them delivering to someone.

Write Fiction

8. Start a short story. Browse the structures, and choose one. Write a kernel essay from the point of view of a made-up person who is younger or older than you. Continue their story from there.
9. Write fan fiction. Imagine a character you already know from a book, movie, or television show in a new situation. Use one of the essay structures to write a kernel essay about this character.

Starting With the Source Document

Starting With the Document

1. Look at the opening and closing. Rewrite either.
2. Hunt for the rhetorical devices, especially in speeches before large crowds.
3. Do a figurative language hunt (for metaphors, alliteration, etc.).
4. Examine the transitions. Highlight them, and then use them in your own essay.
5. Check the punctuation in the original document.
6. Rewrite part of the source document, deleting all the punctuation. Read it aloud.
7. Use the source document for a hunt for any grammatical constructions you've studied in language arts class (nouns? prepositional phrases? compound sentences? items in a series?).
8. Choose the best sentence. Copy these onto small posters for the room. Use those sentences as patterns to emulate.

Appendix II

More Ways to Use the Lessons for Academic Play in a Social Studies or History Classroom

1. Write a prequel to the source document. What conversations came before this message?
2. Imagine the author of this piece was speaking to students aloud. Have them write a response to the speaker.
3. Write a response to the speaker, opposing him or her in some way.
4. Write a response to the speaker, asking questions.
5. Draw the speaker. Write one line from the speaker's kernel essay into a word bubble. Draw a thought bubble, and show the speaker's thoughts. Include several historical details in the background of the drawing.
6. Compare the speaker to the person(s) he or she is speaking to. Draw a T-chart to show how they are alike and different.
7. Draw the characters in the room or present at that time. Identify them with word bubbles or thought bubbles over their heads, showing their reactions.
8. Do some situational research. Find out about the speaker at the moment that they delivered this piece. How old were they? How healthy? Where were they? What family members were nearby? Who were their best friends?
9. Draw the speaker's overnight bag, satchel, or purse. What does this person carry with him or her at all times? Draw five items. Label and justify.
10. Write the heckler speech, to be performed along with the original, in two voices.
11. If there had been a TV station there back then, write the TV broadcast of the news that night after the piece was delivered.
12. What if the message had gone undelivered? If that speaker had not been there at that moment (or ever), how would history have changed? Would someone else have delivered the message?
13. Predict the ripples. What do you *think* this message caused to happen? And what *did* it cause to happen? Identify the chain of events.
14. Study one person in history, and do one of the following projects:

   - Make a timeline of his or her life.
   - Choose five different moments from the person's life.
   - Use five different text structures, and write five different pieces about those moments. Who is his or her audience? Why is he or she speaking about and at this particular moment?

(Assignment sheet and tracking sheet follow.)

Appendix 12

Character Project
Assignment and Tracking Sheet

Character Study Project Assignment

**For Research and Imaginative Writing About Any
Character in Contemporary Life, History, or Literature**

1. Create a timeline showing at least five of your character's most important life moments.
2. Create five pieces of writing in five different genres using five different text structures.

A high-scoring piece will have the following:

- May use any (and as many) points of view you'd like (including speaking as your character)
- Will include figurative language (e.g., similes, metaphors, or alliteration)
- Will include rhetorical devices (e.g., enumeration or anaphora)
- Will include specific references to historical information (e.g., people, places, or events)

Allowable genres include the following:

- Print ad
- TV ad script
- Blog
- Character sketch
- Description
- Email
- Cause-and-effect essay
- Opinion essay
- Persuasive essay
- Reflective essay
- Interview
- Job application
- Friendly letter
- Letter of inquiry or request
- Letter of praise
- Letter to solve a problem
- Magazine article
- Memo
- Memoir
- Newspaper editorial
- News article
- Observation report
- Parody
- Play
- Rhymed-verse poem
- Blank-verse poem
- Free-verse poem
- Song lyrics
- Procedure
- Resume
- Speech
- Short story

Character Study Project Tracking Sheet

Your name: _____

Name of your subject: _____ Timeline completion date: _____

Life Moment	Structure (choose from list)	Genre (choose from list)	Kernel essay finished?	Full essay finished?	Color-coded to show required details?	Edited for correctness?	Grade
Example Deciding not to go to college	No, Thank You	Friendly Letter	5/16/15				
1.							
2.							
3.							
4.							
5.							
6.							

Available for download at **https://resources.corwin.com/textstructures**

Copyright © 2016 by Corwin. All rights reserved. Reprinted from *Text Structures From the Masters: 50 Lessons and Nonfiction Mentor Texts to Help Students Write Their Way In and Read Their Way Out of Every Single Imaginable Genre, Grades 6–10* by Gretchen Bernabei and Jennifer Koppe. Thousand Oaks, CA: Corwin, www.corwin.com. Reproduction authorized only for the local school site or nonprofit organization that has purchased this book.

A SAGE Company

Helping educators make the greatest impact

CORWIN HAS ONE MISSION: to enhance education through intentional professional learning.

We build long-term relationships with our authors, educators, clients, and associations who partner with us to develop and continuously improve the best evidence-based practices that establish and support lifelong learning.